THE BLUE SUITCASE

Tragedy and Triumph
in an Immigrant's Life

SHRI THANEDAR

First Edition 2008

ISBN 978-0-615-46729-0

This book is gratefully dedicated to my wife, Shashi,
who helped me put our life back on track,
and to my sons, Neil and Samir,
whose advice I seek first when in doubt.

A man is but the product of his thoughts.
What he thinks, he becomes.

MOHANDAS K. GANDHI

TABLE OF CONTENTS

CHAPTER I

Coming To America

FEBRUARY 7, 1979. We stepped off the plane in New York City and walked through Customs in a daze. We were in the United States! All around us, people were talking very fast, in accents so different I could barely recognize the English. They were wearing heavy clothing, too, wool pullovers that had strips of twisted knitting and, underneath, cotton shirts that came up and covered the entire neck.

I looked ruefully at my thin sweater and sandals as I stood there holding my old blue suitcase. I could feel the air's chill through the large glass windows. Still, my friend Naushil Mehta and I were here. We'd made it. We gave each other tired grins and wove our way through the crowd to check on our connecting flight to Akron.

Naushil pointed up at the electronic board, finding our flight number and running his index finger across to the departure time column … *Departed*? How could our plane have departed already? I grabbed a man's shoulder and asked him, please, what time it was. Our plane had landed just late enough—and the passengers had filed out just slowly enough—that we'd blown our connection.

We were stranded in New York, and we had $20 apiece. That was all the cash we'd been allowed to bring into the country. We walked up to the airline counter, and the clerk took one look at our expressions and smiled in sympathy.

"You missed your flight?"

Naushil nodded, and I burst into a panicked stream of explanation: "We have only $20. Where can we stay? What should we do?"

"No worries," she said cheerfully. "We'll find you a hotel—it's on us—and you can eat dinner at the airport cafeteria." Then she carefully went over the rules about what we could and could not order. Generosity had its limits.

By the time we stepped through the glass doors—they opened automatically when we walked toward them!—it was dark outside and even colder. Horns were blaring, the sound somehow angrier, shriller, than the insistent beeps back home. Out on the highway I could see a necklace of sparkling lights, the headlamps of hundreds of cars whizzing along, one right behind the other. We stood shivering on the pavement, waiting for the shuttle to take us to the hotel.

"Are you sure we're in the right place?" I asked Naushil, and he shrugged. With so many signs and arrows pointing in so many different directions, there seemed no point in even trying to figure it out. We'd just stand there and hope.

I wrapped my sweater tighter around me and rested one sandal on top of the other, warming my toes. I toyed with the idea of opening my trusted old blue suitcase right there on the sidewalk and swapping my sandals for the one pair of shoes I had packed. I decided that it might look strange. We hadn't known what the weather would be like—it wasn't as if you could Google it back then. The only snow and ice I'd ever seen were in Bollywood movies, where the hero and heroine are in Mumbai one minute and then all of a sudden they're daydreaming, dancing in the snow in some exotic European city.

Hardly preparation.

I closed my eyes for a minute, feeling the hot sun on my shoulders as I stepped into my taxi in Belgaum. That was just a few days ago … and a whole world away.

Suddenly dizzy, I pushed all thoughts of home from my mind. Later that night, I fell into the hotel bed and slept so hard, I remember nothing until the wakeup call shrilled at 5:30 a.m. We made it back to the airport, teeth chattering, and caught the flight to our new home: Akron, Ohio.

All I knew about Akron was that it was close to Cincinnati—or was it Cleveland? Akron was supposed to be a wholesome city, although I suspected that my mother and father—Inni and Kaka—would not think so. Akron was also, judging from what the pilot was saying as we came in for the landing, even colder than New York. But it had its own art museum, and the university had archives of the history of American psychology. At least, if I went nuts, I'd be in the right place.

The university would be smaller than Mumbai University, I reminded myself. But would everyone be as solemn and careful? How ambitious *were* American kids? Were they spoiled and silly, or as fiercely idealistic as Howard Roark, the protagonist in Ayn Rand's *The Fountainhead*, which we had read? Naushil and I started speculating aloud, distracting each other with bizarre scenarios.

Then the wheels bumped twice against the tarmac, the brakes screeched, the plane shuddered, and we were in Akron. We got off the plane last, taking our time and bracing ourselves for our next challenge, finding transport to the university. Then we would have to find a place to stay. We would certainly need help getting around. I was worried: Who would we ask? Who would take the time to help us?

But when we walked down the little tunnel into the airport, a group of four Indian students was standing there, waiting for us!

This was a ritual, it seemed: They always came to welcome new students from India. And they'd brought us winter jackets, because no one who came from India ever realized how cold it would be. Grateful, I fastened every button of my new jacket and pulled the collar up as high as it would go.

Then came the next piece of luck: One of the students, Dilip, asked whether we needed a place to stay.

"Er ... I'm sure we—"

Naushil cut me off: "Yes, we do indeed need a place. Do you have any suggestions for us?"

"Stay with me!" Dilip was smiling warmly, as though he'd expected our question.

"We don't want to inconvenience you," I said quickly, before Naushil's sharp elbow could bruise my ribs.

"It's no trouble at all," Dilip said. "I have a house, and there is plenty of room for you. You can help cook our meals!"

We breathed a sigh of relief and climbed into the car with him. Now it didn't seem so long until the end of the month, when we'd get our first paychecks.

Over the next few weeks, we told Dilip again and again how grateful we were. We did help cook, and we all took our meals together. Our choices were a bit limited, though, because he was a nonsmoking, nondrinking vegetarian. At the market, I sighed over the chicken I'd so recently learned to love.

"I miss *tandoori* chicken," I told Naushil glumly. He nodded. A few hours later, as he passed me in the hall, he hissed, "I'm dying for a cigarette."

"I'd settle for a *beer*," I retorted.

"Me, too," Naushil said. It was a relief to finally admit the tension that had been building between us and Dilip.

Diet and habits were the surface reasons, and they were enough to keep us all on edge. But the deeper reason, I think now, is that Dilip wanted to play older brother, telling us every day where we should go and what we should do. We wanted to explore for ourselves! The first fear and strangeness had worn off, and we were excited to see what the rest of the campus was like, how the chemistry department worked, what people did in the evenings for fun.

American food definitely took some getting used to—it tasted like I'd had Novocain shot into my tongue! I took to carrying a small jar of spicy Indian pickle with me to add to whatever I was eating and make it more pungent. I spent hours at the Akron library, which for me was like Ali Baba's cave. I checked out books on Dadaism and Surrealism and Impressionism. Only after I'd grabbed all those new books did I look to see what kind of Indian books and music they had. I looked only out of curiosity; I wasn't the least bit interested in surrounding myself with my homeland's culture. I had a new country to explore.

Dilip's friends, on the other hand, seemed almost afraid of American culture. They worked all the time, except for Friday evenings, when they got together, cooked curry, and watched Bollywood movies in Hindi with no subtitles, because there were no Americans around. They socialized only with other Indian students, and they gossiped a lot. They often sounded petty or jealous.

I found myself drawn more to the American students. Yes, I missed India's classical music and theater—but I found Abstract Expressionism fascinating. Yes, I missed curry—but I decided that I really liked pasta. There was something very comforting about all those noodles in sweet tomato sauce or melted cheese.

Soon, I felt a bit of strain not only with Dilip but also—and this came as a shock—with Naushil. I think we were both so overwhelmed by the US, and our reactions to everything were so different, that we didn't feel the need to be tied to each other any longer. Each of us wanted to set out on his own, experience things for himself.

Unfortunately, working in the chemistry department, teaching, doing research, and getting a PhD weren't high on the priority list for either one of us. Dr. Michael Farona, the department chair, had shown us around and introduced us to our new colleagues and professors ... but the art, literature, and film societies were much more compelling than our chemistry classes! We did the bare minimum—or, at least, I did. Naushil did even less.

Like two logs thrown into an ocean, we began to drift apart. After a time, Naushil left and went to New York. (He eventually came back to Akron, but when he did he knew for sure what he'd long guessed and tried to tell his parents: Chemistry was *not* what he wanted to do.)

As for me, this whole language business—the different accents, pronunciations, uses of words and phrases—was causing problems. I was having a terrible time understanding my students and they me. I called the elevator a "lift," and people chuckled. I had no idea what a "restroom" was for, if not for napping. When kids joked about "making out," my brow furrowed. Huh? I knew what it meant to "make" something, and I knew what the word "out" meant, but I couldn't imagine what the combination might mean, especially in relation to a girl.

One day I walked into McDonald's. I'd heard people talking about something they called a Big Mac, and it sounded pretty good. After teaching all morning, I was ravenous. So I stepped right up to the shiny aluminum counter and announced that I wanted "a Big Mac and a Coke." The young woman punched some keys on the cash register and named a price; apparently I'd made myself clear in a single try. I breathed a sigh of relief.

Then, as she turned to get my order, she called over her shoulder, "For here or to go?"

For here or to go. For here or to go. What in God's name did she mean?

I stared at her blankly. Finally she held up a paper bag in one hand and a brown plastic tray in the other, cocking her head. Oh! I pointed to the tray. "I am so sorry," I said. Then I said it again. I took the tray, now loaded with paper cup and burger, and hurried to the farthest corner of the restaurant, sliding along the hard, curved plastic bench until I was next to the window, sheltered from staring eyes.

"If I can't even understand five simple words, how am I ever going to manage here?" I asked myself. I slowly unwrapped the Big Mac—it was, indeed, formidable, but I barely tasted it. That night I dreamed that I was surrounded by hundreds of people, all holding up different objects and pointing and saying things in gibberish, waiting impatiently for me to choose. It was not a pleasant dream, to say the least.

For weeks the language barrier kept me tense. Finally I decided on a clown's approach: I would relax, listen carefully to others, and mimic

6

what they said. I kept my ears open and confined my attempts to simple sentences. It worked.

My teaching improved with my English, but my own classes weren't going terribly well. Dr. Farona, who had so generously helped Naushil and I get over our immigration hurdles when we were trying to get visas in India, had turned out to be a very nice, pudgy Italian man in his mid-40s. He had dark hair and gold-rimmed glasses, a jovial manner and a passion for college football. I liked him immensely. But I couldn't concentrate in his special chemistry class. I failed it in my first semester—which embarrassed me and shocked him. I wasn't who he'd thought I was.

I promised him that things would change—and, sure enough, the second semester was better. Now I was starting to understand spoken English. It was as though the words were puzzle pieces people kept tossing at me, and they were finally settling into place. I could answer back clearly and be helpful, and my students reacted much better to me.

I found a rooming house and moved in. My room cost only $80 a month, and I shared a kitchen with about a hundred other people. I was getting the hang of learning chemistry at the doctoral level, though, and the foggy mysteries of American social life were starting to clear.

Smiles, for example. I'd walk down the street, and a pretty girl would smile at me, maybe even say, "Hi!" I'd stop dead in my tracks. Was she making a pass at me? Were American women so bold and flirtatious as to hit up a stranger? Was I supposed to ask her out? Then I'd turn around, only to watch as she walked away.

That happy illusion ended when I noticed, riding the bus, that gray-haired grandmothers and balding men with beer bellies were just as friendly. It was always a "Hi!" or a "Hello!" or even a "Hey!" Americans greeted strangers as though they knew them. Back home, you didn't even acknowledge a stranger as you passed. If you smiled, it would be regarded as a little weird, even suspicious. People were guarded with each other. Here, all guard was let down.

The biggest helps in understanding the culture were all the art films, plays, and concerts I went to. Nearly always I left understanding a little bit more. I also liked comedies, though, so one night an American friend took me to see a Richard Pryor movie.

I didn't understand a word of it. Between my own accent, which seemed to filter even the words I heard, and Pryor's African-American accent and slang, I probably caught about three words in the entire movie. He might as well have been talking in Portuguese! I felt lonely and awkward, sitting there listening to everybody else laughing loudly.

I fared better watching Marcel Marceau, the French mime. What a relief—no English required! Tickets to his performances were expensive, but a new friend of mine worked at the theater and he let us in for free after the intermission.

As I relaxed, I stopped wearing dress shirts with my jeans. I traded my crisp button-downs for soft, washed-out T-shirts, loving their rock group logos and irreverent messages. My Indian sandals were fine in warm weather, but I bought tennis shoes for the rest of the year.

Now I was dressing and living just like my American friends, who worked hard all week so they could play all weekend. A huge keg of beer, nice loud music, and people to talk to—that was all you needed to have a party. On weekends we would go from one apartment or frat house to the next, partying all over town.

We also went hiking and on canoe trips, experiences I'd never had before. I caught my breath the first time we paddled through the rapids, but soon the thrill made me laugh out loud. It was never exactly white-water, just gentle rushes of the river, and we'd dash into other canoes to capsize them, just for fun, or flip our own and splash in the cool of the river.

We played music and danced in the evenings or just drank beer and talked heart to heart, for hours on end, about anything and everything. One day I realized with a jolt that I was beginning to think and dream in English. I almost felt disloyal. But then one of my friends would ask a question, and I'd talk for hours about the wonderful street food back home, or the festivals, and the old sense of belonging would flood back.

My new friends didn't know anything about India, and they'd listen in fascination as I told them about cultural norms and traditions.

"How come you Indians marry without love?" they'd ask.

"We fall in love *after* we marry—that's why our marriages last longer," I'd jokingly respond.

They'd stare at me, trying to figure it out.

Then I'd drive it home, asking: "If you Americans don't marry without first falling in love, how come your marriages break so often?"

What I *didn't* tell my American friends was that I was becoming very interested in one of the young women who lived in my rooming house. Merlyn wasn't going to college. She was about 19, and she'd run away from an abusive stepfather three years earlier and gotten into drugs. Now she was working as a waitress, but she still smoked marijuana, and I worried about her.

We began a friendship, and I think I surprised her, because all the men she'd ever met had wanted only to take advantage of her: men in her family, men on the street, her drug friends. My approach was more respectful. I think that when she realized it was genuine, she started becoming very attracted to me.

I was too naïve to feel the shift, at first. But she soon made her desires plain. Our rooms were next to each other, and she started knocking on my door late in the evening to chat. In the privacy of my room I usually just wrapped a piece of light cloth around my waist, and it hung from my navel to the ground, loose and comfortable. When Merlyn started coming over in nightgowns, I realized that I had better switch to pants—the fabric would be thicker and, well, less revealing.

She wasn't the least bit modest; she tickled my belly or tugged playfully at my sarong, and her gowns were almost transparent. Even I couldn't miss the message.

But it threw me for, as my American friends would say, a loop. I had never been intimate with a woman and didn't know the first thing about it.

My only big experience with women had come in India when I was 16, hanging out with my guy friends in one of their bedrooms, looking across into an open window in the next house. It was about 40 feet away, but we could see a girl watching us. After a time, I noticed that it was always me she stared at. If I was the only one watching, she stood in front of the mirror in her room and braided her hair. Or she brushed it back off her shoulder, tilted her head, and fastened an earring. As she did this, she looked to me for a reaction. After some weeks of this, I got bold and began suggesting in sign language whether she should do a single or double braid and which earrings she should wear. Occasionally late in the evening she would change her clothes, revealing her beautiful young body, the memories of which would keep me awake all night.

We knew we liked each other, but I never dared close that 40-foot distance. Sometimes she saw me in the marketplace when she was shopping with her mother, but on those occasions she avoided looking at me.

So, not counting the young woman in the window, Merlyn was the first relationship I'd ever had. Soon we became physically intimate. I was 24, not an unusual age for a young Hindu man to lose his virginity.

But the fire of my obsession with her nearly consumed me. Once more, I couldn't keep my mind on my studies. I couldn't even keep my mind on pouring cereal or tying my shoelaces. I thought of nothing but Merlyn.

Our relationship went on for more than a year, and I eventually calmed down enough to study again. But I hadn't even begun my research project, which was ironic, because while I was ignoring my own studies I was doing all I could to persuade Merlyn to finish hers.

I was also trying to persuade her to give up alcohol and drugs. I even found a doctor who would help her. She took lithium on and off, starting when her mood blackened and then stopping because it made her feel fuzzy and lethargic. But even when she was taking the lithium she drank or smoked pot, which alarmed me. Once, partly out of curiosity and partly to jolt her back to reality, I tried one of her lithium pills. It knocked me on my back for 24 hours.

Whenever Merlyn slid back into her addiction, she got furious and uncontrollable, tearing herself away from me and drinking or drugging herself into a stupor. When the binge ended, she'd come back remorseful and conscience stricken. She'd talk about how she wanted to die, or say she'd never done anything good, never made her parents love her or given them a reason to be proud.

"Now I'm letting *you* down," she'd say. "Never again, Shri! This is the last time!"

It never was. But I didn't lose hope. I don't know whether she'd ever intended to really fall in love with me, but I'd fallen in love with her, and I wasn't going to give up.

We talked a lot, but she always kept the conversation light. I'd try to talk about religion or life's deepest meaning, and she'd laugh and say, "Live for the moment. It's all we have!" She teased me constantly, making fun of my skinny legs when I bought my first pair of shorts, mocking my Indian curries. "Come have some real American food," she'd say, dragging me down to the common kitchen and cooking me pasta or a hamburger.

I'd always drunk only beer, but Merlyn introduced me to cocktails. She mixed me a screwdriver and she made me taste bourbon, because it was invented in America.

She also insisted that I listen to the Top 40 hits on the radio, and we danced in my room. I liked American pop music a lot. Drinking and dancing on a weekend evening, I could almost forget my academic obligations. But on Monday mornings I'd awaken with a jolt, determined to start my dissertation project *now*.

I didn't even have to worry about coming up with a topic. Dr. Farona had given me an excellent idea for a research project: I would work on developing polymers for new batteries that would be very powerful but also very safe, with no acid. They might have specialized factory applications, especially in electronics, so it was an exciting project.

But I just couldn't concentrate on it. Merlyn had become my primary project.

Somehow I was convinced that if I spent all my time with Merlyn, I could take care of her and keep her sober. Granted, she didn't really *want* me to spend all my time with her. In India, with any hint of a relationship, there is a tendency for us to think immediately about marriage—so of course I'd begun thinking about marrying Merlyn, ignoring all our differences. I talked easily and often about the possibility, imagining aloud what our future together could be.

I thought that talking about marriage would steady her and bring comfort and give her a reason to let go of alcohol and drugs. But it didn't work.

The more I talked, the more nervous she seemed. She let me speak, but she'd pull away from my arms. If we were in bed, she'd get up and start pacing around the room. Marriage just didn't seem as possible to her, and the more serious I grew, the more uncomfortable she felt. "Let's just have *fun*," she urged me.

Of course, the more Merlyn pulled away, the harder I worked to convince her we could be happy together. I grew more and more confused. This wasn't romance the way I'd envisioned it. But she made me feel such powerful emotions that I was convinced that she was my destiny.

She was certainly my distraction.

Teaching was fine, because it was a clear-cut job I could do at the appointed times. I cared about making my students understand, because I knew so well what it felt like to be bewildered!

I was well into my second semester of being a teaching assistant when we had a big symposium, with undergraduates as well as graduate students invited. The guest speaker was a Nobel laureate, and I was eager to hear him speak. But first Dr. Farona went to the podium to announce the recipient of the Outstanding Teaching Assistant Award.

"Yeah, okay, let's get on to the lecture," I thought. And then I heard my name!

My face went hot. Out of dozens of TAs, many of them American-born, I'd been chosen for the award! All I could think of was how embarrassed I'd been, just months before, when I thought that I would never be able to make my students understand me and that I'd never understand them. Obviously I'd made progress.

But my own work was a different story.

Again it was Dr. Farona who called me back to reality. He was well aware that Naushil's heart wasn't in his work, but he'd thought that I was different. In some areas, I excelled—even with Merlyn around!—and my grades were high now. Yet all the students who'd begun when I did already had their research well under way. Without original data from a series of experiments, I could not write my dissertation. And without the dissertation, I could not earn my PhD.

I panicked at regular intervals. Then Merlyn would knock on my door and step into my arms, and I'd forget everything in the world but her.

One afternoon, we were lying in bed, and we heard a knock on the door. It was another TA with a message: Dr. Farona wanted to talk to me. I threw on some clothes, combed my hair, and jogged across campus, wondering why he'd sent for me. What did he want? Was it really important? By the time I made it to his office, my heart was beating in my throat.

I gave my trademark knock, *dum-da-da-dum*, but he didn't look up with his usual grin. He asked me to close the door behind me, then gestured me to a chair. This was odd. Then he stood up, walked around his desk, and leaned against it, facing me, arms folded across his chest.

He began very gently. "Look, Shri, you took all this trouble to come here," he said, "and I'm not seeing any effort from you on your research." He looked straight into my eyes. "I'm not sure we will be able to keep you as a graduate student," he said, a real sadness in his voice.

The room spun. I saw Inni, and the rest of my family, and I thought of all the sacrifices gone to nothing. I was a complete failure!

13

I looked at him and said, "I promise that you will be proud of me." Then I turned and bolted.

I hurried down the sidewalk, and without even registering the people and buildings I passed, I made my way to an isolated corner of the campus, a garden with a single bench.

I sat down hard on the cold concrete. How had I let things get to this point?

"He's absolutely right," I thought. "What have I done in the past 18 months? What have I achieved? Did I come to America just for fun? For sex? For theater and cinema? To enjoy the American lifestyle?" I thought again of Inni and Kaka. I realized, with a pang, how sorry Dr. Farona must be for bringing me to his university, even writing all those nice words to the immigration office to help me get my visa.

I had to change. I had to fix things. There was no other option. The very next morning, I dove into my research.

Two months later, I woke up to find Merlyn gone.

It shouldn't have surprised me when she left, but it did. I don't think I'd ever fully realized how intense her discomfort was, or how sure she was that she *didn't* want to marry me. Merlyn was a wanderer, uncertain and restless at heart. She left a note:

I am sorry, Shri! I have realized that we cannot stay together and even if we do so, we won't be happy. You are leading a different life than me. My life has been totally different, and I will continue to live like that. I sincerely tried to be a part of your life, but it's impossible for me. I am going back to my world, from there I can't look back. Thanks for everything. Good luck and goodbye!

Merlyn

I was heartbroken. I started spending late evenings at the research lab. I worked hard and made a lot of progress, but inside I was shaken by Merlyn's departure. The weeks went by, flat and dull and productive. Every month I sent money home.

Then it was summer, and my paychecks stopped coming. There were no labs for us to teach in during the summer, and because of immigration rules we were not allowed to work off campus, either. I had absolutely no money.

My first summer job was as an extra waiter, called in to serve at banquets and receptions whenever a group rented the campus dining hall. It was all very formal, and I had to wear a white shirt and black pants. I learned by the copycat method, as I'd learned English. I saw how the other waiters talked to the customers, took orders, and brought the right food to the right person at each table. Some of the experienced waiters used to bring 10 plates at a time, arranged one above the next like a tower. I held my breath, watching. It sounds silly, but I admired their skill as much as I admired the top scientists in our department!

One day, I decided to try the same trick. I practiced with two plates, then three, and increased until the day arrived when I had 10 plates balanced, just like they did. I was proud as I walked, balancing the 10 plates.

"Waiting tables isn't so hard," I told myself. "Look, I've already mastered this. It looked so impressive, but it was just a skill to be learned. Now I'll—"

Somebody banged through the door behind me, and I lost my concentration. Down came the plates, crashing to the ground. I saw a spray of food, then sharp bits of ceramic and splotches of meat and potatoes all over the floor. I straightened, sighing, and turned—to find myself in front of the blotchy red face of my very angry manager.

"What the hell have you done?" he asked. "Don't play around until you know what you're doing! These plates cost money!"

I began my drama of apology. I told him I was only trying to do a good job and would be more careful. Somehow it worked. It was pure good luck that he forgave me and didn't ask me to pay for the damage. I was still broke from the previous winter.

I'd left the rooming house for a small apartment, and my heating and electric bills were so high, they stunned me. I hadn't been able to pay them for two months. I expected that I'd have to pay some kind of late fees, making the burden on me even heavier, but it was worse than I thought.

One evening that spring—an unusually cold spring—I came home to a dark, chilly apartment. I flipped the switch—no light. Checked the thermostat—no hum. My utilities had been cut off, and the only food I had left was a bit of stale *naan* and the universal grad student food: cellophane packages of ramen noodles.

I tried sleeping under my thrift-store coat, but it was cold enough that there was frost *inside* the windows. My hands were too numb to hold my toothbrush. Finally I went to a place I'd heard about, a shelter for homeless people. They served soup and other hot food and gave people beds. I stayed there for a few days, miserable but warm, before returning to my apartment.

Even after the nights warmed up, I couldn't afford to get the electricity turned back on. What was I going to do? Paying the rent would mean not eating.

Then I realized: I could sleep in my car!

Earlier in the year, I'd bought a sky-blue '69 Chevy Impala for $200 from a Chinese student. I didn't have the slightest idea how to drive a car when I bought it. When I saw the ad for the car and then bought it, I asked the guy to come and leave the car in my parking lot, pretending that it would simply be convenient for me.

There it sat, just like one of the buffalo people in our village used to buy and tether in a stable. Every morning before I went to work, I went outside and looked at it, beaming. When I came home, I paused on my way in to stare lovingly at my beautiful buffalo. But I didn't dare touch it.

It took me three weeks just to believe I owned a car. Then I opened the driver's door and sat behind the steering wheel. I just sat there, looking at all the knobs and dials, caressing the dashboard with my hands. I was awed.

The next night, I turned the ignition key. The engine roared to life, and instantly I switched it off again.

That was my first driving lesson.

A week later, I was an expert in switching the ignition on and off. So I shifted the gear to roll my Impala a few feet forward, then tried reversing the same distance. I practiced that for another week.

I decided I should get a driver's license. After much agonizing, I finally gathered my nerve and went to get a temporary driving permit. I received it on my second try, but only by the grace of the kind lady at the Department of Motor Vehicles, who hinted at a few of the answers. I think she felt a lot of sympathy for me.

When my friends realized that I had no clue how to drive, they came over and taught me. They wound up yelling at each other, because everybody had a different idea of how to do things and what the rules were. But I heard enough to decide that now I, too, could drive.

The Department of Motor Vehicles had a different opinion. I failed the driving test. Twice. I also found out that the insurance for my $200 car would cost $200—and I didn't have another $200. I still didn't have a license, either.

So I said, "To hell with the insurance and the license!"

I now realize how foolish this was, but what to do? I honestly couldn't afford the insurance. I couldn't even afford car repairs, and, as it turned out, the buffalo needed quite a few. One day I was driving Merlyn somewhere, and I smelled gasoline. "We've got to get out, *now!*" I yelled, and we scrambled out just in time to see flames shoot from the front of the car.

The mechanic showed me what was wrong: The fuel pipe was leaking, and it would cost $200 to replace. *Another* $200? I thought for a minute, and what flashed in front of my eyes were all those rubber hoses and clamps we used in the lab. I took that metal pipe out and put in a rubber tube with two clamps on the side, and the car ran just fine.

What I didn't know was the effect that gasoline would have, over time, on the rubber.

Slowly my wonderful hose was eaten away. I solved that problem easily, though: As soon as I started to smell gasoline, I simply replaced it with a fresh rubber tube.

Eventually I saved enough money for insurance, and I got my license. Instantly I became a better driver. I'd been tense and jumpy before, because every time I had to maneuver the car in some tricky way, all I could think was "illegal driver."

Even after I was legal, though, I collected quite a lot of tickets for parking in no-parking zones. Many times my Impala kissed other cars gently as I was backing up, and for this I also paid heavy compensation. But I was quite happy with my car—especially when I had to move out of my apartment because I couldn't afford the rent.

The summer started out just fine. I spent my days in the nicely air-conditioned chemistry department, and I spent my nights asleep in my car.

Alas, the buffalo was a little cramped, and I had nowhere to bathe properly. One day I was in the lab, rubbing a bit of grime off my wrist—it showed up better against the white lab coat—when I heard a rush of water above the ceiling. I followed that sound like a lion stalking prey: out the lab door, up the stairs, and down the hall to … a locker room with showers! It turned out that on the third floor, where they conducted animal experiments, they actually had showers so the lab techs could clean up afterward. And as I stood outside the locker room, listening jealously to the hot running water, I couldn't help but notice that there was also a large seminar room on that floor. The walls of that room were lined with large cabinets.

I watched that room for a week. No one ever used it. I devised my plan.

One evening I brought my blue suitcase, which still held all my possessions, and a little sleeping bag, and I stowed them in one of the cabinets. That night, I slept in the seminar room.

I was in heaven. The building was air-conditioned, and very quiet at night. I slept better than I had in a long time. Early the next morning,

I rolled up my sleeping bag, showered, and walked down to my lab to work. No one knew and no harm was done. No more sleeping in the car, no more rent to pay.

Pretty soon, Dr. Farona was very happy with me: I was making such wonderful progress, I'd passed up all the students who'd started their research before I had.

Everything went smoothly—and then came the fateful day. Late in the evening, after I'd snuggled into my sleeping bag, a senior faculty member walked into the room to prepare for a meeting the next day. As he moved through the room, he saw the lump of my sleeping bag, and I swear I felt his eyes burn through me. I stumbled to my feet, hugely embarrassed, and apologized. Then I rolled up the sleeping bag, stuffing things inside it willy-nilly, and rushed out of the room as fast as I could.

I went outside and crawled back into my car to sleep. All night I lay there rigid, wondering what the professor would do. Would he have me kicked out of the program?

The next morning, a friend came to me and said yes, the department chairman had been told someone was sleeping in the seminar room. Fortunately, no punishment was meted out. But my days of cozy sleep and morning showers were over. I was back to the buffalo.

Comfort is a powerful lure, though. As soon as things got quiet again, I gathered my nerve and tiptoed back into the seminar room. I slept there the rest of the summer, undisturbed.

My car and I were getting along just fine now—until the day one of my friends asked for a lift to college. With the ownership of a vehicle, my social status had risen, and I proudly offered lifts whenever necessary. Before he could even finish his request, I'd reached over and unlocked the door.

We rolled away from the curb and were cruising along, complaining about one of our courses, when I happened to glance down. Smoke was curling around my feet! I braked the car to a screeching halt, and we jumped out to see what was wrong.

19

Before we could even decide how to diagnose the problem, flames burst from the engine area. "Run!" I yelled, and within seconds the car exploded. Burning fragments flew through the air.

I watched this terrifying scene as if it were a stunt in some action movie. Then reality sank in. My beloved car was no more. All that was left was a pile of rubble and ash.

The police made an inquiry, and their report noted: "The accident occurred as a result of the melting of the fuel pipe." The case was closed.

I told no one about my stupid experiment with the fuel pipe. I was terrified that I'd be thrown in jail for endangering the public safety—and rightly so. I vowed never to meddle with any car again.

The car was what Americans call totaled. A junkyard bought it for $20.

That fall, I started dating again. My sadness over Merlyn had softened. I'd realized that Merlyn had helped me understand America. She wasn't just a young woman with problems, and she wasn't just a romantic fling—which was how my friends tried to brush her off when they comforted me. No, she had tremendous influence on me. Through Merlyn, I got comfortable with America. Being with her made me feel that I understood other Americans as well; being close to her showed me that beneath the superficial differences we are still the same people.

The ease I found in those months with Merlyn was, ultimately, what convinced me: This was the country where I wanted to be. Not in the way of other immigrants, who became Americans professionally but not culturally, socially, or emotionally. I wanted to be as truly American as I was Indian. And she had shown me that it was possible.

Now I felt able to date other women, and they, too, taught me about my new country. One lesson came about tragically, when a girlfriend's father died. She called and, between sobs, asked me to take her shopping, because she didn't have a car and she needed a new dress for the funeral.

A new dress for a funeral? This struck me as bizarre, even heartless. In India, you dress up for happy occasions; you dress *down* for a funeral, because you don't want to show off on such a sad occasion.

I'm sure I looked puzzled—especially when she told me that I'd need a new suit, too. Why wasn't everyone preoccupied with the sadness of the event? I obediently bought the new suit and went to pick her up, concealing my private feelings.

But during the wake and Catholic funeral, I realized that this was just a different way of showing grief. It was more about celebrating the life of the person who had died. And there was a lot of dignity in the ritual. In India, funerals are very melodramatic, and you are expected to be hysterical. "Just because someone is falling on the floor or pulling out her hair doesn't necessarily mean she really cared about the person who died," I reflected.

My girlfriend was obviously very sad, but the way she handled herself and supported her family was amazing. And people's behavior at the funeral didn't make me uncomfortable, even as someone who didn't know the family very well. I was impressed, and I wrote my friends in India about it.

I dated a few other girls, too—nothing serious. Then I ran into a former student, Virginia, on my way to the grocery store one evening. She was a joyous, energetic young woman with a precise, melodious British accent. She used to flirt with me, smiling and standing very close, wearing short skirts and sometimes sitting in a manner that would distract me. At the time, though, I was dating Merlyn. Besides, Virginia was a student! Now, however, she'd finished her chemistry requirement and was focused on her nursing classes, and Merlyn was no longer part of my life.

As we stood on the sidewalk talking, I noticed for the first time her dreamy hazel eyes. "Shall we have dinner together?" I asked, amazed to hear myself ask.

She agreed right away. I bought some lentils for *dal* and some wine that was rich in alcohol, and we went back to my room, and I cooked her an Indian dinner. She kept touching my arm, standing close, but

I felt shy and constrained. I was still a little sad about Merlyn, a little hesitant.

"I want to show you a place," Virginia said suddenly. "It's pretty."

We drove out of the city, and she directed me down narrow country roads until we reached an open field. I parked at the edge, and she led me by the hand through the field, then along some old railroad tracks. Around midnight, we reached the place she wanted to show me: a small, peaceful lake hidden by the trees.

We sat on a big rock at the lake's edge, watching the moonlight ripple across the water. We started talking about what we believed. Virginia was a deeply spiritual person, and she was interested in Hinduism. She loved the idea of purifying the mind and body, and she was intrigued by the teachings on reincarnation. We got into the kind of conversation I'd tried so many times to have with Merlyn. I was so absorbed, I didn't even realize that two hours had passed.

She leaned her head on my shoulder, and we sat like that for a long time. Then I put my hand against her cheek, turned her face toward mine, and kissed her.

We kissed, nothing more, for an hour or so. Afterward, we held hands and walked through the trees. We weren't ready to drive back to the city yet, so we climbed up the side of the cliff and sat looking at the stars.

I have to admit, I was a little scared that night, the two of us alone in the pitch-black countryside, but Virginia was absolutely fearless. It was refreshing just to be with her. I sensed a very pure soul. "Maybe," I told myself, half afraid even to think it—"maybe she will be the one I can share my life with."

I might have been nervous in the countryside late at night, but in other areas I was fearless—some might even say foolhardy. Take Dr. H. A. Kuska, for example. A tall, grave man, he walked with his back straight, absorbed in his own thoughts, oblivious to the world around him. If you greeted him on the sidewalk, he responded with a cold stare. Dr. Kuska chose his words carefully and used them as sparingly as saffron. His reputation preceded him, and word in the hallways was that he was a stickler for rules and order and it was best not to get on his bad side.

Dr. Kuska taught quantum chemistry and relied heavily on textbooks. I'd never been able to afford textbooks, so I'd always just studied in the library, reading as many viewpoints as possible on whatever subject I was studying. I'd jot down notes during lectures and go later to the library to extract references and additional notes from other books.

My method had worked beautifully for six years in India. But when I got to Akron, I realized that American professors regularly said things like, "Read pages 28-92 before the next class." So just about everybody went and bought the books ... except me.

One day I walked into class, and here was Dr. Kuska telling everybody, "Okay, everybody, open up to page 34." He saw right away that I didn't have a textbook.

"Where is your book?" he asked sharply. "Don't forget it next time."

The next class, he saw that I still didn't have a book. "*Where ... is ... your... book?*" he asked, deliberately spacing out the words.

I told him the truth: "Sir, I don't have one."

"How can you take my class without a textbook?" he sputtered.

"Sir, I don't feel that the book is necessary, because I never study from only one book," I said. "I go to the library and take not just one textbook but all the books I can find on the subject. I don't just rely on one author."

His cheeks were spotted red, he was so angry. He said—keeping his voice quiet, which made it all the more ominous—"If you don't bring your book I will not let you into this class."

"I am a student of this university," I flashed back, tired of being treated like a child. "I have the right to attend class, and you should not prevent me from attending class for such a flimsy reason."

He stared at me for a long cold minute, then pivoted and resumed his lecture. Word spread around campus that I'd clashed with Kuska and had invoked students' rights. The American students thumped me on the back. The Indian students cautioned me: "Be careful with Professor Kuska! He is dangerous—if he gets angry, you may never graduate. Why do you pick an unnecessary argument with him?"

The next class was the midterm exam—no textbooks allowed—so I knew that I was safe. The class afterward, he started by handing back our exams. Quantum chemistry is a tough subject, very hard to comprehend, and Dr. Kuska wasn't the most patient teacher. He scowled as he handed the exams back. His habit was to tell us the highest and lowest scores and the curve. But this time he didn't volunteer much information. I looked down at my paper. I'd done very well, something like 98 of 100. So I stood up and asked, "What was the highest grade?"

As I suspected, it was mine.

"What was the next highest?" I couldn't resist asking.

"It was a 72," he said, and hurried into his lecture.

After that, he never once mentioned my not having a textbook.

Toward the end of my coursework, Dr. Farona urged me to have Dr. Kuska on my dissertation committee. My friends strongly urged me not to agree. *Nobody* wanted Dr. Kuska on his committee, because the man was so fierce.

But I said, "Well, I will take him. What can he do to me?"

Dr. Kuska agreed to serve on my committee, and my friends panicked again: "Shri, don't be crazy! He will settle the score with you, and you will be in a mess again." But somehow, I felt, he was too honorable to take revenge. I was sure that he would evaluate my thesis impartially.

Meanwhile, my relationship with Virginia had grown as serious as my relationship with Merlyn—and this time the feelings were mutual. When Virginia's mother arrived on campus for a visit, I was eager to meet her and make a good impression.

They dragged me to a square dance.

Virginia's parents went square dancing all the time. I'd never seen such a thing, and I soon realized that the rules were very complicated. But

Virginia's mother insisted that I dance, and I didn't want to say no. An incredibly awkward two hours later, I said good night.

Something I said or did that evening must have offended Virginia's mother—that, or my utter inability to *do-si-do*. After that visit, Virginia seemed a little distant. That summer, after she graduated, she took a job at a clinic in Mexico.

When she came back, a few months later, she seemed entirely changed. She said that she wanted to talk to me, so we went for a walk. But it was nothing like that first walk. We sat down in the middle of a field, and she told me that she'd fallen in love with a doctor in Mexico and they were going to get married. We held each other, and we both cried.

Another heartbreak.

At least I'd seen this one coming. I tried to focus on my academic triumph instead: I was about to complete my PhD in three-and-a-half years, which was a record for an international student. Even Dr. Kuska had approved my thesis without reservation. I would soon be *Dr.* Shri Thanedar, not *Mr.* Shri Thanedar. I couldn't wait to see Inni's face.

In August of 1982, I graduated. I had already started applying for jobs.

Do you have any idea how hard it is to apply for a job in the midst of a recession when you happen to be a foreign student with a visa that's about to expire? I sent out 150 résumés for jobs all over the country. I didn't get a nibble. Zero.

I was bone tired, and heartsick over Virginia, and I needed to send more money home to my family. "What am I going to do?" I asked myself, over and over.

In the middle of all this soul-searching, I was invited to make a presentation about my research at a chemical society meeting in Michigan. I went over the material almost on autopilot, describing the findings in my doctoral dissertation. I talked about how the special polymers I made could produce long-life batteries. After I spoke, I answered questions from the audience, fielding them with a few crisp sentences.

At one point, an older gentleman in the back of the room raised his hand. I nodded to him, and he asked me a really tough question. I answered, and he asked another. As my talk drew to a close, he challenged my conclusions. Roused from my daze, I defended them in detail, and he nodded, although he didn't seem persuaded.

After the presentation, the man approached me. He introduced himself as David Curtis, chair of the chemistry department at the University of Michigan–Ann Arbor.

"You've finished your PhD?" he asked.

"Yes," I said, and waited. Was he going to tell me that my work did not merit the degree?

"Do you have a job?"

"No, I do not," I admitted.

"In this economy, nobody's going to give you one," Dr. Curtis said, "but I have a research position that might interest you."

He was warm and jovial, now that he wasn't trying to poke holes in my research, and I liked his manner. Besides, he was right—what other options did I have?

I said yes on the spot.

My American undergraduate friends threw me a going-away party, with a big keg of beer and loud music. With a sigh, I gave one friend the treasured encyclopedia set I'd bought at a garage sale. It was just too big and heavy to bring with me. By then I'd bought another car, a gold 1973 Mazda 626, for $325. It was a bit newer than my Impala, and its fuel pipe seemed just fine. I threw my blue suitcase in the trunk and my chemistry books in the back seat. My worldly goods no longer fit into a single suitcase.

Ann Arbor was not the plum job in industry I'd hoped for.

But it was a solution.

I had never planned on doing more research—to be honest, I was sick of it. The fact was, I needed a way to stay in the country, now that I was no longer a student. "We'll be happy to sponsor you for a green card," Dr. Curtis had said. That was all I needed to hear. I started my postdoctoral research in the fall of 1982. The University of Michigan was of a much higher caliber than Akron, and, just by working there, I learned a lot.

Still, I was tired of starting over, and I was beginning to feel the distance. I worried constantly about my father's health. He was diabetic, and he'd had several strokes by then. Every time I read a letter from home telling me of another stroke, all I could do was fold up the piece of paper and worry. I couldn't bring him trays and fuss over him; I couldn't talk to his doctors; I couldn't even put my arm around my mother. Every month I wrote and sent a check, but I missed hearing Inni's voice, and talking by phone was very expensive. Besides, my family had to use the phone of a distant neighbor, and that neighbor didn't always want to be disturbed.

I ached to go home. I just wanted to be someplace familiar, even if it was only for a week. I wanted to see bright red tropical flowers instead of those pale pink ruffled begonias and silly little white flowers the university planted everywhere. When somebody told me they were called impatiens, I smiled wryly. I walked, slept, and breathed impatience. But until my green card had been processed, I couldn't leave the country.

Meanwhile, the two relationships I had hoped would turn into marriage had both broken apart. My life had no immediate purpose. I didn't even have a big problem to solve! After five years of struggle and excitement, I felt empty inside, aimless. It was an odd feeling for me, and I didn't like it.

I needed something to fill up my life.

One day, bored and restless as usual, I stood reading a bulletin board, scanning all the ads from people looking to buy and sell and rent things. Next to a tricycle and bassinet for sale—would I ever have children of my own?—I saw a notice seeking volunteers for a place called Ozone House. It was a center for teenage runaways, and it made me think of Merlyn. Ozone House provided teenagers like her food and shelter and counseling.

Reading the plea for volunteers at the bottom of the page, I tore off one of the little paper strips. The minute I got home, I called the phone number.

"We'd *love* to have you volunteer," a female voice told me warmly. They wanted people to answer the calls on their suicide-prevention hotline. I went that weekend for the first time, thrilled just to have something new to do. They put me through training, explaining how to listen when a kid called the hotline, and what to say. The main thing was to encourage the caller to open up, to get the caller talking—and that set me thinking.

I came from a culture where no one ever spoke of deep despair. Suicide was so taboo, people avoided even using the word. Here I was, showing up for six-hour shifts on the hotline, listening eagerly while kids, monosyllabic at first, started pouring their hearts out. Half the time, the problem was that they felt they couldn't talk to their parents, and their parents weren't honest with them. Everybody kept their feelings in tight compartments, sealed off from each other.

As I learned how to help these kids open up, I became more open, too. I found myself spending more and more time at Ozone House, trying to help kids make their way back to a meaningful life. I liked this kind of problem-solving, and I found that the kids related to me.

Then one day I was offered a job there. The director asked whether I'd be willing to take a paid position training and supervising other volunteers. I took it gladly.

And then I fell in love with one of them.

Roberta was Jewish, with curly black hair and big glasses. She wasn't what you'd call pretty, but she had a great sense of humor and a sort of little-kid innocence about her. We'd go someplace, and suddenly one of us would say, "Let's race!" and we'd tear off. We pulled pranks, too; our friends at Ozone House never knew what to expect next, and it broke some of the tension in that stressed-out place.

My relationship with Roberta was different from anything I'd ever experienced—it was lighter and happier. It set something free inside me.

Again I started thinking of marriage. I could easily imagine sharing the rest of my life with Roberta, teasing each other out of sadness, feeling carefree in each other's company.

Alas, it was not to be. Her parents were Orthodox Jews. They did not like my background, and they made that clear. Roberta was to marry the proverbial nice Jewish boy.

"Here we go again," I thought glumly. "Will I never find someone I can love and *marry?*"

I moped around for weeks. "You take these things too hard," one of my American friends informed me. "You always read too much into them. It's just *dating,* man!"

I couldn't be that casual, though. Not when I knew what I ultimately wanted.

My only distraction, in those weeks after Roberta, was waiting for my green card to arrive. Every day I checked the kitchen table. That's where the mail landed for all 17 residents of the rooming house, and it was a mess. The whole place was a mess—there were two or three refrigerators in the kitchen, and we all name-tagged our food. Even so, you never knew who would guzzle your beer or gulp your orange juice.

I went to the kitchen every day as early as I could and carefully sifted through all the tuition bills, Victoria's Secret catalogs, grocery circulars, and other people's love letters.

No green card.

Two months passed. Three months passed. I was getting more and more nervous. Finally I decided to just go to the immigration office in Detroit. Some things had to happen in person.

I went in the minute the office opened and introduced myself to the receptionist.

"Who is your agent?" she asked.

"Mary."

"Mary is out on maternity leave."

I groaned, remembering her smocked top. "When will she be back?"

"Not for a month and a half. She just extended her leave."

"Er … can't someone else help me?"

"Well, it's her case. She has to process it further."

By now I was in a somewhat heated discussion with this clerk. Out of the corner of my eye, I saw a man walk by and stop to listen, looking mildly interested.

"Are you an agent?" I asked him, breaking off in the middle of my rambling explanation. "Can I talk to you for a minute?"

The clerk interrupted. "I *told* you, you can't *talk* to anybody here! This will be taken care of when Mary comes back."

The guy held up his hand to quiet her and said, "Give me a minute." He vanished inside. I stood there examining the leaves of the ficus tree, the weave of the synthetic carpet—anything to avoid meeting the clerk's eyes. Finally the man came back.

"Your case was all approved," he said. "All it needed was the routine FBI paperwork. I've just forwarded that form, so you should receive your card in about a month."

I left happy! Now everything seemed more bearable. I did my research, volunteered at Ozone House—Roberta had stopped volunteering there; maybe she was upset, too—and started watching the mail again for my green card.

The football games distracted me: In Ann Arbor, the whole town goes crazy on the day of a game. Everything's festooned in blue and maize, and the celebration starts hours before the game and lasts hours after. I started getting into the spirit of the thing, and after a few cold, sunny afternoons up in the cheap seats of the Big House—the Michigan stadium—the game's strategies and patterns started to make sense to me.

A month went by, pleasantly enough. But when another month and a half went by, I started to worry again.

I went back to Detroit.

The same woman was at the front desk. "Mary hasn't come back; she extended her leave again." She tapped a few keys on her computer, peered at the screen and said, "The card was mailed 30 days ago."

"I never got it!"

"Obviously it got lost. Fill out this form; you'll have to apply again. In another 30 to 60 days, you'll get your card."

Ninety days after that, I got my card. I slid it very, very carefully from the envelope. Then I kissed it.

While I'd waited, I'd gone ahead and started applying for jobs, telling people that the arrival of my green card was imminent. By the time it came, in March 1984, I already had three job offers. One was from Texaco, in a small town in upstate New York—very, very cold winters, which was a major negative for me. Another was from Dow Corning in Midland, Michigan—also a small town, also very cold winters. The third was from a smaller company I'd never heard of, Petrolite, in St. Louis, Missouri. A big city, farther south.

I took it.

I told my new boss in St. Louis that I couldn't start until June, because I intended to spend two months in India. I had not seen my family in five years! He gave his consent immediately, and I booked my flight.

I was, of course, still broke, but I was finally debt free. I'd paid back the entire Mumbai loan I had taken before coming to America, and, better yet, now I had credit cards. I charged my plane ticket on one of them. My new salary would be several times what I'd made at the university; I could pay off the credit card easily once I started working.

Now I had a job and a green card. I wanted a wife.

I was 29 years old, more than ready to settle down. I thought back on all the relationships that had ended, letting the filmstrip play in my memory. I'd so loved the American way of choosing a partner, the emphasis on compatibility and not just height, weight, class, and family background. In America, marriage was based on liking, compatibility, and, ultimately, true love. That's how I saw my American friends getting married. Granted, it sometimes took a while—but it always eventually happened.

31

Now, after three heartbreaks, I was beginning to wonder whether I needed to go back to the Indian system. Maybe because of who I was, my background and my culture, the American way would never work. I was disappointed when I reached this conclusion, but once I accepted it I got excited. Maybe I could go home to India and find a wife.

I was not the same young man who'd left Belgaum. I'd become American in so many ways. English came easily now, even its slang. I'd earned the highest degree in the American education system. I had American friends, and even though I hadn't managed to marry I'd had three serious relationships. I'd even landed a decent job.

My heart, though, was still in India. My native land's brilliant colors and spices shaped my preferences, my taste, my definition of beauty. Maybe only an Indian woman would ever understand me fully. And if I found her, maybe we could—if she was willing—have the best of both worlds: careers with all the scope and freedom America offered, a close family, and an inner life with the richness of our Indian culture.

At the airport, waiting for my plane, I dreamed about this double life. Then a more immediate excitement took over. In just 19 hours, I'd see my parents again! And my sisters, and the little brother I barely knew, and then my childhood friends, and all my aunts and cousins … I couldn't wait to hug Inni and hear her play the proud mother and introduce me to her friends as Dr. Shri. I wanted to spend a lot of time with Kaka, too, making sure he was taking good care of himself, and the money I sent home was helping ease his life. "That's worth all the heartaches and embarrassments, all the stiff necks from sleeping in my car, all the little battles I had to fight just to fit in," I told myself.

Then I grinned. "All those problems and distractions," I thought, listing another dozen, "and still I made it."

They called out boarding instructions, and as I walked up the ramp to the plane, a happy, proud feeling welled up inside me.

I had done what I came here to do.

CHAPTER 2

The Boy from Belgaum

WHEN HE SAW the date and time of my birth, the astrologer raised an eyebrow. The date was February 22, 1955, and it was the darkest day of a dark moon. In our Hindu religious calendar, the new moon is a powerful time. It signals a new beginning—with an uncertain outcome.

"This one," the astrologer told my mother, "will be either a genius or a *dacoit*."

A dacoit was a thief of the worst kind, a thug who knocked people down and robbed them.

Ever since that day, my mother never missed a chance to remind me which choice I should make.

I was her first son, you see, with girls before me and girls after me. She had made an offering at the temple before I was born, promising that if I was a boy she would name me Prasad, "offering for the god." *That* name, as you might guess, was used only within the family.

To the outside world, I was Shrinivas Thanedar—Shri for short. And my mother, a tiny woman with dark hair parted precisely and pulled into a bun, was bent on making sure that Shri did not become a thug.

I gave her some bad moments. One day when I was 4 I saw everybody rushing around getting ready for a big festival. Inni (our nickname for our mother) had taken special jewelry—necklaces, earrings, bangles—out of her safe for the girls to wear, and they had left it carefully arranged

33

on the kitchen table, one pile for each girl, while they bathed. Bored, I walked through the kitchen. A flash of gold stopped me: sunlight, bouncing off one of the bangles.

Just that fast, the idea came to me.

Quickly I slid all of the bangles onto my arm, looped up the necklaces, and stuffed the earrings in my pocket. Then I scampered up the ladder to the attic. It was open to the kitchen, and I could hear the grownups moving back and forth below me.

I waited, holding my breath. One of my sisters called to the others. Footsteps sped up, zigzagging all over the house. My oldest sister, Rajani, began to wail: "We can't find Shri—and all the ornaments have vanished!"

I giggled, then clapped my hand over my mouth, not wanting to get caught.

Finally I saw my older sister Veda pass below me. "C'mere," I hissed. "See? This is a trick on Inni!"

I waited. She didn't climb up to the attic. She didn't even answer me.

"Vedakka!" I whispered again, trying to make my voice urgent but not loud.

Her footsteps were moving away. Soon I heard a rumble of grownup voices, then a huge stomping, as my parents and sisters all came to stand under the attic. Uh-oh.

My stomach did a somersault.

"Shri, you come down here *right now*!" Inni called. My trick didn't seem so funny as I scrambled down the ladder.

"We were frantic!" my father told me. His gentle voice was rough with worry. "We thought someone had stolen the jewelry and kidnapped you!"

No, *I'd* been the dacoit. And oh, did I get spanked! True, we didn't have lots of money, but we were a respectable family—my father, Pandurang Thanedar, was a senior clerk in a civil court—and we did *not* play silly and alarming pranks. My father, whom I called Kaka, made sure I got the message.

The experience did not sober me completely, but my later pranks were often carried out with noble intentions (and we all know what paves the road to hell!).

One day, for example, I saw a man outside in the street, carrying a basket of colorful saris on his head. He was calling loudly to passersby, advertising the extraordinary beauty of his wares. I went to the door and waved him in, sweeping my arm grandly, as I imagined a man of ease and wealth might do. I was only a kid, but I could play grownup.

"My mother's birthday is coming up," I informed him, "and I want to give her something very beautiful."

It was the truth. Inni had only a few saris, but they were always perfectly matched to the blouses she wore with them, and she selected them very carefully. I wanted to give her something new and special to wear. I picked out two of the most brilliant saris, holding them up to the light and studying the details the way I'd seen her do.

After examining them, I nodded to the merchant, the way I'd seen men nod in the bazaars. These would do. When he smiled and bobbed his head, reaching for the saris I'd chosen, I felt a rush of excitement. This buying business was fun—I didn't want to stop.

So I kept going. I picked out a sari for each of my sisters, and then I picked out one for my grandmother. Soon there was a pile of silken saris in front of me. I picked them up again, one by one, and let them slowly fall into shimmering folds, the sunlight making the reds and oranges glow.

The merchant waited, watching me. He knew this could be the big sale of the day for him. The second I had let the final sari fall from my hands, he complimented my choices and told me he would strike me a bargain and then quoted me a package price.

"Oh, I don't have any money," I told him. "But soon I will have a job, and then I will pay you the entire sum."

Just then Inni, who'd been outside gardening, came into the room. The man took her aside and started speaking to her, his voice getting louder as he gestured toward me. She frowned at me and hurried away to make him tea.

Then, to my dismay, he packed up all the saris I'd so carefully selected and took them away with him.

Inni didn't have the heart to scold me. In a way, I was glad that she hadn't been stuck with the bill for all those saris.

Ah, but I had a few genius moments, too, the first when I was only 4. I was watching Inni stir lentils over the stove, round and round, when suddenly she bent double, gasping for air.

"Mommy!" I ran over to her, tugging on the arm she had wrapped around her chubby middle. "What's wrong?"

"I was just having a little pain," she said, still short of breath. She patted my shoulder, but I was too alarmed to feel reassured. I marched outside into the street, stood in front of the first car that came and yelled, "Stop! My mother needs to go to the hospital!"

The driver braked and pulled over. I grabbed his hand and tugged him out of his car, up our sidewalk and into the house. He took one look at my mother and helped her out to his car, and they drove away.

I watched the car until I couldn't see it anymore, and then I sat down on our steps and hugged myself, kind of the way she'd hugged her tummy.

Soon everyone in my family knew, and Kaka stayed with my mother at the hospital. That night, Kaka came home very late. Yawning, but seeming very happy, he told us everything was fine and gave us all hugs before he stretched out and fell asleep.

Two days later, an auto-rickshaw brought Inni home. I ran outside, ready to throw myself at her for a big hug. She stepped out—with a baby in her arms! I took two steps back, stunned.

"This is your new little sister, Veena," she said, raising the blanket so I could see the baby's face. Then she tucked the baby close to her again and, with her free hand, touched my cheek. "You helped me so much, Shri!"

Kaka came to stand next to her. "Yes, my son, you did, and we are very proud of you."

I felt happier that day than I'd ever felt. I still wasn't quite sure how I'd made a baby happen, but I knew I'd done something good. I'd taken action, and a problem—a sick mother—had turned into something magical that made us all very happy.

At least, that is, until the baby started wailing in the middle of the night.

I was born in Chikodi, a tiny village just outside Belgaum. Growing up, I always had red clay under my fingernails; Belgaum is famous for its fiery earth. A fine red dust covers everything—the cows, the street vendors' carts, the bicycles and rickshaws that crisscross in the narrow streets. Inni was always telling me to bring things inside—and wipe them off first!

I grew up lulled by conversation—everywhere I went, it surrounded me. Every morning, while Kaka pumped bathing water from the well, I went with Inni to fetch the drinking water. By the time I was 5, we had drinking-water taps at the end of every lane. We'd wave to our neighbors and stand there and chat—Inni could talk forever—while we filled up big narrow-mouthed brass pots that even I couldn't spill.

At home, there was no such thing as knocking on the door. People came in and out all day, gossiping and exchanging favors. Inni and the other moms cooked together, blending dry lentils with spices so they would be ready to cook when guests came.

Sometimes they'd make a sweetened wheat dough and then gather in the afternoon to pull it into thin threads of vermicelli, called *sheveya*. We kids were their audience, and there was a lot of joking and happiness—especially the next day, when we cooked the noodles in a sea of milk, sugar and sweet spices, and slurped them down.

Summer started in March, and by May it was very humid. We'd prop the door of our house open, because we had no air-conditioning. We didn't close that door until 10 at night, when we went to sleep. The heat felt like a wool blanket draped over your shoulders. The wells were drying out, and the gardens and farmers' fields desperately needed rain.

And everybody waited for the monsoons to cool the air and water the crops.

When the clouds finally burst, usually in that first week of June, we kids would play in the streets, and the vendors would close up shop, and everybody, especially the farmers, would celebrate. I loved how the wet earth smelled, how the rain sounded when it hit the roof. The roof was so close to us, it was almost like living outdoors.

Then the storms would start, crashing thunder and lightning, and I'd dive under my pillow. This didn't feel like peaceful nature; it felt like angry gods were inside the house with us. I'd count the seconds between the thunder and lightning, trying to be scientific about it, so I wasn't so scared.

By morning there were large puddles everywhere, and we'd go out and splash around, knee-deep in water, and I'd forget the night's terrors.

After three months of constant rain, though, we were ready for the monsoons to end. Our whole family had to share a single umbrella and my sisters were always grabbing for it, so I was always soaking wet. Kaka would have pots and pans out to catch the water from the spots where our roof leaked. He could never find anybody to fix the roof tiles, because only a few people had the skill and everybody had leaks.

With September's cooler, drier air came the festival season. One of the first was the Ganapati festival, in honor of Lord Ganesha. He was always one of my favorite gods because he's so cool—he has an elephant's head—and because he's a problem-solver. You worship him when you're trying to figure something out or you're about to tackle a big new project. He is the remover of obstacles, the lord of new beginnings.

Neighborhoods competed to have the best decorations, and I loved walking through town, looking at the elaborately decorated tents on each street corner. For the festival, my father always ordered the biggest, brightest statue of Ganesha he could find. We had to tell the statue-maker our requirements—for example, whether Kaka wanted the trunk swinging on the right or the left side, because each position held a different meaning. Then we all put on our nicest clothes and played musical instruments—I loved to ring the bells—as we made a mini-procession to bring the statue home.

Inni, meanwhile, had made *modak*, a special food that Lord Ganesha likes. She'd form round balls from rice flour and fill them with coconut, spices, and *jaggery*, unrefined whole cane sugar. In my opinion, the modak were the best part of the festival!

In November came Diwali, the festival of lights, which was a lot like Christmas. Diwali celebrates the return of Rama, the legendary king of Ayodhya, from exile and the beginning of a reign of 11,000 peaceful, happy years. It's a time of gift-giving, and because we had so little money our presents were always boringly practical. I had two shirts and two pair of pants always, one set I was wearing and the other hanging up wet, and whenever I outgrew a shirt or pair of pants I had to wait for Diwali to get one that fit. The minute I opened my present, I put it on and wore it all day. I could move my arms and legs again!

The few times we went from our village into the city, I was always excited and thrilled. I would stare in amazement at the houses and factories, all jumbled together. Inni showed us the buildings where women spun and dyed fabric by hand. The silk I'd stroked when I'd picked out the saris had come from one of those places.

Other people worked at the sweater factories, the factories making *ghee* (clarified butter), and the grain and flour mills. We walked past many large school buildings, even a very famous medical college that Inni made sure I noticed. "Someday you may study there, Shri," she said lightly.

The city was crowded, though, and scary, and I was always glad to go back to the village. Even though we moved periodically to wherever Kaka was stationed, it was always a village. Every time we moved, we rented a small house, and they were all so similar, it was hard to remember where we were. The house was always set right on the road, with no front yard to buffer the street noise. There were no footpaths, so everybody shared the streets at once: people walking or driving rickshaws, cars honking as they tried to pass each other, stray dogs barking, buses chugging uphill, kids running across the road, bicycles crashing into each other.

Despite the chaos, people generally remained calm and went about their business. The chaotic nature of street life was normal.

What I remember most are the everyday things, like going to the river for drinking water. We'd dig in the sand on the banks and wait for water to bubble up. It was pure spring water, and I'd cup my hands and drink it in great gulps while Inni was trying to fill her urn.

I remember, too, how we collected dried cow dung from the streets, after which the women used it to wash the walls, giving them a smooth texture and making them look cleaner. For fun, we would throw stones at trees until their little round soft fruits fell, and then we would eat the fruits, spitting out the seeds and sucking in the sweetness.

When I was 7, we moved to Hindwadi. The house we rented there was squeezed tightly between two other houses, like kids crowding close to see a circus. Under the front step ran a gutter—there was no underground sewage system—and I would sit and watch bits of trash float by.

Our neighborhood was full of mango trees and coconut trees and bright tropical flowers, but there were no big, green, open spaces where you could draw a deep breath. It was the same inside our house: crowded, with no doors to close, no private bedrooms. We would bring out the mattresses every night at 10 and lay them all over the place.

We were a respectable family of the Brahmin caste, which values education and does not engage in manual labor—or, at least, that's what our parents kept telling us. "So why don't we have more money?" I wondered, but I didn't dare ask this out loud. When I got older I'd realize that, as a clerk in the courts, my father made only a modest salary. And the clincher? He had six daughters. That meant he'd have to pay for six big weddings and set aside money for six dowries. A dowry is money, property, or goods that a bride brings to her husband in marriage. Although the dowry was officially outlawed in India in the '60s, it has not been eliminated in practice.

As a kid, I didn't understand any of that. All I knew was that I was the only boy in a sea of sisters. The eldest still at home was Rajani, and she was the bossiest. She kept a close eye on my pranks, even dragging me through the streets to school when I tried to play hooky.

Veda, the second oldest, was gentler, and I adored her. She took care of me, but she didn't order me around the way Rajani did.

They both spoiled me because I was their only brother. During the Diwali festival, brothers give their sisters gifts, and in return the sisters do nice favors for their brothers. Rajani and Veda went all out. They would give me a bath and rub scented oils into my skin and make me special food and light candles to bless me. Even on ordinary days, they read to me or played games with me. Their games were too quiet, though, and they had to improvise, because we could not afford to buy games.

Usually they played board games, drawing the board on a slate stone in our back yard. They would throw dice made of beans, cut in half so there was a darker outside and a lighter inside. They'd fill their palms with eight of those half-beans, shake them, and throw them onto the ground. Then they'd count the number that fell with the light side face up, and that would be the number of places they could advance on the "board."

We boys played in the middle of the street, moving to make way every time a car or rickshaw came, and cheerfully slapping the cows that trudged by. We made up our games, too; nothing was ever bought from a store. We'd start with a round stone, then find an inner tube from an old bicycle tire and cut it into small rubber bands. Then we'd tie the bands around the stone, layer after layer, until it started bouncing. In one of our games, you had to make sure you didn't get hit by the bouncing ball, because that meant you were "out." In another, we stacked flat stones and then stood 20 feet away and threw the ball, trying to knock them down. Or we'd find a thick tree branch, shave it off, and make a cricket bat of it.

"It doesn't take much to make a game fun," I once informed little Veena. "You just have to be resourceful—and find a way to win."

In the monsoon season, sometimes it rained too hard for us to play outside. On those days, Veda and I used to make up little dramas. The theme was always that one of us was a rich person and the other was a poor person, and we showed how the rich person took care of his money, buying all sorts of things, and how the poor person was struggling.

I suspect that this was my idea; I've never found anyone who remembers playing that particular game. I know that Veda would always play the poor person and I'd play the rich person. There was never any doubt in my mind which I wanted to be. Our neighbors came to watch, and sometimes our cousins, and always Inni. No matter how silly we got, she would clap for us, laughing at our antics.

She wasn't the least bit surprised that I wanted to be the rich person. "You've wanted that since you were 4 years old," she laughed.

That was when we lived in Tilakwadi, right across the railroad tracks from the biggest, nicest bungalow in the village. It was owned by Mr. B. M. Gogte, who owned mines. Inni said that I used to stand near the tracks that divided us and stare at that house, just stare.

"You told me, 'Someday I am going to live in a house just like that one!'" she said, still laughing. Then she pulled me close, tousling my hair. "You know what, little Shri? I think someday you will!"

Inni was the strong one in our family. I think I always knew that. Everybody, even my father, turned to her for guidance. I can only remember a few times when he put his foot down to overrule her. On those rare occasions, she backed down immediately. But in everyday things, he nearly always let her decide.

Inni was the most confident person I'd ever known. She was never shy about anything. It didn't matter who she was with—rich or poor, normal or famous—she was always the same. Other kids' parents acted goofy when they were trying to impress somebody. Inni was just herself.

She was beautiful, too, with slender, fine features I had to sharpen my charcoal to draw. Her smile lit up the air. And she told great stories—she had one for every occasion, and she remembered everything exactly right: what colors the parrot's feathers were, how the giant's voice boomed. She even made the stories of our family life exciting. They were so vivid in my mind, years later I wouldn't know if I was remembering something as it happened or as she told it in her story!

You could feel a room change when Inni walked in; she lightened people's minds. I saw her sad only a few times and never for more than a few minutes. All of a sudden she'd stand very straight, brush her lap as though to whisk away the pity, and started taking care of the situation.

She was a born problem-solver. That's probably why, in the villages where we lived, Inni was always the one who helped arrange and fix marriages—and other kinds of relationships, too. When people came to her troubled, she'd invite them in, set aside her cooking or sweeping, shush us, and make the visitor a cup of tea. We'd pretend to play, but we'd be listening, and by the time the tea was sweetened the guest would be pouring out his or her heartache.

In the morning a mother-in-law might come, furious at slights made by her daughter-in-law. Inni would calm her and give advice in the form of a question.

"Your daughter-in-law is blunt, but she speaks well of you and she likes you. Why don't you try to understand her and see how things change?"

Then, in the afternoon, the daughter-in-law would come, hysterical about injustices perpetrated by her mother-in-law. Inni would listen sympathetically and say, "You're right. Older people might not understand what the new generation thinks. But look at it from your mother-in-law's point of view." At that, the daughter-in-law would start stirring her tea impatiently, but Inni would continue softly:

"She has witnessed a lot of ups and downs in her life while bringing up your husband, and now she feels she should be respected for that hard work. She always tells me a lot of good things about you—do you know that?" At that the stirring would stop, and the daughter-in-law would look up, startled.

"Remember one thing in life," Inni would finish. "Always appreciate good qualities and ignore the ones you don't like." Smiling, the daughter-in-law would thank her and leave with a light step.

My mother was not only a counselor but also a master negotiator.

Her skills came in handy when it was time to spend money. She did her shopping at the bazaar, walking up and down the dusty street. Farmers and their wives would sit on the steps with their vegetables spread out in front of them. Inni would walk through maybe half a mile of sellers, and I'd trot alongside her, carrying our cloth bags. Every third or fourth vendor, Inni would pause, finger something, and ask, "How much?" At the answer, she would look appalled and murmur something like "Oh my goodness!"

She would move on to the next vendor right away, to see what the going rate was. Then, in due time, she would go back, as though she were considering the purchase. She would hesitate, maybe weigh a plump mango in her palm or sift a handful of lentils. Then she would start walking away again … ever so slowly … until the seller called her back. She'd be offered a lower price.

I learned some useful lessons at that market. Inni made things happen her way. She never took no for an answer. Instead, she came up with strategies to get what her family needed. My father sat quietly and made his peace with whatever fate doled out, but Inni *managed* our lives.

I knew, even as a child, which approach I preferred.

Kaka had no vices. Never drank, never ate meat. His only indulgence was eating *paan*, and that was a very ceremonial thing: He would prepare a little pouch of two betel leaves, with betel nuts and spices and lime paste inside, and put it inside his mouth and gently chew on it. The lines on his face would smooth and his shoulders would drop from their usual slight hunch as he leaned back and gave a sigh of contentment. He did this once in the afternoon and once after dinner. He also drank tea, but only at teatime.

Slight, soft-spoken and gentle, Kaka was faithful to his routines. He had rituals that ordered his day and paced his daily life.

First thing every morning, he listened to the news on his beloved radio. Then he washed off the stones in our tiny back yard—which got terribly muddy in the rainy season—and drew water from the well. Chores done, he worshiped at the shrine he'd built in the back yard. On special holy days he would clean his statue of Lord Krishna, dress it in clothes, put flowers in front of it, circle it while holding a lighted lamp, and offer it a sweet.

I watched closely, because if he ever fell ill it would be my responsibility, as the oldest son, to do these things in his place. After he prayed, he would eat a little, go to work around 10 a.m. on his skinny black bicycle—which was a bit too tall for him and had nothing fancy except brakes— and come home around 5:30 p.m. He did this for 30 years.

As quiet and solitary as my mother was social, Kaka expected very little from life. His greatest pleasure was reading newspapers—in Marathi, Hindi, and English—and listening to the news on his radio. It was brown, with huge chrome knobs, eight screws, and rows of little lighted bulbs inside. Every week I watched him carefully undo each screw, remove the back, and clean each little bulb.

One day I decided to surprise him: I would clean his radio for him!

Rushing to finish before he got home from work, I turned the screws too hard and widened the little groove, making it harder to keep the screwdriver in place. After denting the back a bit—"He'll never notice," I lied to myself—I pried it off. Just a few scratches where the screwdriver slipped—again, he wouldn't notice. I started wiping the bulbs—and one shattered.

That he'd notice.

By the time Kaka came home, I was almost in tears, and there were bits of his precious radio all around me. At least it was Kaka, I thought. Inni would have raged, but Kaka was so gentle ...

He started yelling. "How dare you touch my radio?" he blazed. "What the *hell* did you think you were doing?"

Kaka never cussed.

I started stammering, trying to explain. He must have seen something in my reaction that touched him. All of a sudden his face softened, and he pulled me close. I kept my body stiff, not sure what to expect.

"I'm sorry, Shri," he said softly. "I know you were trying to help."

At that, I relaxed into his arms and started blubbering. "I'll never touch it again, Kaka!" I swore again and again.

And I never did. That was the one and only time my father ever yelled at me like that.

On the first of every month, when Kaka got paid, he and Inni would go out together. "Sulochana," he would call in a singsong way when he came home, using her married name. "Are you ready? Come, let's go out for a walk!"

She was always freshly bathed and wearing a new sari, with flowers in her hair. They'd walk together, and sometimes they'd stop to eat at a restaurant.

We'd wait up for them, of course, because on the way home they always stopped to buy some small treat for us. Nothing luxurious—maybe just a couple of apples we could cut up and share—but it always felt special. Sometimes they would even bring one of us with them on their "date," carefully rotating whose turn it was.

How Inni and Kaka met was a story I learned as I grew older.

Inni had come from a poor family in Kolhapur, a larger town in the state of Maharashtra. Her father was a Hindu priest—a freelance job whose benefits were mainly spiritual. He went from family to family, performing ritual ceremonies, and they paid him what they could.

46

Alas, of his eight children seven were daughters. He had no money to educate them, and he most definitely had no money to give them dowries. So when a village elder came to him and said, "There is a man looking for a wife, and he does not expect a dowry," Inni's father said yes instantly.

Kaka came to the home, and her family "showed" him Inni. That is literally the translation in Marathi: It was *dakavane,* the day to "show" the girl to the prospective groom.

Inni was 17; Kaka was 14 years older. His wife had died just two weeks earlier, and he was in mourning, his head completely shaved as is the custom for a mourning husband. But he was desperate to find a mother for his two daughters, ages 11 and 9. So as soon as the intermediary said it was okay, Kaka just showed up, without the usual elaborate prior arrangements, and said that he needed a bride.

If things had been done in the usual way, Inni would have been expected to make his family food, to show that she could cook. She would have to serve the food, to show that she could walk and serve with grace. She might be asked to sing or show some other talent. And then she would have to sit, rather awkwardly, on a chair far from the men, with her eyes on her feet. Eventually she would be released to join the women in another room. But even there she would not be allowed to talk much.

Kaka cut right through all that ritual. And Inni, who was already very practical, agreed without protest.

She knew that this was a good match for her family's sake, and she knew that her father had no money. But one day, when I was starting to become interested in girls, she confided in me that she hadn't fully understood the seriousness of what was happening. She said she'd been a bit of a tomboy, not yet interested in what happened to a woman when she married.

What *Inni* had wanted was to go to school, and, now that she was married, she would have no opportunity. Still, she was bolder than most girls of her day, not shy at all. She took charge of her new husband's life, and she even won over his daughters. That part wasn't easy; the younger girl was only seven years younger than Inni and very feisty. She did *not* want a new mother. But Inni held fast, and in time they grew close. In later years, when the second daughter fell ill, she came to live with Inni, who took tender care of her.

I didn't know my stepsisters very well; they were both married by the time I was five. The big sisters I grew up with were Rajani and Veda. Then came me, and then my two little sisters, Veena and Vandana. My little brother, Ravi, wasn't born until I was 10 years old.

By then I'd already been through my sacred thread ceremony, a Hindu boy's rite of passage.

"Nothing will be the same after this," my aunts and uncles told me, adding little comments about my "going away to learn about the Brahmin caste."

"Away where?" I asked, panicked. "What are you talking about?"

They wouldn't say anything more, just chuckled knowingly. I would run to ask Inni.

"You are 8 now, a big boy, and it is time for you to learn what is important," she'd say, adding that we would go to Narsinhwadi, and there would be a big party for me, and I would wear the sacred threads.

I didn't have the nerve to ask her whether I was being sent away forever. "Inni and Kaka would never do that to me," I told myself. But it seemed like they were hugging me closer, looking at me more thoughtfully. I was terrified.

"I don't want to go away," I finally blurted.

"Oh, but Narsinhwadi is a very beautiful place, a holy city," Inni said, misunderstanding. "Two of your aunts live there. And"—she drew me close—"it was in Narsinhwadi's big temple that I prayed to the god Datta for a son. He sent you to me! So now I want to thank him and honor him by bringing you to his temple for your thread ceremony."

Was I going to be some kind of sacrifice? What if Inni left me alone in the temple all night in the dark? Maybe Datta would not like the way I'd grown up and would vent his fury on me. What did gods do when they were angry?

Without saying why, I asked Inni what Datta was like.

"He came to show us the universality of religion," she said. "He is always shown with animals, like the Christians' St. Francis. He is very gentle, and I have always loved him specially."

Kaka, meanwhile, was preparing me for the ceremony. "When you wear the sacred thread," he said, "you are supposed to be pure in thought, word, and deed." I would go from being a little kid who was basically innocent—he didn't mention the way I'd torn his radio apart—to being an older boy with serious responsibilities in the adult world.

He showed me what I would wear for the ceremony, stretching a band across my forehead and tying it in back of my head so two strings of pearls dangled down, one above each eye. He said that my aunt's husband, who was a Hindu priest, would wrap a long thread (only one knot was allowed) around my body so that it fell from my left shoulder and crossed under my right arm. "The thread will be 96 times as wide as your four fingers," Kaka said, placing his hand across mine, "and each finger symbolizes a soul state." He picked my fingers up one by one as he ticked them off: "Waking, dreaming, dreamless sleep, and knowledge of the absolute."

None of this made much sense to me. I tried to focus on the fun part: a big party just for me! There would be gifts and wonderful things to eat—sweets made from chickpea flour or fried puffed dough. But every time I started to get excited, one of my relatives would say something that would shatter everything.

"You are going to be sent away from your parents." *What?*

They would say it very seriously, and then they would laugh with each other, and I couldn't figure out whether they were laughing because it

49

was a funny joke or because I didn't know what strange things fate had in store for me. The week before the ceremony, I lay awake every night for hours, trying to puzzle it out.

"It doesn't matter," I told myself. "Even if they do send me away, I'll be brave. I'm grown up now."

But as we drove the five hours to Narsinhwadi, I kept studying Inni's face, trying to make sure that she wasn't really going to send me away. "Maybe they're just scaring me to make me tough," I thought. I knew there was a point in the ceremony where I could eat only what was given to me; I had to beg for my food. The message was pretty obvious: It was time for me to learn to fend for myself.

On the day of the ceremony, my parents hired a *photowallah*, a photographer, to take my picture for the occasion. A photograph was rare and a really big deal. He told us that his camera needed strong light, and the only place he could take the picture was with me standing on the roof of my aunt's house.

I went with him reluctantly—maybe this was the part where somebody grabbed me and took me away!

My head had been shaved for the ceremony and I was wearing formal clothes, but my feet were bare, as they always were indoors. Yow! It wasn't exactly the hot tin roof of American movies, but it was hot clay tile, so the look on my face in my first photograph is of a squinty-eyed, wincing, desperately impatient sort of misery.

I got through the ceremony, and everybody came up to hug me, and there was party food and music, and I was still there!

Later I learned the story behind all that joking about sending me away. In ancient times, there were no schools. After his thread ceremony, a boy went off to a small hut in the hills to live with wise men, sages, until he was 18. He grew all his own food, and he learned about religion, work, and self-reliance. In my day, boys weren't sent away anymore—we had schools—but people still teased about it, and the hazing was its own rite of passage.

50

After the ceremony, I kept reminding myself of what Kaka had told me: "It is time to become independent and self-sufficient." I didn't have to leave home, thank God.

But something *had* changed. I was no longer a little kid. The rite of passage was over.

I started acting with maturity—or what I assumed maturity to be. I took on new household responsibilities and helped with the shopping. I was the first son, and I was now preparing for my role in the family.

The thread ceremony *should* have marked the beginning of my formal education, but I'd long since started school, because Inni had registered me as two years older than I really was! She did the same with my little sister.

"Grow up as fast as you can," she urged us, "and get educated as fast as you can." Inni had never even finished high school, and she was in a hurry to give us what she hadn't had. For me, the goal was to get a good job. My sisters had cooking and household wisdom drummed into their heads to prepare them for the day of showing.

Nobody seemed to notice how young we were, so we just did what the other kids did.

Then one day I came home and found our teacher, Mrs. Taskar, talking to Inni. She lowered her voice when I came inside. So of course I stood close to the front-room wall so I could hear what they said.

"Forgive me for asking such a personal question," Mrs. Taskar said, "but how can Shri be only a few months older than Veena?"

Inni's scheme was blown. She hadn't done the math.

Nobody changed our places, though; we were doing the work just fine. Our school was a great big abandoned house, which the villagers believed was infested with ghosts; others used the house to store grain for animal feed. We called it the Ghost's Castle, *Bhoot Wada*, but we weren't scared to go there; somehow we'd convinced ourselves that ghosts would never come out in daylight.

The classrooms were divided by low walls so the teacher could keep an eye on several classes at once. The work made my brain fall asleep: over and over, the same questions. I especially hated the way we had to do the same things every day at the same times, and I could never speak my mind, and nobody really cared about any of it.

I was never fond of structured regimens; I wanted grownups to trust me and give me a chance to show them what I could do. Besides, there were always bullies, and I was very thin and not very strong. I teased the bullies anyway, because I couldn't stand how mean they were. Then, when they came after me, I hid!

On days when I just didn't have the energy to deal with the bullies and recite for my teachers, I came up with a long line of excuses—splitting headaches and stomachaches, mainly—that got me out of school. Figuring out what to tell Inni once I got home was the hard part; she was a lot shrewder than any of my teachers.

One day when I was about 9, I got creative: I'd heard everyone discussing "Pandit Nehru's illness." I didn't know much about this Pandit Nehru fellow, except that he was a well-known personality and lived somewhere in Delhi. I entered the house with a gloomy face.

"Oh! What's the new story today?" Inni said. "What happened, Shri?"

Making my face look even sadder, I said very slowly, "Nehru is no more."

"Nehru died?" Inni screamed. "My God!"

The minute people heard her, the house was thrown into chaos. She ran to a neighbor's house—our neighbor must be a friend of Mr. Nehru, I thought. The neighbors told more neighbors, and my news spread like wildfire. Somebody switched on the radio, and somebody else went to find a phone to confirm the news.

People wept and wailed like this fellow was a god. "Our first prime minister!" they kept saying, making long lists of his virtues.

By evening, when they had found nothing to confirm Nehru's death, people began to grow suspicious that this was just a rumor. The neighbors who had gathered in the street dispersed, and Inni came back inside.

Without a word, she took hold of my ear and twisted it, hard. "You embarrassed me in front of my friends," she said, "and you lied." She was angrier than I'd ever seen her. "With this kind of behavior," she spat, "you just *might* become a dacoit!"

I was upset that I'd gotten caught, but I was also upset that I had disappointed Inni. She was always talking about honesty and respect, and I'd shown neither. I went out to the back yard and sat alone, ashamed that I'd let her down.

Then I came in and swept the kitchen and tried to make her tea, to show her I was sorry.

A few days later, Nehru really did die. The day was declared a national holiday, and all the schoolchildren went home.

I walked straight home, went inside, and set my slate down, but I didn't dare utter the words "Nehru is no more." Never again would I say that sentence—not even to explain why I was home from school.

I told Inni I had a stomachache and went and sat quietly in a corner.

Until fourth grade, all I had to write on was a black slate, framed in wood. I used a long piece of white chalk, which kept breaking, and the slate kept cracking. I'd wind up chalking my letters and numbers as small as I could make them on a jagged little piece of slate.

In the fifth grade I went to a city-owned school and, from there, to Chintamanrao High School. The other kids weren't very smart or ambitious; many of them were poor, and their parents didn't even read. So there I was, at the top of the class—and I don't care what that astrologer said, I was no genius!

I graduated in 1969, at the age of 14. I barely made a B grade on the statewide final exam, and my percentage was only 55, but it was one of the better scores from my school. I was thrilled—until I found out that my friends who went to expensive schools were graduating with 70 and 80 percent marks. The brief illusion that I was a clever student was wiped from my mind.

But that didn't erase my ambitions.

I read the *Tarun Bharat* newspaper every day, like my father. For years my mind had buzzed with letters to the editor. I was convinced that I could write as well as the adults who were getting published, and I loved the idea of seeing my name in print. So at the age of 11, I'd written my first letter to the editor. I knew that no one would take me seriously, so I carried the letter into the newspaper office early in the morning, before any of the reporters arrived, and put it on the editor's desk.

I repeated that process now and again for the next five years. Then, after graduating from high school, I decided to raise my game. I wrote a conservative op-ed piece about women's role—and signed my sister's married name! I wrote:

There is alarming increase in the number of women leaving their houses for the purpose of their jobs. Children are not brought up properly as a result of parent's negligence. If everyone decides to run after the money then, who will look after the children? If both father and mother cannot spare time for children then, how can they bring them up well?
Mrs. Vidya Vasant Kulkarni

The next morning, I opened the newspaper with my heart racing. They had printed my article!

Veda's in-laws were surprised and shocked by her article. As for Veda, she kept saying, "I didn't write it!" When I went to her house, she, my mother, and another sister were all chattering about it indignantly.

Inni only needed one look at the grin on my face and the newspaper in my hand.

"Shri!"

We had a good laugh, and the next day I wrote a response above my own name, criticizing the writer for being so old-fashioned. "It is surprising to know that a woman has stated views which are not only conventional but also detrimental to the freedom of women today," I wrote, and went on from there. I signed the piece "Shrinivas Thanedar."

They published my response, too, but I didn't dare to go to Veda's house and show her *that* edition.

For months afterward I continued to write articles—now under my own name—and leave them secretly on the editor's desk. I wrote about road conditions, politics, women's issues, anything else I had an opinion about. The editor printed maybe one in every 10.

Every time I saw my name in print, I felt the same thrill. I could do adult things; I could speak and be heard. With that knowledge, a new confidence grew in me.

My world was getting bigger, and so was the part I could play.

The year I graduated from high school was the year money started to matter.

The tidal wave of my sisters' marriages was about to hit—just when my father had to retire from his job. He'd been a court clerk for 30 years, and in India the mandatory retirement age from a government position was then 55. (It has since been raised.)

Because Kaka had a pension of only 20,000 rupees—and four daughters left to marry off—he started looking for a new job. Finally he found a private job with a moneylender. But he came home every night looking gloomy and distressed. He never spoke with an open heart, but we all knew something was bothering him.

We took turns questioning him, and finally the truth came out: The moneylender was cruel and filthy-mouthed, and he insulted Kaka constantly.

"Why do you tolerate him?" Inni asked angrily. "Leave that job! We will manage!"

I saw relief flash across my father's face. He asked several times whether she was sure, but it was only a courtesy; as we all knew, Inni never said anything she wasn't sure about! So he gladly deferred to her wisdom and quit the job.

Inni had promised him that she would manage, and so she did, even though we now didn't even have money for food. She searched all her brass storage pots and found some bran in the bottom, and she added spices and salt and boiled it into a hot *kanher*, or gruel, to fill our tummies.

As I sipped that gruel, it dawned on me that until I started earning money our family was going to suffer. As the oldest son, I was now my family's great hope—which is quite a sobering realization when you're 14.

Still, Inni had been subtly preparing me for this all my life, and I was looking forward to the responsibility. It made me feel serious and important, because I had a duty to my family, and they were looking to me to take care of them.

So that was my next challenge, and I started thinking about it non-stop.

Meanwhile, my father had decided to use his pension to buy us a house. We had lived in rental homes all our lives—that's what families of modest income did—so we were all very excited.

But I felt a jolt of fear: "Kaka, if you spend it all on a house, what will we do for income?"

Somehow, that problem had to be solved. Soon enough, I had a brainwave—a way to own our own house and solve our money problems at the same time. I leaned forward and grabbed my father's arm:

"Why don't we buy *two* small houses and rent one of them?"

To my amazement, Kaka listened closely while I explained my idea. He and Inni then started discussing the possibility, raising questions. Inni saw the logic of two small houses instantly, and she begged him to consider it.

Thrilled to be taken seriously, I started looking for *two* houses. Instead of doing the usual thing and consulting a real estate agent—who would then take a big chunk of money as commission—I asked all sorts of people, even strangers, for advice. I read the newspaper line by line. I walked all over town looking for sale signs.

Weeks went by, and I'd found nothing. Maybe this wasn't such a great idea after all. I played it down at home, saying I had a few lines on something but it might not amount to much. I didn't want Kaka to dismiss the idea entirely and throw all his money into one house—but I was no longer so sure I could find him a better option.

Once people did own a house, they never sold. The house stayed in their family for generations, because no one ever moved. It was almost a bad omen to sell your house, a blow to the family's pride.

Still, I kept asking, and one day I heard of a gentleman named Mr. Patil who had fallen into financial difficulties and could no longer afford to keep his two houses. They stood side by side on Mirapur Galli, a narrow lane in a town called Shahapur, not far from my old high school. Both houses were in terrible shape, their loosely tied bamboo roofs rotting.

On the roofs, the bamboo sticks were covered with slanting, hollow half-cylinders of black clay, to let the monsoon waters drain down. These pipes were supposed to be laid tightly together in overlapping layers. But often bunches of monkeys would come to town from the jungle and jump up and down on the roof, eating fruit, throwing the pits, chasing each other. Cracked or broken cylinders needed to be repaired regularly, and these roofs hadn't been fixed in years. I could see sunlight through the bare spots, and I knew that when it rained, it would rain indoors as well as out.

Still, the price was definitely right: We could have both of Mr. Patil's houses for 17,000 rupees total. Heading home to tell my father, I started to whoop with joy, but my fist stopped halfway into the air. We would be taking away a man's property, his respectability. Was that fair?

"Yes, because we will be helping him," I answered myself. "He needs the money more than he needs those houses." I raced home.

Kaka came right away to see the houses, but his brow soon furrowed. "They are in really bad shape, Shri," he murmured.

By then he had found a house that was really nice, and I could tell he wanted to go ahead and buy it.

"We will fix them!" I promised, and Inni joined in, helping me convince him. To my amazement, he agreed to the plan.

We paid 17,000 rupees and spent 2,000 rupees on repairs. I hired workers who would charge a very low amount, and I went to the market and bought the sand, cement, and paint myself, loading it onto Kaka's black bicycle in relays.

Soon the repairs were finished, and we moved into the nicer of the two houses. It was like a tiny toy train: its three rooms were lined up in a row, front to back, like train cars hooked together. The walls were thick, so it wasn't as noisy as our earlier homes, and it had an extra room. The toilet was outside, with no running water to flush it, but there was a tub inside, and a really big kitchen.

While we were doing the rehab work, I found piles of newspapers in the houses and sold them to the recyclers for money. Old newspapers are very valuable in India. Then I used the profit to buy the contents of a grocery store that was going out of business. Now we had bulk groceries to fill our larder, enough to last a year, with some left over to sell. We rented out the other house right away and collected money from the renters every month, just the way we used to pay.

My mother was thrilled. She'd been worried sick that Kaka would spend all our money on a house and she'd have nothing left to pay bills. From then on, whenever my father seemed hesitant about something she brought me into the conversation and asked for my opinion. Inni started confiding in me regularly, and I began to feel that I really was capable of being a provider for my family.

If both my parents trusted me with our family's shelter and finances, I *must* be almost grown up!

Soon it came time for Rajani, my bossy older sister, to marry. She was about five-foot-one, very pretty, and a little bit rebellious: She liked to listen to lyrics my mother didn't quite approve of, romantic songs in which a man expressed his love for a woman. My mother thought such music a little … cheap … for a daughter of hers to listen to, and they were still arguing as they prepared for Rajani's wedding.

The "showing" had begun. Unfortunately, we had shown her to two men already who hadn't chosen her, which is always a bad moment for a family. Each time, Rajani was a little sad and quiet for a week or so, and then she'd perk up. Her romantic dreams kept her hopeful.

Now a man was interested, and he was very handsome.

But there was a problem. He was in the navy, stationed far from our home, in southern India. We all worried about Rajani's going so far away. So from our family's perspective, he was not a desirable man for that reason, and he probably had difficulty finding a girl. On the other hand, Rajani was lovely and full of personality, but she wasn't a great catch, either. Our family didn't have money, and she didn't have much education. She'd gone to college for a year and hated every minute.

The man's family was brusque and formal, not warm at all. We talked about them every night at dinner: Would they like Rajani? Was her skin too dark? Should she be bubbly or quiet when they met her?

On the initial visit, the *dakavane*, the women brought food, and we men sat, talking a little stiffly. Rajani sat with us for a while, then left to rejoin the women. I watched the boy's father when she left, trying to read his expression.

In general, the girl's side is usually not that picky; very rarely do they say no. The boy's side has the upper hand. This made no sense to me, but I wasn't one to fight tradition. I just wanted to manipulate it a bit, to get what was best for my family. It was important that Rajani get married, and at the least cost possible. Kaka and I really wanted this boy for her.

After the initial meeting, the intermediary came to give us the other family's verdict. (The two families don't communicate directly at this stage.) We saw her coming and hurried to get ready; we were all a little nervous. By the time she left, we would either be glum or jubilant—which would it be? Was Rajani's fate decided?

Small talk, more small talk, endless small talk. My mother gave the intermediary a little snack and a cup of coffee. Finally, she smiled and gave the news.

"Yes, they liked Rajani."

This would allow us to go to the next stage: financial negotiations. This intermediary was kind of playing both sides. She said to us, "Oh, it's a good family, he is a nice guy, look how wealthy they are, they will treat your daughter well."

Inni nodded and said, "Fine," then started preparing the intermediary to lower the other family's expectations. "We have six girls, four still unwed," she pointed out, "and my husband is retired. But we will come and visit again with them."

The second visit was, as customary, at the man's house, on his family's turf. Before we went, Inni coolly assessed the situation and began to prep us. My father and I would be in the room with the other men, and she would have to go and sit with the women, away from the negotiations.

That is exactly what they would be: hardcore financial negotiations. The "yes" had already been said, but anything could throw a monkey wrench into the delicate money talk that would now begin.

"Don't tell them how much gold we have," Inni warned Kaka, who had a tendency to show his cards and might have blurted that we had 100 grams. She turned to me. "Make sure he says, 'With her older sister we only gave 20 grams.'"

"They will say, 'But we want our daughter-in-law to look good; she has to look worthy of our family,'" Inni predicted next. "A woman," she reminded us, "is judged by the gold she wears."

As for me, she said I had to be careful on our visit: I couldn't talk too much, because I was still just a kid, but I could whisper a comment to Kaka to jog his memory, and every once in a while it would be okay for me to make a comment. "I'll do my best," I promised.

The day came, and Kaka and I made it through the gold negotiations. I could almost feel Inni straining to overhear the conversation; the walls were just thin enough.

Next came the cash issue, and this was where it could all fall apart fast. We waited for them to bring up the subject, and, sure enough, the boy's father cut straight to the chase.

"We want 2,000 rupees," he said flatly.

I quickly calculated our expenses and nodded to Kaka. What they were asking was fair, and we could manage it. *Whew*. We all smiled and nodded and reached for our tea.

Next we would decide how we were to honor our new relatives. This would have its own costs. The negotiations always came in spurts, with pleasantries in between. First the gold, then the money, then the family obligations—gifts and showings of respect. To honor the groom's sisters, for example, we had to give each a nice sari. It could not be cheap, because it would be from the look of the saris that the guests would gauge how much we appreciated our new relatives.

They wanted a water cooler, too, as one of their gifts, which almost made me giggle. And then they said, "Oh, don't give us the boy's clothes; give us money for that and we'll take care of it."

As each item was agreed upon, a man from the village wrote it down to keep account. Through it all, food was being served. I found the entire process a little strange but quite enjoyable. I only hated the moments when we had to concede and give things we couldn't afford, just for Rajani to have the privilege of becoming this boy's wife.

That gender-based imbalance of power was engraved in everyone's mind, had been for centuries. By now it was a common habit, a necessary evil. We couldn't say no; that would leave Rajani husbandless. I thought it unfair: A boy and a girl should be equal and of equal worth to each other's families. Still, I told myself, this boy's family was not too demanding. It could have been much, much worse.

Next we had to plan the ceremony. How many guests? They said 80;

Kaka said 50; they met in the middle—well, almost the middle—at 70. What would the menu be? We suggested something simple, and they said, "No, no, no, the dessert at least has to be a little fancier than that."

When the last detail had been worked out, and we'd reached a million compromises both sides decided they could live with, the deal was sealed: My sister's fiancé called her to the room and presented her with a sari and a necklace. Rajani was supposed to go put on the sari and then come and greet everybody.

From that point, everybody relaxed, and the visit actually became fun. We all went home happy, Rajani chatting excitedly about how handsome her future husband was. She was nervous, I knew, about going so far from home. But she was also excited about her new life!

In the next few days, Inni continued schooling us for the first family wedding. I took responsibility for a lot of the etiquette, because I knew how much it mattered. The groom's side had certain expectations about how we would treat them, and if we failed I knew they would say, "Your side didn't respect us; you didn't even come and greet us when we came into the hall." And my sister would never be forgiven.

My father was pretty clueless about the social niceties; he usually left them to Inni. Still, in a wedding there were certain things only the man could do. If he was not waiting in the door when the groom's family arrived, to help carry their bags, for example, it would not show respect. I was really good at those little gestures; I knew that they were important for my sister's sake. So I made sure to do all kinds of chores to please the groom's family.

I also took charge of the wedding preparations and immediately went about saving money. I knew that if I could buy all the ingredients myself and hire the cooks, instead of hiring a caterer, it would be a lot cheaper. First I found the cooks, and then the head cook told me how much of everything to buy—25 coconuts, 6 kilos of sugar, and so on— and I wrote it all down. I rode on my bicycle to the market and bought all the freshest ingredients for them, making several trips to carry it all.

The day of the wedding, everything went smoothly—and, to my huge relief, the food was delicious!

Rajani, on the other hand, was a little sad and stressed. She took me aside and whispered, "Oh, Shri, I am so worried! What if I am not able to be a proper wife? What if I do everything all wrong?"

"What you don't know, you will learn," I promised her—as calmly as if I knew! She nodded slowly, not quite convinced.

Two days after the wedding, Inni sent me to Rajani's in-laws' house to check up on my sister and make sure all was well. I was eager to see her, to see how she was faring in her new life. I hoped that my advice had been right.

Her father welcomed me but seemed a little distant, as he'd been at the very start of our negotiations. When he offered me tea, I felt suddenly nervous.

"Is Rajani at home?"

"Yes," he said, and left the room. I waited for 10 minutes, then 20. After half an hour had passed, I was a wreck. I had expected Rajani to come running out to meet me and talk to me. Were they holding her captive? Had her new husband beaten her and left bruises? In an arranged marriage, you always have to worry that maybe there is something wrong with the family that you don't know about. Now there was no sign of her anywhere, her father-in-law had left, and nobody was speaking to me. I felt so alone and helpless that tears came to my eyes.

Just as I was about to lose control completely, Rajani's brother-in-law came in. "What happened to you?" he asked, seeing the look on my face. His tone was so light, it seemed almost mean. I just shook my head, not trusting my voice. He left the room and then, finally, Rajani came in, wiping her hair dry.

She was startled when she saw me crying. "Shri! What happened?"

"Why did you take so much time?" I fired back.

"I was having my bath," she explained. "But what's the reason for your crying?"

Now sulking, I admitted, "I thought you were being harassed and ill treated and that was why you came out late."

Rajani burst out laughing. She ruffled my hair and said fondly, "You are crazy." And those three words reminded me: I was still a child. I could negotiate business with grown men, but when it came to the rest of life, I was far from understanding its nuances.

After we paid all the bills for Rajani's wedding, we no longer had money for milk or sugar. I remember seeing the wealthy kids across the street, who lived in a fancy two-story bungalow and looked down their noses at me, go off all crisply dressed to their private school. *They* had milk and sugar for their *chai*. *Their* father, a sari merchant, didn't go around with his shoulders bent in worry. "I've got to get this family out of this situation," I kept telling myself.

Then came time for soft-hearted Veda to marry. *More* bills.

Veda, my favorite, was somewhat frail, light-skinned, and delicate looking, as though she'd snap if you bent her. Because she didn't look healthy and strong, she had much more difficulty than Rajani in finding a match. Nine or ten boys met her and said no, which was very stressful for all of us. I could see the emotional toll it took on Veda.

Each time, the intermediary would come and take a copy of Veda's horoscope. Then she would distribute that to maybe 15 different boys, and of that group maybe two would say that there could be a match.

It was like sending out 100 applications for a job, hoping to get an interview someplace.

Finally Inni and Kaka found a man who was considerably older than Veda. His family agreed to consider Veda, so Inni and I launched our usual strategy session. Kaka would have to go alone this time; the negotiations were to be only among the older men. Even Veda was not invited.

After Kaka left, our advice pelting him all the way down the road, Inni and I looked at each other. How would he do? He was so soft-hearted—would he cave in to every demand?

64

Hours later, he came home, his step heavy. This had been a much harder negotiation.

He said, "I agreed to 10,000 rupees and 60 grams of gold," and Inni gasped.

"Go tell them that we are not going to go through with it!" she burst. "You didn't negotiate well!" They argued until midnight. Kaka kept saying, "Look, this is what they asked for. I couldn't do any less. I had to give. It is important that she gets married." And Inni kept saying, "We still have two more daughters to marry! How could you give away all that we have?" What she thought we had saved for three weddings was now gone.

I listened to both of them, back and forth, over and over again. I glanced over at Veda. She was sitting in the corner, weeping quietly. She had already been turned down by so many boys.

When I couldn't stand it any longer, I stopped Inni. "Don't *worry* about the other two girls. I will be earning too, and they are still young. I'll take care of it. What Kaka did is right. This is the best for our sister. I don't want him to go back and tell them we are going to walk away from this deal."

I paused, but nobody said anything. "This is a happy event," I said. "Why are we all sad?"

Still no answer, from Inni *or* Kaka. "Look, nobody's looking at the main news," I said, figuring that I might as well keep going. "Veda's going to get married! We've been waiting for this for the last three years! The money is not important. If they want a little *more*, we could have given it to them. This event has to happen. It's one of the happiest moments for our family—let's *celebrate* it."

I hoped that would change their mood, but when Inni finally found her voice, it was to argue with me, too. "I don't even know when you'll get a job," she said. "You're only 16. He's spent everything—"

I said, in a tone so firm it surprised even me, "Kaka did a great job. Kaka, don't feel bad about what you did." Then I told Inni, "This was the hardest wedding, and you have taken care of it. The other two, I will take care of."

Maybe she was just exhausted, but she gave me a small smile and then a nod. With that, the mood lifted and we all began to smile a bit, even Veda, who started speculating happily about what her new life as a married woman would be like.

After Veda's wedding, we had to pawn the rest of our gold for money. We had lost our security, and there were many bills to pay. The money collector would come on a bicycle; we could see him coming from afar as we stood on the front steps of the house.

Just seeing my father's eyes as he watched that guy pedal closer and closer made my heart hurt. The shame of the family was beginning to get to me, and the only thing I could do was go to college, graduate as soon as possible—just as Inni had always urged!—and get a good job.

But what?

Kaka wanted to sell his last investment, the house next door, and send me to the prestigious medical school in Belgaum. I knew that Inni liked the idea, too; she had, ever since she showed me the school when I was a little boy. And they had a point: Becoming a doctor would have promised me a very successful life, and money would have ceased to be an issue for any of us.

But I couldn't bring myself to take Kaka's nest egg. Besides, it would only pay tuition, not my living expenses and not my family's expenses.

"You've never had a burning drive to be a physician anyway," I told myself as I went back and forth between my parents' plans and my doubts. "What you want is to succeed, simple as that. So go do something you're good at."

I'd always been good at chemistry. That's it! I made my decision without further thought.

I chose Govindram Seksaria Science College, a school in Belgaum well known for chemistry and physics. Now the only trick was that I would have to study hard. Even in the chemical industry the job market was very competitive, and I would need to get top marks.

I did my best—I thought—but I finished my first year only third-class (C-minus), with marks of 45 percent. At the end of the second year my grades had not improved much.

I would have to earn better than 60 percent in the next two years if I wanted to graduate first class, with honors.

But how could I concentrate on my studies in our crowded little train house? We had so many people in our family and Inni's friends coming in and out all the time. I knew what I needed: a quiet place with no distractions. This was my new problem, and I had to find a way to solve it.

As was my habit, I thought about my problem nonstop; instead of studying, I kept thinking about how to find a place to study. One day, as I puzzled it over, I found it right before my eyes.

I was in our high-ceilinged kitchen, thinking hard and glanced up at the mezzanine. It was about 12 feet high, so you had to have a ladder to get up there, and it was cobwebbed and being used for storage, so it was full of junk—broken chairs and other stray objects we didn't have the heart to throw away. But the space was about 6 feet by 8: plenty of room for a desk and bookshelves.

I took a simple ladder—two bamboo sticks, with holes for rungs—and climbed up there. I took everything out of that space and then hoisted a bucket of water and rags up there and started cleaning.

At first it made me dizzy to be so high, because it was open to the kitchen below, with no railing. But as I polished the skylight—a windowpane in the roof where the bamboo had been cut away—everything started to sparkle. I felt almost giddy with joy. I made myself a little bed on the floor with old rugs and clothes, and a desk from wood I'd found, and I was set.

I read and studied up in my garret for hours, with no one to bother me. The place was mine and mine alone, and it gave me my first sense of freedom, solitude, and independence. Sitting up in my aerie, I felt like a king.

At the end of that year, I earned a mark of 62 percent on the exam. The following year, I would earn 70 percent.

Problem solved.

My college years were going fine. I majored in chemistry and minored in physics, both of which came easily to me. Luckily, after the first two years my grades in literature and poetry—which did *not* come as easily—no longer counted toward my final results.

But my family was still struggling. Our tenants never paid their rent on time, and the rent money wasn't much anyway. Inni pawned her gold jewelry and rationed milk: Only the youngest child in the house could drink milk. At Diwali, the neighbors were out in the streets celebrating, sharing the sweet treats they had prepared. We stayed inside, because we had no money for sweets and nothing to share. I could hear the fireworks as I fell asleep, and it seemed very lonely to have nothing.

"This is no way to live," I told myself. "We are so careful, never spendthrift, yet there is never enough coming in to let us really enjoy our lives. That has to change—and it's up to me to change it."

That night, as the Diwali firecrackers faded into the night, I resolved to find a job. I told neither Inni nor Kaka, because I knew that they would try to stop me. Kaka hadn't sold his plot of land outright, but he'd mortgaged it to pay my college tuition. He did not want me to work; he kept saying, "Your job right now is only to study."

Surreptitiously I asked people I could trust whether they'd heard of any job openings. Eventually someone told me that the boy assisting Dr. Apte, a dentist in Belgaum, had left his job. I went to his clinic and asked very casually, "Where is that boy who used to work with you?"

"It is very sad," Dr. Apte replied. "Nowadays I find it difficult to get good people to work."

This was the opening I was waiting for. "Can I work as your assistant?" I asked.

He looked astonished. "Really? Would you be willing to do that?"

"Yes, certainly," I assured him. "I have lots of spare time after my college courses end each day. This will help me use my time and also collect some money for tuition."

He explained the nature of the work and said, "I will pay 200 rupees a month." That was 200 rupees more than my family had, I figured, so I accepted.

I showed up for work the next day. Soon I was down on my hands and knees with a bucket of soapy water and a rag—there were no mops in those days—cleaning spatters from his clinic floor. I knew I couldn't miss a single spot, or he would notice.

There was a lot of blood, which made me a little woozy, especially when I had to sterilize his instruments in boiling water. Otherwise, though the work was quite manageable. When Dr. Apte arrived, I carried his bag upstairs to his office—the clinic was in a two-story building with a steep staircase—then helped him while he was treating patients. Afterward I cleaned the table and his instruments so everything was ready before the next appointment.

Dr. Apte was in his mid-thirties and very handsome; he had very light skin, which in India is considered a sign of beauty. One day I found a stack of love letters in his office: an affair he either had finished or was in the middle of. While he was busy filling cavities, I read a few of those letters, struck by the difference between their torrid passion and the businesslike negotiations we had conducted for my sisters' marriages.

I was curious about Dr. Apte's life, but we were not on equal terms. I was merely a worker, and he was a doctor. Our conversations were limited to "Hey, come here and take care of this" or "Don't set it there" or "How come you didn't…?" I couldn't talk back to him, of course; all I could say was, "Yes, sir" or "Sorry, sir" or "Right away, sir."

So there was no real talk; it was just "I'm paying you—get this done." And he did pay my salary in cash faithfully, even though his practice wasn't exactly lucrative. Dr. Apte was a good dentist, but people in Belgaum still looked at going to a dentist as something optional, almost a luxury. If you were missing a tooth, you were missing a tooth—so what?

My parents would have been horrified at what I was doing, because it was not "work fit for a Brahmin." In their minds, I was to be studying now, acquiring knowledge for a professional job, not scrubbing floors and washing dental tools.

Personally, I couldn't have cared less about such silly rules. But I knew better than to be open about my job. Every time I worked, I told my family I was going to a friend's house to study.

In the first weeks, my heart pounded every time I left home for the clinic. But when time passed, and the job became familiar, and I hadn't been caught, I relaxed a little.

Then one of Inni's friends showed up at Dr. Apte's clinic to have her teeth cleaned.

When I peeped through the door and saw her, I bolted. I came back two hours later to find Dr. Apte furious and ready to fire me. Ashamed, I confessed that I didn't want my family to know about my job and explained how important it was for me to earn money for them.

To my surprise, Dr. Apte turned instantly sympathetic. For the next three years he conspired with me to keep my job a secret. His attitude toward me also loosened up considerably; he was a lot nicer. He wouldn't say it in so many words, but I could tell that he respected what I was trying to do.

Part of every paycheck from Dr. Apte I used for household expenses, but Inni never knew. She would give me a few rupees to buy groceries, and I would add more money from my pocket. She marveled at my knack for finding bargains.

I held a little money back, though, for myself. In the evenings I would go out with a group of friends. Often we'd walk to the temple outside of town, just to get away from everything familiar and claustrophobic. We'd joke around, talk about life. Occasionally we'd smoke cigarettes and drink beer or eat meat, all activities forbidden for a Brahmin, which made me feel very daring, because my parents would certainly be upset if they found out. I was beginning to rebel, quietly, against my parents' countless rules.

The three biggest rules, which Inni repeated almost daily, were not to eat meat, not to smoke, and not to see movies. Now I was doing all three— and enjoying them! I kept waiting to feel unclean or guilty, but nothing happened. I felt a tiny bit disloyal. But, more than anything, I felt free.

I graduated with distinction, my degree a bachelor's of science in chemistry. I'd started school in a ghosts' castle, and at age 18, I'd finished college in the top 5 percent of my class.

That was the first time I really felt sure I was not destined merely to be ordinary and to live a humdrum life. "I could do something really important," I told myself.

Getting that first-class award had given me a fresh burst of confidence, something very different from the solid, practical resourcefulness I'd felt doing things for my family. Now I was being measured by the outside world's standards, and I'd proved that I really did have some ability.

I wasn't about to settle for an ordinary future.

But what was my next step? I had no elaborate career plans. I just wanted a job. That was easier said than done, though; the economy was lousy, and no science jobs were opening up. So, in the fall of 1973, I began working on a master's degree in inorganic chemistry at Dharwad University, which was about 50 miles south from Belgaum.

This would be my first experience living away from home, away from the reassuring bustle of my family's common life.

I dug out my suitcase, a boxy light-blue case with black bands and chrome hardware.

The suitcase had been a gift from Rajani's in-laws, my reward for slogging through all those wedding preparations. I grinned, remembering how, during the ceremony, my official role had been to take the groom's ear and twist it, saying, in essence, "You'd better take care of my sister."

It was at that point that he had turned around and handed me the little blue suitcase. I'd thanked Rajani's in-laws, privately sure that I'd never have need of a suitcase, and tucked it away on the mezzanine.

Now I dusted it off and started packing it with my belongings. I felt that I had to pack everything I wanted and liked into that suitcase.

Little did I know that over the years that little blue suitcase would become the repository for everything that was precious to me, that it would become my trusted companion, and that I would grow attached to it as I traveled over land and sea to places near and far.

I took the bus to Dharwad, and I settled in pretty well there. I was just a tiny bit homesick, but I enjoyed being someplace new. There was just one problem: The classes bored me to tears.

Many days, I sneaked away and took up small jobs to help my family. I wasn't worried about the consequences, because I'd already hatched a strategy. After a few weeks of sitting through those monotone lectures, I'd thought to myself, "Well, I could do this all semester like everybody else, read every chapter, go over all the notes, and memorize as much as possible, or ... I could use my head."

I did a little research on past tests. First I requested the previous 10 years of exams and scanned them for patterns, looking to see when certain topics rose or fell in importance and, using the results of that analysis, jotted down notes about what this year's questions might cover.

My classmates did not use any strategy at all. They just studied everything. But I ignored big chunks and focused on certain topics. I was pretty sure, for example, that the exams would have a heavy emphasis on certain kinds of organic reactions, or questions on chemical kinetics.

When I got the exam, the questions were almost exactly what I expected. Everything I had anticipated showed up. My analysis was perfect, and I aced the fall exams.

That February, I received word that a cashier's job had opened up at the State Bank in Vijapur. My family needed the money, so I could not turn down the opportunity. I went to the head of my department, Dr. Nataraj, and said, "Sir, I have to go to Vijapur."

"What about your studies?"

"I will miss only my labs, but I will make it up later," I assured him. "I will definitely appear at the final examination."

He looked at me for a long moment, then shook his head. "I cannot allow you to sit for examination if you take a break."

As is customary in traditional Indian culture, I had been taught to respect all teachers as though they are gods. I used to touch their feet in respect when we met on the road; I used to bow down to take their blessings. But this was ridiculous! "He might be godlike," I told myself, "but he can't see how serious I am."

So I went around him.

I met with the dean of the college, Dr. Badami, and begged him to let me sit for the examination. "I have to help my family," I told him. "Please just let me take the break to work at the bank. I will bear the responsibility of the results."

He hesitated, then grudgingly consented.

I tore back to my room and jammed all my textbooks and notebooks into my blue suitcase, glad that I didn't have many clothes. Another bus ride, another new experience.

I was afraid that working in a bank might be as boring as sitting through those chemistry lectures, but I loved my new job. Vijapur was still a small town then, and people came to know and respect me as the cashier of the State Bank. I loved the responsibility and the thrill of counting out hundreds of thousands of rupees, even when it was not my own money.

As for my salary, it felt like a king's ransom. My family only needed about 200 rupees to survive, and I was getting 450 rupees. I could rent a little place for myself and buy gifts for my family every time I visited them.

Suddenly things were really good for my family. By earning money, I had solved their immediate problems. For the next three months, I savored that feeling.

And then, with a cold clutch of fear, I remembered: my master's degree!

It was May already. I had only a few weeks to study and get back to Dharwad for the final examination. I went to my boss at the bank.

"Sir, I want leave for 15 days to appear for my examination."

"Thanedar, you have not even been here six months. How can I grant you 15 days' leave? I can't do that."

Again I dove in, explaining and arguing, trying to persuade him, but he would not relent. Four more days had passed. I had only eight days before the exams.

I told my manager I was leaving anyway, to take my exams.

"You may lose your job," he called after me. But I felt I had no choice. I rushed to the college hostel at Dharwad, where my friend Divakar gave me his notes to study. I had eight days to absorb an entire semester that I'd missed.

I locked myself in the hostel room and slept only one hour at a time, instructing my friends to wake me at the end of that hour no matter what it took. Several times it took buckets of water, which they thoroughly enjoyed dumping over my head. I read as much as I could, then picked one important topic for each exam and focused hard on that topic. I was guessing they'd ask a lot about metal complexes that are used as catalysts. So I mastered that first.

I was taking a huge risk; I could study maybe only 40 or 50 percent of the material. I could have just glanced over all of the study material, but instead I picked and chose the topics I thought were important and mastered them.

On the seventh day of studying, I received a letter in the mail from the bank. My position had been terminated.

I should have expected this, but the news still hit me hard, because I badly needed my salary. I sat on the side of my hard cot, stunned, rereading the letter. Then I gave myself a little shake, just the way Inni used to do. I had no time to worry about this.

I went back to my books.

On the eighth day, I was barely aware that it was exam day. I took my notes in my hand and walked the mile and a half to the exam hall in a daze, reading with one eye on the traffic.

I passed my first-year exams with a first-class and distinction.

Afterward, I went home to Belgaum.

Inni was proud of my exam results, but she wasn't happy at what I'd done. "How could you lose that bank job?" she asked. "People are dying for those jobs, and you got one, and you gave it *away*?"

At first I shrugged off her words, but as the days went by and I was no longer getting a salary, our financial problems crept back. Inni and I went back and forth about what was more important: playing it safe or thinking long-term. Of course, we each had a different definition of long-term. I admitted that I hadn't thought that my manager would be so aggressive, but what was done was done. She sighed and shook her head, exasperated that I wasn't taking this seriously enough.

Deep down, I really was starting to wonder whether I'd done the right thing. I tried to be nonchalant and show her how confident I was about my—our—future. I'd applied to several research centers; surely one would need a chemist …

Two more weeks went by. One morning Inni was saying for the hundredth time, as she sorted through the post, what a mistake it had been to jeopardize my job at the bank. Then she glanced down, and I saw her expression change. Wordlessly, she handed me the envelope. Return address: Bhabha Atomic Research Centre in Bombay, now renamed Mumbai. I quickly slit it open, then handed it to Inni, grinning.

They wanted me to come for an interview for a position as a scientific assistant.

If I got the job, my salary would be 800 rupees—almost *twice* my salary at the bank. *Now* what did Inni have to say?

She read the letter slowly, let out a long breath—then went back to arguing. "This is good that you got that letter, but it's in Bombay!" she exclaimed. "We don't know anybody in Bombay!"

I threw up my hands. "Stop *worrying*," I told her. "I will be all right."

"But why do you want to go so far from home?"

"Inni, I'm a scientist," I said, with a young man's grandeur. "I can't just work at a bank for the rest of my life. I need to explore, try different things." Her face was set; nothing I said was making any difference.

I wondered whether I really did have the courage to leave home, if it meant my parents' disapproval. Would they soften in time? Would our relationships change for the worse? Would they ever forgive me?

To my relief, Kaka came to my aid. "My dear, try to understand the situation from his point of view," he told Inni. "Whatever decision he has taken must have been with proper deliberation. We must support him happily for the sake of his future." She pressed her lips together and said no more.

I couldn't show Inni how much I wanted to go to Mumbai, because I didn't want to hurt her feelings. But deep down I was terribly excited. Mumbai was one of the biggest cities in the world. It was a far cry from the tiny villages around Belgaum where I'd spent my childhood. It seemed like a very natural next step in my journey.

The BARC interview would be fiercely competitive: For every position, they were interviewing about six people, and they wouldn't be asking softball questions like "What are your long-term career goals?" No, they would ask technical questions, and I had better be ready. I laundered my best clothes, trying to look as professional as I could. On the train to Mumbai, I studied everything I could find on radiochemistry.

I got off at the Victoria Terminus, the famed central train station in Mumbai, my head swimming with neutrons and atomic particles, and found myself trapped in a crowd of people, everyone pushing in a different direction. I stood still for a minute, panicked by the crowd and wishing that I, too, knew which way I was going.

Finally I'd had enough of being jostled. I shoved my way to a ticket window and tried to ask the best way to get to BARC. I had a job interview, I explained, thinking that the guy would take pity on me and help me figure out a route.

Instead, he said, "Make up your mind. I can't sit here and talk to you all day." A line was forming behind me, and people were starting to mutter.

I went back to look at the route maps again. Eventually I figured out that I didn't need another train after all; I needed three buses. I found the closest bus stop and waited, memorizing the name of the first bus I needed and checking each bus that arrived, my heart pounding.

Finally my bus came, almost an hour late. When I climbed on, I asked again, to be sure, and the driver said I needed to go in the opposite direction, so I should have been waiting on the other side of the street. I was already late, and now I wasn't even on the right bus yet?

I was furious with myself. My one big chance, and I was going to lose it because I'd waited for the wrong *bus*? I scrambled down the steep bus steps and sprang to the ground. I was moving so fast, I didn't expect the ground to sink when I landed. I lost my balance and fell into the wet monsoon mud.

I got up, the legs of my white pants coated in mud, and shook it off as best I could. I clenched my teeth, resolved that by God I'd at least make it to the blasted interview, even if it was only to get laughed out of the room.

When I arrived—seven minutes late and looking like a half-drowned muskrat—I was rushed into my interview. Across the table were eight scientists. Their style, I realized later, was to ask scientific questions until you couldn't answer any more, then ask easy questions.

"What's your favorite subject?" one of them asked me.

"Radiochemistry," I said instinctively, and their faces lit up.

I cursed myself.

That was *their* subject; they knew it better than anyone. Radiochemistry was one of the subjects I had chosen not to study for my exams, but I had crammed on the train because I expected them to ask about it, and now I'd gone and guaranteed it.

I sat there like an unarmed soldier while eight captains of radiochemistry fired questions at me. Why hadn't I said polymers, which really was my favorite subject, and to heck with what they wanted?

I did my best to answer every question—although later I couldn't remember anything I'd said. Exhausted, I got back on the bus, and by the time I was on the train for Belgaum I was thoroughly depressed and half asleep.

Days and then weeks went by, with no word from BARC. About a month after the interview, I received a letter. Despite my mud splatters, despite my nervous babblings about radiochemistry, I had been appointed to a position as a scientific assistant in the health physics department. I would be responsible for keeping workers safe from radioactive exposure.

I packed my blue suitcase for Mumbai.

CHAPTER 3

Mumbai

BELGAUM WAS A SMALL town, and everybody around me seemed content to just live from day to day, eating, gossiping, doing things in the same leisurely way they'd always done them. Not me. I burned with energy. I wanted to experience more, move faster, *get* somewhere.

Well, now I had. Here I was in Mumbai, surrounded by 14 million strangers, all in a rush. I felt as slow and hesitant as a grandmother. I'd dreamed of seeing big-city skyscrapers, but Mumbai's sidewalks were so jammed with people, I didn't dare look up. And crossing the street! Cars whizzed by without a break, and the tall, red double-decker buses spewed foul blue smoke, and the drivers of the black-and-yellow taxis honked at anybody who dared cut in front of them.

I felt a little dizzy.

How would I find my way around here? I'd already tried asking a few people for directions, but they'd turned away, not even bothering to answer. Hordes of people hurried past me, like whitewater rushing around a big rock. They all knew where they were going. They weren't about to stop for a minute and listen to a stranger.

I looked down. My familiar old clothes and sandals looked awkward and out of place to me. And my blue suitcase clearly identified me as an out-of-towner. My Marathi language sounded strange, too—all I heard around me was Hindi and, every once in a while, a bit of English. Twice

I stumbled around, trying to use a few Hindi phrases to ask a question, and both times the person looked right through me as if I didn't even exist.

That would never have happened back in Belgaum.

I realized with a jolt that I had come to a place where I could not count on people to be kind.

A huge lump of fear filled my stomach, taking away even the hunger. Where in God's name was I going to sleep tonight? I saw beggars everywhere, weaving in and out of the well-dressed crowd. Would I become one of them? I was already starving, and I hadn't even seen a street vendor yet. Didn't these people *eat?*

I walked around Mumbai for hours, feeling overwhelmed and wondering whether I should turn around and just go home. Life moved fast here, and I could get swindled or stolen from at any second. I had heard that there were pickpockets on every street in Mumbai, even kids with little razors who would slice your pocket with one hand, grab your wallet in the other, and disappear into the crowd before you felt anything.

The sun was starting to set, and I still had no place to sleep. I sat down on some steps to think. If I had to, I could find a dark alley, roll up my extra shirt as a pillow, sleep with my suitcase under my arm so nobody stole it ... I shuddered, thinking of what Inni would say. I stood up again and started walking briskly—where, I still wasn't sure, but I was determined to find a place to stay.

Finally I found a room—well, one-fourth of a room—at a cheap hostel called the Krishna Lodge. I locked all my possessions inside my blue suitcase and fell into a deep sleep, twisting with nightmares. I woke up groggy. It was barely dawn, and one of my new roommates was chanting his prayers at the top of his voice. I groaned and fell back to sleep.

Soon I was able to move to a room on the BARC campus, in the suburb of Trombay. A family who lived in a one-bedroom apartment sublet the bedroom to me and another BARC worker for extra cash. It was cramped but easy on my wallet—and a definite step up from the hostel.

It was fun to work at BARC, because everybody I met in Mumbai had heard of it—it was, after all, India's main nuclear research facility, and it was in the news all the time. My job wasn't hard at all. I tested different types of radiation from the reactors to make sure the researchers and the guys who did maintenance on the reactors weren't getting overexposed.

By my second week in Mumbai, I felt comfortable with my daily routine, and I started to look around the city a little more calmly.

That Saturday, I went exploring. First I found a roadside newsstand with five or six Marathi newspapers, five more in English, and one in Gujarati. Kaka would have been thrilled! I bought a couple of papers and tucked them under my arm. Then I found a cheap restaurant, which, I discovered, I really liked. I started eating there whenever I could, and soon the owner was greeting me by name.

On my evenings and weekends, I came upon one thing after another that I wanted to experience—movies, restaurants, shops, plays, concerts, museums, even the zoo. But to make time to do it all, I had to move quickly. I'd wondered, when I first arrived in Mumbai, where everybody was going; what could possibly be that urgent? Now I knew. Soon I found myself scurrying around like everyone else, hopping from trains to metros, eating on the run, going hungrily to see experimental theater and listen to concerts.

After a month of this, I had mastered Mumbai. I could now get around faster than people who'd lived in the city their whole lives. I knew exactly what routes to take and how to time them, so I could cram as much fun and culture into my day as possible. Back in Belgaum, we had four movie theaters, total. Movies came there two years after they opened in Mumbai. Now, all I had to do was walk a few blocks and I'd find a theater, with new releases every Friday. I saw Bollywood films I never would have dared to watch at home, films that exposed more of a woman's body than I'd ever seen. Kissing wasn't allowed, of course, but there were plenty of curvy bodies in tight-fitting dresses and wet saris to catch my breath.

In Belgaum, a movie with an actress wearing a two-piece swimsuit was enough to make my mother gasp. We were to see only decent movies with good morals—and not too many of those! Drinking alcohol was just as bad; it meant that you were wild and decadent and headed for trouble. The goal was to lead a pure life.

And here I was, watching risqué movies, chugging beer, smoking cigarettes and eating meat! Back in college, beer hadn't even tasted that good and smoke had made me cough. I'd tried it all in college, with my friends, but, to be honest, it was only thrilling because it was forbidden.

Now I began to actually enjoy the strong tastes. My parents would have been mortified—but, because they weren't there to see me, it almost felt like it didn't count. As someone once said, what they didn't know wouldn't hurt them. No guilty feelings ruined my fun.

Because my job at BARC was stable and paid a good salary, I could send money home and still have enough left over for my new pleasures. For a few months, I was supremely content.

And then I got bored. I'd learned my job backward and forward, but I kept thinking, "What's out there that I *haven't* learned? What can I do that will get me more money or make my life better?"

It was the same old restlessness: I'd mastered a challenge, and now I needed a new one.

And then it hit me: finishing my master's degree. I'd done well in the first year of the master's program at Dharwad, and that meant I was already halfway through. Receiving my graduate degree in chemistry from the University of Mumbai—one of the largest universities in the world, established in 1857—would look great on my résumé. That was it!

I immediately called the admissions office on the Kalina campus and explained my background. I was excited at the prospect of completing my master's in one year. But they gave me bad news: None of my work in Dharwad would count! I would have to appear for my first-year examinations all over again in Mumbai before I could go on.

I hung up the phone and sat there for a minute. That test I'd crammed for with such panic? Eight days with water splashed on my head and text swimming before my eyes, for *nothing*? I took a deep breath. "Okay, fine," I said out loud. "I did it once. I'll just do it again."

I'd wanted another challenge, and now I had one.

The next step was to fill out the paperwork, and, because I was working for the government, I needed permission from the head of my department. That would be Mr. Soman. Surely he would admire my ambition. I was glad I'd have a chance to finally talk with him for more than two minutes.

But the next morning, when Narayan, a friend at BARC, heard me chattering about my plans, he looked worried. "Don't even try," Narayan warned me. "Mr. Soman is very rude. He will only insult you—and if he is unhappy with you, you are doomed."

The other guys in the department joined in, saying I should stay off Mr. Soman's radar entirely.

I did a double-take: "But how will I get my master's?"

"Don't upset him, not while you're in this department," Narayan repeated. "Make sure he doesn't even know you *exist*. If you piss off Mr. Soman, you'll never get anywhere in BARC."

I'd seen Mr. Soman scolding other workers, so I knew that they had a point. He was as rigid as a steel beam, and he definitely liked showing who was boss. Everyone was intimidated by him.

But I felt that I had an advantage: He was a Maharashtrian, like me. So I brushed off the warnings and made an appointment. When the time came, I knocked on his heavy door, first lightly, and then with more conviction. "May I come in?" I called, speaking in Marathi.

He said yes, very curtly, in English. I walked in and looked around at a huge room filled with mahogany furniture. Mr. Soman wasn't even wearing a jacket, just a short-sleeved shirt, untucked. He didn't acknowledge me, just kept working on his papers, studying the fine print through little reading glasses. I stayed quiet, waiting for him to make eye contact. Finally he snapped, still not looking up, "What do you want?"

"I want to complete my master's degree in chemistry," I answered in our native tongue.

"What?" he said impatiently, still speaking in English. "Don't you have a job? Don't you have to work? Don't you have a salary?"

Yes, I said, three times. I told him I wanted to work night shifts and go to classes during the day.

"And how are you going to do justice to *this* job?" he asked. Then he set aside his papers and rose slowly from his chair.

The scourge of BARC was a small man, no more than five-foot-two! I stifled a nervous laugh. I'm not very tall, and I had at least three inches on him.

"I have no wife or children," I said firmly. "I can work nights. I won't let my work here suffer. In fact, my learning will be good for the company."

I waited. I was hoping he'd soften.

"I cannot approve it," he said with finality, "and if I do not approve it, it cannot happen."

I left Mr. Soman's office without another word. In the hallway, I ran into Narayan and blurted out everything Mr. Soman had said.

"He will remember this, and now you will never get anywhere in this company," Narayan warned me.

"Okay," I said, shrugging. The shock had worn off.

"So what are you going to do, Shri?" he asked, sensing a change in me.

"I'm going to do it anyway."

And I did.

I wasn't angry at Mr. Soman. He was all puffed up with his own authority, and he was convinced that he was just doing his job. But I couldn't let him stop me from doing what I wanted. Getting my master's degree was the right thing to do, I was sure of it. I had my path all mapped out, and Mr. Soman was like a jagged boulder blocking my way. He represented "the system." And so what if the system didn't approve my path?

Oddly enough, Mr. Soman's rigidity had only strengthened my resolve.

I proceeded to execute my plan. I needed to trade shifts with someone who worked nights—that way, no one could complain. I had plenty of married friends who wanted their nights free, so I had no problem trading shifts. I enrolled at the University of Mumbai.

My daily routine became hectic. In the morning, when my shift ended, I'd ride the BARC bus to my living quarters, take a quick shower, change clothes, nap for an hour if I had time. Then I'd take the 352 bus from Trombay to Sion. It was always crowded, so I had to stand the entire 20 minutes, holding onto the straps overhead and swaying. At Sion I got off and speed-walked 10 minutes to the subway station. I needed the Central train, which left from a platform on the far side of the station, and I'd hear it coming as I clattered down the long subway stairs.

Every time, it was a toss-up: Would I get there in time? I'd run alongside the train and hop on. When it slowed down at my station, I'd jump out before it screeched to a stop. I had to make sure that I got out already running, so I learned how to balance and land without falling. Everything had to be done perfectly, you see, or I would have had to wait 10 minutes for the next train, and then I'd have been late. If I was late for class, I'd have to make up the class. I had no time to make up the class. My grade would fall. I might even get kicked out of the program.

All these things ran through my head as I raced for that train every day. I nearly always made it. The Central train took me to Dadar, which was a huge terminal with trains coming and going all the time. There, I'd run up 50 stairs and across the bridge over the tracks and down again to catch the Western train to Jogeshwari. Then I had another 10-minute walk or, in monsoon season, a covered rickshaw ride to my college. All morning, I worked in the lab. Afternoons, I attended lectures all over the city. Then I squeezed in sleep, dinner, and often a movie or a play before reporting for work at 11 p.m.

Amidst all this craziness, a really wonderful thing happened: I met Naushil Mehta. And he opened up a whole new world for me.

We were in a chemistry class together, but we couldn't have been more different. I was five-foot-five, with dark skin and a little beard; he was six-foot-two, very fair and handsome. Naushil smoked fancy British-made Dunhill International cigarettes and drank imported Scotch. He went everywhere by taxi and ate at the restaurants in five-star hotels. I didn't even know which fork to use first at a nice restaurant, and I'd never been *inside* a five-star hotel. Yet somehow—I still don't understand it—we became good friends. We'd play fierce games of chess, not speaking for hours, or drink beer and make fun of melodramatic, overacted Hindi movie musicals.

Naushil read Nietzsche, Jean-Paul Sartre, and Sigmund Freud for fun. A true artist, he was only studying chemistry to please his parents. Until I met him, I'd never read any English literature at all, and the only plays I'd seen were *sangeet natak*, the Marathi musical dramas. Bollywood had already started to feel a little silly to me, its love stories utterly predictable. It was great fun to mock them with Naushil. But then he started taking me to see independent art films from all over the world. *One Flew Over the Cuckoo's Nest, Equus,* all the films of Fellini and Ingmar Bergman. Each film surprised me in some way, made me think about something differently. Afterward, I couldn't wait to talk about it.

Naushil was writing and directing a play, so I went to the rehearsals, too, and hung out with the actors. One day I met Naushil's friend Prabodh Parikh, who'd lived in America and was now a philosophy professor at Mithibai College in Mumbai. When Naushil took me to Prabodh's home, I walked in and stopped short. Every inch of every wall was covered with books, and the few empty spots held paintings. "Prabodh did that," Naushil whispered as he pointed to a painting, "and that one, and that one …" That night, after we left, he told me that Prabodh's paintings fell somewhere between Surrealism and Abstract Expressionism. All I knew was that the shapes sometimes suggested the human body, but not always. Sometimes they just danced. And the colors were so intense, they shone.

Modern art had always seemed meaningless to me. Now I looked and listened intently as Prabodh said things like, "The painting doesn't have just one meaning. Here's what I read into this particular painting ..." He opened my eyes and broadened my mind. Soon I was reading everything I could find about modern art, existential literature, and philosophy. I had trouble understanding English poetry, so Prabodh would read it to me, and from his tone of voice I could get a sense of the rhythm and the emotion. He read Samuel Beckett's plays out loud, too, and he introduced me to American jazz and blues, as well as classical Indian music.

I even struggled through Nietzsche, just because it was such a treat to be exposed to all these new ideas. But the books that hit me clear and hard were Ayn Rand's *The Fountainhead* and *Atlas Shrugged*. She wrote about the wonders of the free market, and I think that's when the seed of capitalism first took root in me. Rand's philosophy was individualism— you against the world—which was exactly how I'd always felt. Nobody around me talked that way; everything was collective in India, and there were certain norms that everybody followed without question. Now I could finally admit to myself that I didn't conform to all the values and rules in my own culture. More to the point, I didn't *want* to. Rand's fictional architect, Howard Roark, had taught me that it was okay to be different, to have your own ideas about how to live and not to compromise your ideals or vision.

Suddenly the world seemed much bigger—but also closer, more immediate. Life was full of possibilities, and nearly all of them were open to me. I felt like somebody had sliced through a tangle of knots, and my mind was moving freely for the first time.

Thinking had more power than I'd realized.

I finished my master's degree with a first-class distinction and won a gold medal.

It was time to seek a promotion at BARC. Once more, I knocked on Mr. Soman's door. This time, I felt confident. I'd accomplished my goal; surely now he would relax and smile. Maybe he'd offer me the raise right away. Maybe he'd tell me I could have a new job title, and I would have to prove myself for a few months.

Or maybe he'd throw me out.

With Mr. Soman, anything was possible. Palms damp, I knocked. "Come," he snapped, and I gently pushed the door open and entered his office.

Once more, he pretended to be busy with files and ignored my presence. I gave up on the Marathi-speaking tactic this time. In English, I announced that I now had my master's degree.

He looked up. He was furious. "This is a government service!" he said. "You need to obey orders! You cannot do things without authorization! Your master's was not authorized!"

"But I already have it," I pointed out.

"Why are you coming to tell me this? What do you want?" His voice had risen a bit.

"Sir, I have not neglected my work," I said defiantly. "I studied on my own time, and I took honors, and now I'd like you to consider me for either a raise or a promotion."

"I cannot consider it!" he thundered. "No promotion for you!"

Speechless, I mumbled, "Thank you"—I'm not sure for what—and left the office. His words kept ringing in my ears: *No promotion for you!*

I was truly frustrated. I had worked hard, and I had hoped against hope that Mr. Soman would change his mind now that I already had my degree. My work hadn't suffered! Why couldn't he be a little more human? All I was asking for was a well-deserved promotion, or at least a small raise.

I tried every angle, even going to other departments at BARC to see whether I could transfer into a better position. But I could do nothing without Mr. Soman's permission, because he was the head of my department. Now I really *was* stuck. I wanted to get my PhD, and that meant I needed a better job so I could afford the tuition.

I could start over again at another company—but the thought exhausted me.

Then I had it! What if I went abroad? The minute the idea flashed into my head, it felt like fate. I knew instantly where I would go: the United States.

All my life, the words "United States" meant freedom, hope, and success. Every Indian I knew felt the same way. I didn't know anyone who'd ever actually gone to the US, but now I'd read Ayn Rand—that was encouragement enough. In the US, I could get the education I wanted and make the money my family needed without having to fight my way through a million suffocating rules, traditions, customs, and conventions.

I was feeling less and less comfortable in my own culture because everyone wanted me to play it safe. I wanted to be in a place where talent and skill were what mattered, not obeying bureaucrats. In Mumbai, I would always be one of the anonymous millions. In the US, I could succeed or fail by my *own* efforts, not wait for somebody in authority to approve of me. Hard work and courage would count, not caste or inheritance, bribery or connections. There I would succeed, I was sure of it. And then I could *really* help my family.

I called Naushil and told him my idea.

"That's brilliant, Shri! You've gotta do it!" he said, and he was so enthusiastic, I had a brainstorm.

"Naushil, you have to come with me! Think what fun it would be! Think of all the adventures we could have in America!"

Relieved at the idea of going with a friend, I worked hard to convince him.

He wouldn't budge. He was happy in Mumbai, in his own world of art, theater, and literature. Still, he didn't say no outright. I asked at regular intervals, and every time he just said, "We'll see."

I went straight to the United States Information Agency office and collected the address of every university with a doctoral program in chemistry.

My enthusiasm must have been contagious, because Naushil joined me in writing to as many American universities as possible. It was a lot of paperwork to prepare meticulously, but we were on a mission and sent off a whole bunch of these applications.

Soon big fat envelopes started arriving by air mail from admissions offices. I'd tear open the envelope and find not a scholarship but instead an invitation to a PhD program, along with brochures and course catalogs and other forms. That was very nice, thank you very much, but I had no money! And even though Naushil came from a wealthy family, he wanted to pay his own way. We could not afford US tuition without scholarships.

Finally the University of Akron—a world leader in polymer research—offered us both teaching assistantships, beginning in autumn. "Polymers," I told Naushil, gloating. "That is *the* thing to research. Plastics are the new high-performance materials—scientists are finding all sorts of new uses for them!" I sounded like Mr. Robinson from *The Graduate*, giving Dustin Hoffman's character advice on his future!

Naushil couldn't have cared less. "Do they have theater in Akron?" he asked.

"Yes, yes, they have theater," I told him, although I didn't have a clue. "This is great! Now all we have to do is get our passports."

I got us both passport applications and started to fill mine out right away. Almost immediately, I hit a stumbling block: They needed a birth certificate, and I didn't have one. Small hospitals in India don't automatically provide you with tidy legal records. I would have to go back to the tiny town where I was born and look through all of the birth records until I found mine.

This I did. At the end of a long, hot day locked in a suffocating records office, going through box after box after box, I found the piece of paper some doctor had signed the day I was born. I left with a copy, which then had to be certified by a government officer. Next I had to prove my residence and document that my parents were my parents, all on special stamped paper. Then there were the notarizations to get—and pay for.

Little by little, I worked through everything they needed. Then I reached a blank in the form that I hadn't noticed before. I read it twice, and my hand started to shake.

I was still a government employee, so I needed the signature of my employer.

Mr. Soman.

When the shock wore off, I figured out why: In those days, there was a fear that government servants might take secrets to foreign countries. Relations were already tense between India and Pakistan, and I'd had access to all sorts of information about India's nuclear reactors.

I knew why they needed his signature. But what I didn't know was how Mr. Soman would respond. The last two times I had asked something of him, he had flatly denied my requests. Yet I had no choice but to try—I *wanted* to go to America!

I braved his office the next morning. "Sir," I began, "I have a scholarship for a PhD from an American university. I need your signature on the passport application."

"But who told you to apply?" he asked sternly, and for the next 10 minutes he berated me for being "an irresponsible brat."

"Look at you!" he said. "You look like a drug addict! Unkempt, untidy, disorderly, and clumsy." My beard hadn't been trimmed in months, and I rarely combed my hair with any thoroughness. Hanging out with Naushil's theater crowd, I'd begun to wear jeans and ragged T-shirts, looking rough almost as a badge of pride.

Mr. Soman continued to scold me. I think he would have gone on all day. But at the first break in his tirade I gave it one more try, begging him: "Sir, please! I won't get the passport if you don't sign!"

He turned his head away, but I could see that he was still watching me out of the corner of his eye.

"I will give you the signature on one condition."

"Yes?" I leaned forward.

"You must resign from your position immediately."

My shoulders slumped. My salary was helping support my family, not just me. Inni's face flashed into my mind, then Kaka's tired eyes. Veena's eager smile. Little Ravi tugging at my sleeve for a story. If I had no job, I would be letting them all down.

I stood up, ready to walk out.

Then I hesitated. What choice did I really have? I certainly couldn't approach Mr. Soman about getting a PhD in India!

"Fine," I said quietly. "I'll resign."

Determined not to show any hesitation, I reached for a piece of paper and quickly scribbled my letter of resignation, and signed it. I handed it to Mr. Soman.

Now it was Mr. Soman who had no choice. He signed the application, and handed it to me. I rushed out of his office feeling like a hero who just won an epic battle.

I hurried home and sent off the passport application immediately. I was worried sick—what would I do for money?—but elated, too. I called Naushil.

"Now we just get a visa and *go*," I told him. "It's that simple."

Or, at least, that's what I thought.

We'd have to hurry and get the visas. It was already August, and the autumn term began in September. So far, we'd told no one of our plans. Now I had to go to Belgaum and break the news to my family.

Granted, nothing they said was going to stop me. Once again, I knew I was doing the right thing. I wasn't going there to ask for permission. Still, my news would hit them hard, and I had to soften it somehow. I was their biggest support (and they were mine). Somehow

I had to make them comfortable with the idea of my leaving the country.

I wasn't entirely comfortable with it myself, even though I was determined to go. What if someone in my family got sick or was injured? What if we changed so much, we could no longer talk easily, filling in the gaps in each other's sentences? I stopped myself right there. My job was to calm my family, not think wild, panicky thoughts. I considered everything I would say very carefully, even planning the order in which I would make various points. I rehearsed the whole thing in my head numerous times.

Then I showed up at their door in Belgaum without announcing my visit.

My sisters raced to hug me; Inni kissed my forehead; Kaka was beaming; Ravi wanted to hear stories of Mumbai. I gulped, forgot all of the points I'd carefully rehearsed, and blurted it out.

"I'm going to America."

The room went dead quiet. Then Inni burst into tears. "Why do you want to go to the USA and leave the golden opportunity you grabbed in Mumbai? What's the *reason*?"

I talked fast and hard, explaining my line of thinking. Kaka listened carefully. Then he turned to my mother.

"Let him go, Inni," he said gently. "How can we object to this?"

In the end, it was Kaka who persuaded her to agree. When she heard the uncharacteristic firmness in his voice—and saw the determination in my eyes—she gave in gracefully and consented. Then she got all practical on me: I'd need warm clothes; I'd need snacks for the trip to the airport…

My family visit ended with tears—in my eyes as well as Inni's. But she smiled at me as she wiped her face. "I have always known you would be a genius!" she teased, and hugged me again.

By the time I arrived back in Mumbai, all our friends had heard the news: "Thanedar and Mehta are going to America." They threw so many send-off parties, I almost forgot the big move that was drawing closer. Naushil and I couldn't completely relax, though—we still needed money for the airfare. We started applying for student loans.

Luckily, I won two interest-free loans of 10,000 rupees each. At the time, the exchange rate was 10 rupees to the dollar. I started calculating furiously: Airfare was about 10,000 rupees, and my salary would be about $300 a month. That meant one of the 10,000 rupees loan was surplus and I could repay it from America quickly, and then begin sending some money home each month.

I blew the extra money on expenses and parties. By the time I got my passport, we had only eight days left in India if we wanted to arrive at the university in time for the first day of classes.

All that remained was the formality of stamping the visa on our passports.

By 6 a.m. the next morning, we were standing in line at the American consulate—in a clammy, humid rainstorm—to get the necessary forms. I hadn't slept at all the night before; I was too excited. We filed through the security check and then, one by one, we were called into the room where the interviews were being conducted.

Our interrogator was a white American woman, middle-aged, with blondish-gray hair that was pulled back tightly and tied at the base of her neck. She wore glasses and a navy blue suit and seemed very businesslike. I squinted, trying not to be obvious, and read the name on the laminated badge that was tucked into her jacket pocket: Virginia.

About 10 minutes later, Miss Virginia called my name. I drew a deep breath, stood up and went to sit in the chair across from her desk. I couldn't understand a lot of the questions she asked me because of her accent. But one I could definitely understand, because she asked it over and over again: "Why would you want to come back to India?"

The American government was very worried that people would enter the US on a student visa and then apply to change it to permanent residency and bring over their entire families. So Miss Virginia wanted cast-iron assurance that I was only going to America to study and would return to India the second my studies were done.

I explained that I was the oldest son, and I fully intended to come back to take care of my parents, sisters and brother, as that was my responsibility.

Miss Virginia looked me up and down. I folded my hands tighter and sat very still.

She asked again, "What is the guarantee that you will come back?"

"I have a nonimmigrant visa," I said. "I will come back as soon as I complete my education."

I smiled at her, hoping she could read the sincerity in my face. I really did intend to come home to my family; I just wanted my PhD and, along with it, the chance to work and make money—which Mr. Soman refused to let me do.

She stared back at me for a long time. She was seeing, I'm sure, my lack of money and sophistication. She knew what awaited me across the ocean.

Finally she glanced down at the forms and said briskly, "I'm not convinced that you will come back. I'm going to deny your visa."

I was so stunned, I collapsed. Completely lost consciousness, fell down right there on Miss Virginia's floor.

When I woke up, she had called staff members to bring me a pillow and water. She was kind enough to help me stand up, but she had not changed her mind. No visa.

I walked out, my face an ashen brown, and found Naushil in the corridor. I gave him the terrible news.

"Even mine was rejected," he said with a shrug. "We were sailing in the same boat, and now, we are sinking in the same boat!" He burst out laughing and patted my shoulder. "Let's forget it. Come on, cheer up, we'll go home."

I followed him slowly, unable to let go of my dream so easily. For a few days, I sank into a muddle. I had resigned from my BARC job already.

Now what was I going to do? Work in some little company in Belgaum for the rest of my life, never able to really help my family? The thought devastated me.

Once again, I had hit a wall. But after a few days of moping around, I felt my usual energy flood back. "It's just a part of life," I told myself. "I will try again."

I thought long and hard about the question Miss Virginia had asked: *What's the guarantee you will come back?* She wanted a logical answer, something definite and convincing. I could appreciate that; I liked logical answers myself. So I contacted several people who had been to America and asked them how I could allay her doubts.

"You need evidence that your financial position is good," one man told me. "If you can show a fat bank balance or immovable property as your asset, perhaps you will be granted your visa."

A "fat bank balance" was out of the question because I was always broke. But my father did have a small plot of land at Digraj, in the Sangli district. I collected all the papers, met the land surveyor there, got a letter from him and an affidavit from my parents, and I took them back to the American consulate. This time all I could do was push my stack of papers through the window.

"Come back at 4 p.m., and we will tell you what happened," the clerk said. So I wandered around town, drank some tea, paced the sidewalk outside the consulate. Would the property documents satisfy her of my intention to come back? Was there something else I could have done to convince her?

At 4 o'clock sharp, I was at the window. They handed me my papers, and right there on the top sheet was Miss Virginia's signature, under the words "Evidence not sufficient. Rejected."

I was disappointed again, and I asked around again for advice on what else I could do. "If you have a letter saying you will have a job when you return, maybe that will help," another friend said.

Back I went, knocking on Mr. Soman's door. I needed him to give me a letter saying BARC would hire me back when I returned with my PhD "Sir, we have a particular rule in our office," I began, telling him about the provision of reemploying someone who has left if a vacancy is created.

"So what?"

"Sir, can you give me a letter stating that BARC would provide me a job when I complete my PhD and return to India?"

For a minute he was speechless. Then he burst, "You are impossible! Are you trying to tell me the rules of my office? I will not give you any such letter. You may go now."

I gave up on Mr. Soman – but not on getting a letter. I managed to get one from a friend who owned a chemical company. I was delighted; this time it would be a sure-shot approval. We had already missed the fall semester, but we could make it in time for the spring semester.

I was lighthearted as I went again to the American consulate. I handed my papers in through the window, went back out and wandered around and returned at 4 o'clock sharp.

Same answer: "Evidence not sufficient. Rejected"

Miss Virginia and I were now at war—and I needed high-powered ammunition. I decided to call Dr. Farona, the department head at the University of Akron, and tell him we were having trouble getting our visas and ask if he could intervene and perhaps put some pressure on Miss Virginia.

Making an international call was not an easy task at the time. In fact, it was a bit of an ordeal.

Naushil and I had to go to Mumbai's central post office, a large place where they had a little area for all long-distance calls. First you had to book the call and pay the deposit. Then the operator tried to schedule the call, and it could take four to five hours before the connection was made. You had to wait nearby—close enough to dive into the phone booth when the call came—or else you would miss the call!

97

We arrived at the post office around 8 p.m. because of the nearly 10-hour time difference. Around midnight our connection came through, and we rushed into a little phone booth to talk. Dr. Farona's accent was difficult to understand, and he couldn't make out what I was saying, either. We had only paid for three minutes, so I thrust the phone at Naushil, who was a little better in English. Several other calls were waiting, and people were lined up behind us. We talked faster and faster, which only made us harder to understand, and on top of that, we were talking in what we thought was an American accent!

Somehow, Dr. Farona figured out what we were trying to say, and he promised to help. Whew!

He immediately sent a very nice letter about me and Naushil, saying how smart we were and that we had been offered scholarships and teaching assistantships and the university had been terribly inconvenienced by the delay, and asking that our visas be expedited. I waved the letter triumphantly at Naushil, laid it carefully on top of the application pile, and carried the whole stack with me the next morning. Naushil went with me at 4 o'clock to hear the happy news. This time, we were damn sure we wouldn't be rejected.

But we were: "Evidence not sufficient. Rejected."

For Naushil, that was the last straw. "Shri, I will not apply again. You leave me alone. I neither want a visa nor do I want to go to America, so let's forget it!"

I wondered whether I, too, should make my peace with staying in Mumbai. Maybe going to America was not for me.

Over the next month, my life began to fall apart. I had lost my government job at BARC and I'd used up all my loan money, sending some of it home to help with my sister's wedding. I couldn't bring myself to tell my family I no longer had a job, so I quickly found part-time work tutoring students for their college entrance examinations. But I was broke. I had a bag of rice in my room, some salt, some *ghee* (clarified butter), and a little kerosene stove to cook it on. That's all I ate in the morning, and that's all I ate at night.

One Thursday morning I woke with the sick memory that I'd finished up all the rice and *ghee* the night before. That evening, I had nothing to eat. But at least my tutoring job paid on Friday.

Unfortunately, when I went to tutor the kid that day, I found out that his mother was out of town until Monday, so no payment for me. My luck had run out. Now I had no money even to take the bus home, let alone eat. I sat down at the bus stop anyway, wondering what to do.

A few minutes later, two guys my age came up and said, "Hey, how are you, where've you been?" Not wanting to admit I didn't remember them, I said, "Oh, I'm fine, I've just been busy."

"Come with us and have rice and curry," one said, and his friend hailed a taxi. Mesmerized by the thought of curry, I followed them.

"What's in this bag?" the first guy asked. "It looks heavy."

"Oh, it has books in it," I said.

We all climbed into the taxi. I was still trying to make small talk—and figure out how I knew them—when they told the taxi to stop. We got out in a very dark lane. "Come," the first guy said, gesturing behind a building. In a flash, I realized he had his hand on my briefcase handle, and the other guy was shoving his finger inside my cheap gold watch-band.

"Help!" I shouted, and luckily, a handful of students came running toward us. The two guys jerked away from me and took off. My books spilled out on the road, and my watch fell to the ground, its big round face cracking.

So there I was, in the middle of the road, on my hands and knees, my possessions all around me. I gathered up all my precious books, put my broken watch in my pocket and started walking, thinking that I was not only broke and hungry but stupid.

Then I saw a guy selling *pav bhaji* on the street corner. He would soak very soft bread in butter and grill it until the outside was crispy and dice an assortment of vegetables he was waiting to season and cook to each customer's taste.

"Could I have just a little bit?" I asked him, seeing that he already had some made. "I have no money, but I will pay you on Monday."

"Just eat as much as you want," he said warmly, and I spooned out a huge bowlful, grabbed for a piece of the crisp, buttery bread, and sank down on the curb to eat it. It was delicious!

That Monday, when I got paid, I brought him ten times as much money as the meal cost.

In those days I was living in a room with four other people, my same blue suitcase stashed under my bed. Inside it was the stack of papers I'd been bringing to Miss Virginia. I kept sliding out my suitcase and rifling through that stack, not really even looking at the pages, but waiting for something to jump out at me. I often thought that I should simply throw those papers out and be done with it. But somehow such an action would mean a defeat, and I couldn't get myself to do it.

One day I pulled out my blue suitcase, looked through the papers and decided that I just had to give it one last try. I couldn't give up yet, the way Naushil had. He had his art world in India. For me, the US was the best hope.

I gathered up my stack of papers—I didn't have a single new document to attach—and went back to the familiar window at the American consulate, determined to try my luck with Miss Virginia one more time.

"Come back at 4 o'clock and we will let you know," the clerk said, in a singsong I could have imitated down to the last inflection. I came back, as I had done before, at 4 o'clock sharp, braced for the familiar cover sheet with the word "Rejected" above Miss Virginia's signature.

"Ah, yes, Thanedar," the clerk said. "Hand me your passport."

I stared at him. Then I saw his outstretched hand and came back to my senses. "I didn't bring it," I said.

"If you don't give me your passport, how can I give you a visa?" he asked me, exasperated.

"Does this mean Miss Virginia approved my visa?"

"No, Miss Virginia is on vacation in the United States. Her assistant, Mr. Johnson, approved it."

I raced home, picked up my passport, raced back, and got it stamped. Then I called Naushil. "Great news! I got my visa!"

He thought I was bluffing. "How come?"

"Miss Virginia has gone to America, and Mr. Johnson, who is working in her place, is convinced that both Mr. Thanedar and Mr. Mehta should go to America."

"Are you joking with me?"

"I swear I am not! You'd better hurry up and put in a fresh application tomorrow morning, before Miss Virginia gets back!"

By now it was January, and the second semester had already started. Naushil got his visa the next day, and we went to buy our plane tickets to America. They cost 8,000 rupees apiece. I packed my suitcase and arranged a quick trip home to say goodbye to my family.

But first there was one other person I had to see.

Mr. Soman.

I didn't even bother cleaning up. I walked in with my beard scraggly, wearing an old shirt. He looked at me and frowned as usual.

"You are 24," he said, as though it was news to me. "You don't carry yourself well, and you don't follow procedures." Mr. Soman was a stickler for systems, and was always conscious of the obligations of his position. For me, life was simpler: Yes, I was 24, but I knew exactly what I wanted to do.

"I got my visa," I announced. "I'm going to America."

Then I braced myself.

"Oh, good!" he said.

I waited, wondering if this was sarcasm.

"You must come to dinner," he said, and there was warmth in his voice.

Huh? I was dazed. "Sure, I'll try," I said.

"No, you must come. Tonight."

And so I did. I showered and put on my best clothes, all the while dreading the things he might say when I was trapped inside his home. Why did he want me to come for dinner? But I couldn't have refused. I argued like this inside my head, back and forth, all the way to his house. I had no idea what to expect that evening and I was a little nervous, to say the least.

I knocked on the door of Mr. Soman's house more softly than I'd ever knocked on his office door. His wife opened it with a big smile and invited me inside, and Mr. Soman rushed into the room and shook my hand.

They showed me around—he had a very lovely, simple home—and then Mrs. Soman urged us to sit down for dinner. She had prepared *shrikhand-puri*, fried wheat flatbread with a dessert made with yogurt, cream, sugar, almonds, and cardamoms. It's a special meal you make if you want to treat someone with the best of the best. I ate it with relish and started to relax. We chatted freely, and I found I was enjoying myself.

Toward the end of the evening, as I was thanking Mrs. Soman for the wonderful meal, Mr. Soman rose and left the room. He returned with a beautifully wrapped gold pen set.

"My best wishes to you for a successful career," he said formally.

I touched his feet and thanked him.

What a surprise the world could be.

Once we'd gotten our visas, everything had happened so fast. I'd had only 24 hours back home with my family—which was okay, because that was as long as I could stand to hear Inni weeping. No one in my family had any concept of what my going to America would mean. I sure thought I did. They all squeezed into our living room, and Inni brought food, and everyone talked at once, full of dire warnings and practical advice and maudlin reminiscences.

"I'm not dying," I reminded them a little sharply. "I'm just going to the States for a few years." I kept waiting for them to be happy for me, proud of me. That would have helped me feel less nervous.

"But what if we never see you again?" Veena wailed. Finally I had to face the truth: They had no idea what was coming next or how to feel about it, and they couldn't fake happiness for my sake. All they knew was that I was the oldest boy, they'd relied on me to take care of them, and now I was leaving to go far, far away.

"Don't you think I know that?" I wanted to yell, even though nobody was actually putting these feelings into words. I knew, we all knew, that ultimately this would be the best way I could take care of them. Just a small portion of my pay as teaching assistant would be enough to support my entire family. Still, if they had a problem, or my dad got sick, I couldn't be there overnight.

Nothing would be the same, ever again.

It was an awkward 24 hours for all of us. The next morning, the rickshaw came to take me to the airport. I stepped outside, carrying my blue suitcase, and every member of my family pressed after me and stood on the front steps of our home, right at the edge of the road. One step out, and I'd be in the road.

A thought came into my mind: "It will not be easy for me to just come back here."

Nor would it be easy to stay in touch—trips home were unthinkable on my stipend, and making phone calls would be difficult, because my parents didn't own a phone. The whole way to the airport, my brain raced with situations that might come up, ways I could find to get in touch or get back home.

When I got to Mumbai, Naushil was in a very different mood, much happier. For his family, travel was an adventure, and they had been celebrating his great triumph. When it was time for the two of us to fly out of the country, they came to the Mumbai airport to see him off, which left me feeling even lonelier.

Once we were seated on the plane, I cried for a few minutes, feeling about 5 years old and very much alone.

After an hour or so—and several Indian beers and snacks—I started to feel distinctly different. All through my life I'd carried this sense of obligation like a heavy river stone, lugging it everywhere with me, setting it down only for the briefest times—an extra glass of wine, a trip to the theater—before hoisting it up again. Now it was as though I could float straight up out of my seat, with no weight to hold me in place.

The feeling was so real, I wrapped my fingers around my seat belt to make sure I stayed put. Anything could happen now. I leaned my head against the cool, thick glass of the airplane window and watched fluffy clouds below us. My past was slipping away as the plane flew west into the future.

CHAPTER 4

The Wedding Knot

HERE I WAS, after five years in the US, heading back home—and excited as hell. The journey from Ann Arbor to New York and then all the way to Mumbai was exhausting, and yet I was wide awake. I arrived at the Mumbai airport with a light heart—and heavy suitcases. My trusted blue suitcase was still with me, swelled up with gifts from the land of plenty. I had bought lipsticks and jewelry for my sister, light sweaters for Kaka and my little brother, expensive gold and pearl earrings for Inni, crayons and Barbie dolls for all my young cousins, chocolates and other candies. I was truly happy to be coming home again.

It didn't feel like home, though. To be honest, it felt like arriving in a foreign country. People were hustling me in the airport, and outside, the beggars rushed up to me. I'd grown used to strangers smiling and nodding but respecting my space and privacy. In India, people either ignored you or crowded you.

I was feeling very American, grown-up and a bit of a stranger. Then I heard Rajani call, "There he is!" and my entire family rushed over. They were all dressed up, and they threw garlands of flowers over me and then crushed the flowers with their embraces.

I hugged them all hard, solemnly shook the hand of my little brother, who was now a young man I didn't even recognize. I caught sight of Inni staring with a small frown at my American T-shirt and jeans, and I threw my arm around her and squeezed her shoulders. "Ah, don't worry, Inni, I'm still your son."

She smiled shakily and touched my beard, which she'd never seen before.

That night after what must have been a 12-course dinner, Inni informed me that she and Kaka had found three girls suitable to be my wife. "It is time," she said firmly.

"What? Marriage?" I asked, pretending I was not interested. "Why such haste?"

"One is from the Kanadi Vaishnav caste," Inni said, ignoring my questions. "Her family are nice people, well known in society. Even their house is nice! But before we go there to meet them, you must shower and put on a nice shirt."

I realized with a start that even though I felt very successful, I probably did not look successful to my family.

Nor could I speak easily with them. On the way from the airport, I pointed to a cluster of tiny brown birds and realized I couldn't remember the word for "sparrow" in Marathi. A native tongue more than 1,300 years old, with origins in Sanskrit, and in just five years I had lost so many words!

I reassured my sisters, who were slightly appalled, with what I hoped sounded like calm scientific reasoning: "When you don't use an instrument for a long period, it gathers rust. I have not been speaking our language for years, only writing it; the words will come back." And so they did, within a week or so, to my secret relief.

By then my family had seen that I was the same Shri, and they had lost their strangeness to me. We'd eaten up the brass canisters of festive snacks Inni had prepared for my homecoming, and they'd caught me up on all the gossip.

Only my bride search remained awkward. As Inni told me more about each of the girls she and Kaka had chosen, I said impatiently, "All these things are all right, but I want to know the girl's personality! What are her likes and dislikes? Her ambitions—does she have any? What are her beliefs about marriage and family?"

"We didn't ask so many questions," Inni said, almost reprovingly, "but you can ask, if you insist."

I put my hand out wordlessly for the address of the first girl on their list. Before I left, Inni fussed over my clothes, checked my fingernails, even picked up a washrag and scrubbed the back of my neck to be sure. I felt like I was 5 again—until I knocked at the first door.

The girl's family ushered me in and hurried to bring me a chair. They treated me like a prince, and it felt distinctly odd and uncomfortable. They brought me tea, and the minute I finished it someone appeared to remove the cup from my hand and refill it. Every time I ate something, they urged me to eat more. I drank so much tea and ate so many snacks, I had to use their bathroom, and when I emerged a young man was waiting outside the door to hand me a towel.

The mother had obviously cleaned and polished everything in the house, and she'd filled urns with beautiful flowers. All this was, I knew, because I was the boy—and a boy living in America!—and the burden was on the family of the girl to be extra-hospitable and polite. But instead of enjoying the attention and deferential chit-chat, I felt slightly queasy. It all seemed fake, not honest. They were only telling me things they thought I wanted to hear.

I tried to ignore all the attentions and focus on the girl. She sat several yards away, looking down and playing with the folds of an ornate sari, bending them this way and that way, while I asked her questions.

"Would you like to study further?"

"I will, if you wish."

"Tell me about your plans for a career—do you have any particular field that interests you?"

"I haven't decided yet, but I will work, if you wish."

Brick wall after brick wall. I had no idea what she really thought about

107

anything. Finally I asked her parents, "Would you mind if I talked to your daughter in private for a moment?"

There was a pin-drop silence. No one came out and said, "That is not allowed in our community," but it was obvious from the changed facial expressions around the room that I had shocked them. Finally her father spoke.

"You may talk to each other in this room," he said. "We will move to another room."

Even after they left, the girl did not express herself openly. She was heavily made up, in the traditional way, and she wore so much jewelry, it could have been our wedding day already. I couldn't talk naturally with her.

Her parents returned a few minutes later. Then it was their turn to ask *me* questions, and they fired them off in rapid order.

"How big is your house in America?"

"I was renting a room; when I finished my study, I moved out."

"Oh. I see. What about your belongings?"

"I didn't have much. Just a few daily necessities."

"You must have a fat bank balance by now!"

"Actually, no. I was studying on scholarship, and got paid for the bare necessities only. I paid for my flight with a credit card."

"And your new job, does it have a big salary?"

"It's sufficient, but nothing extravagant. I am just starting out." I could feel the tension in the room, because nobody was hearing what they wanted to hear. I could just imagine what they would say when I left: "The boy has a doctorate and a job, yet he doesn't seem to be either wealthy or well settled." We thanked each other, and I hurried away.

Rajani was disturbed when I recounted my first adventure. "Shri, why did you answer their questions like that?"

"I wanted to tell them the truth," I said, in a tone she knew meant, "Don't push this further."

Inni quickly distracted us: "How was the girl?"

"She *looked* fine, but I couldn't find out what she was like. She didn't express her opinions openly. I'm not even sure she *had* any opinions of her own. She seemed completely inhibited; she didn't look at me once. When I asked her a question, she answered with her head down. Either she was fascinated by her feet or she was terrified."

The next girls were more of the same: rapid-fire question contests, disappointing conclusions.

Inni and Kaka were even more disappointed than I was. Kaka said, "You are the right age to get married. I can't believe someone like you would work so hard and get such an important degree and you can't find a girl that is right for you!"

I couldn't believe it either, but I didn't want them to see how dejected I felt. Finally, I took matters into my own hands. "Stop searching for a bride for me!" I warned everyone in the house. "Let me handle it in my own way."

"But Shri! You can't do this alone!" Inni said, and even Kaka was nodding, his brow furrowed in concern.

"Why not?" I asked. "Is it harder than getting a PhD?"

Privately I was beginning to think it might be. I stayed up all night thinking about it. I thought a lot about the American system that had so attracted me: how it began with dating, followed by love and, only then, marriage. "Unless I like a girl and feel attracted to her, I will not marry," I had decided back in grad school. But it hadn't worked so far. I'd gotten nothing but heartbreak and disappointment. So now I had no alternative but to get married in the traditional Indian way. But, I resolved, I still will not marry unless the woman's thinking and values mesh with my own.

I wanted my wife to be independent in her thinking, confident of herself, capable. I was looking for someone who was down to earth, not someone fascinated by money or American glamour.

In the old days, social networks were big enough and robust enough that marriages were easily arranged. But more and more people were placing "matrimonials," ads in the *Times of India* that spelled out qualifications and prerequisites in precise, if superficial, detail. The Sunday classified section was fat with them, pages and pages with the ads listed by language, religion, or desired profession, and with preferences indicated for such traits as height and complexion.

What I cared about was the quality of the woman's mind and spirit, not how fair or petite she was. Still, I decided I'd place one of these ads myself.

So I did. About 200 replies poured in the following week!

I selected 40 of them, some from the Pune area, some from Mumbai. I settled on Pune, because I had a cousin there, Shaila, with whom I could stay. I had only 15 days left in India, and I really wanted to make a decision by then.

Shaila welcomed me to her home, and we walked around trying to figure out where I should meet with my prospective brides. This would be the romantic equivalent of a job fair: I couldn't go to each woman's house, because I had about 30 interviews to schedule, 10 a day.

Shaila's house had only two rooms: a living room and a worship room. We couldn't use the entry hall, because children, servants, and neighbors would be constantly coming in and leaving.

"The living room?" I said hopefully.

"Absolutely not," Shaila said. "The neighbors might think you're just chatting with girls the whole day."

"Why the hell would they care what I was doing?" I almost blurted. I'd been in America too long. I'd forgotten how nosy people could be. I sighed and resigned myself to the worship room, a tiny windowless space with such dim light, I couldn't even make out the girls' features. They came with their families, and we had warned them all to be on time, because if families overlapped, there was no place for them to sit and wait! I chuckled, thinking, "I should have used that dental clinic where I used to work!"

Then I quickly sobered and set my mind on the matter at hand. It would not do to be too silly about this. I was, after all, setting the course for the rest of my life.

Some of the women were shy and constrained; others were *too* frank, and I found them very choosy and demanding. Only one struck any spark with me: She had a graduate degree in biochemistry, she was lovely, and we had a really interesting conversation. I invited her and her parents to come to our house in Belgaum to finalize the wedding arrangements. I left Shaila's house with my heart light, because I had accomplished what I wanted.

Back in Belgaum, I described the woman to my family, and then I sat and waited for her father to call, scheduling their visit. Eight days went by—no call, no telegram or letter, nothing. Concerned, I called them.

The woman's mother answered. "Call back in a few hours and speak with my husband."

I called back a few hours later and the father answered. "We've been waiting for your phone call," I said, trying not to sound impatient. "Have you decided anything?"

"This marriage is not possible!" he exclaimed.

"But why not?" I asked, startled.

"Your horoscope does not match with my daughter's."

This floored me. I really *had* been in America too long.

"Um … I handed over my horoscope because you asked me, but I don't believe in matching horoscopes for marriage," I said, remembering the silly astrologer who convinced my mother I might end up a thief.

"We believe in it strongly," he said. "I cannot marry my daughter to you."

I hung up, dazed. "Oh for God's sake," I thought. "I'm going back to America."

Then I remembered that of the 40 girls I'd chosen, there were still 10 I'd never met. Most of them were from Mumbai and for one reason or another had not been able to make the trip to Pune. I didn't have much time left to write letters to them, so I decided to try my luck one last time. I went to stay with a distant cousin in Mumbai—I called her Tai, which means "aunt," because she was about 15 years older than I.

It was ironic: Here I was desperate to find a wife, and here was Tai, content because she had taken a vow of celibacy. She read scripture all day and had dedicated her life to her guru; she'd never been married and had no intention of ever marrying. I found myself pouring out all my tribulations to this kind, disinterested cousin. She listened with calm interest and asked good questions, helping me clarify what I really wanted.

By then more responses to my ad had come in, so I added another 15 or so names to my list. I mapped out their addresses and the train lines, covering all of Mumbai as efficiently as I could. Most of the families didn't have phones. I wrote telling them I was going to visit them—but in most cases I arrived before my letter, so I had a bit of explaining to do.

The first woman's father drew himself up and grandly informed me, "My other daughters are married. All my remaining wealth will go to this last daughter, and you will be set up for life." He didn't ask me a single question. He only wanted to have a son-in-law in America, and that made me very uncomfortable.

I moved on. The next door I knocked on was answered by the girl herself.

"Hello. I am Shri Thanedar," I said. "You answered my ad?"

"I most certainly did not." She started to close the door.

"But you did! Look, I have it here!" I fumbled with my file folder; luckily I'd brought all the letters with me. As I was waving hers before her, an older, sharper female voice came from inside the house: "I answered his ad for you."

"You *what*? How dare you?"

I looked beyond the girl and saw a young African man sitting in the living room.

Soon the girl and her mother were screaming at each other so hysterically, they'd forgotten all about me. I murmured an apology for inconveniencing them, slowly backed away from the door and walked as fast as I could down the road. Only after I'd turned two corners—and was far enough away that the mother couldn't come flying after me—did I stop to catch my breath and hail a taxi.

I pressed on, and soon I'd made it through most of my Mumbai list. Not one of the women truly interested me.

I'd mapped out the women's addresses and, to make efficient use of my rapidly dwindling time, arranged my list geographically—not as a ranking of the women's desirability.

Last on the list was a woman named Shamal, who lived near the central Mumbai train station. She was a neurologist, 24 years old, and I remembered really liking her letter. It was clever and thoughtful, skillfully worded, very smart. Above all, I liked what she said: that she was from a modest family and did not care about wealth; that she wanted someone ambitious, like she was. I'd been disappointed when she did not come to Pune. Now, on my last day in Mumbai, I knocked on her family's door. Her mother answered the door.

"I am Shri Thanedar," I said, continuing in a rush: "I had invited your daughter to come to Pune. I'm really sorry to just drop in like this, but there was no time to call. I really liked the letter Shamal wrote ..." I trailed off.

Her mother smiled. "Yes, of course. Please come in. I am sorry that we are in rather a hurry." I noticed that she was wearing a festive sari, and her husband was also dressed for a special occasion. "Our other daughter married two days ago," she explained. Ah, I thought, that's why Shamal did not come to Pune. "Today we are having lunch with her groom's parents, and we are already late. But my sister and her husband are here. Why don't you stay and talk with them? We'll be back in a few hours, and Shamal will be home from the hospital at 5."

Delighted at the thought of learning more about Shamal from her relatives, I agreed instantly. Moreover, I had no other candidates to check out. We drank tea and talked all afternoon. I learned that Shamal was very studious, very serious, dedicated to her patients. On the high school graduation exam, a national standardized test, she stood 48th among at least half-a-million kids throughout the state of Maharashtra.

The house was small, just a kitchen, living room, and toilet, and I sensed that her family was like mine: lower-middle-class, not wealthy, but with strong values. Finally, a few minutes after 5, the door opened and Shamal walked in. She was barely 5 feet tall, and she wore her thick dark hair long, parted in the middle. She took one look at all of us in the living room and headed for the kitchen, where her sisters were chatting.

Minutes passed. Finally, when her mother called out to her, she came into the living room. I saw that she wore no makeup, just a small *bindi*, a simple decorative red dot, on her forehead. She wore nothing in her ears and no necklace. She had on a cotton *kurta* over torn jeans. She didn't look any more like a doctor than I had looked, to my parents, like a doctor of chemistry.

Then she started to talk and revealed something about herself. I could hear the self-assuredness in her voice, the cool ambition and principle. She had just graduated from medical school, and she was not in the least swayed by money, as so many of the other girls had been.

I liked her.

She didn't talk much, but what she did say was open and honest. Her face went blank when I mentioned a few lines from her letter. Finally her father—an advertising copywriter—interrupted and said that he'd written it on her behalf. I scrambled to remember the entire letter—had I just been lured by clever wording? No, I didn't think so. He'd just written, artfully, the very things she was telling me now. A parent writing on behalf of the daughter wasn't unusual; it's considered the parents' responsibility to find their daughters a husband.

That was the *only* traditional aspect of our meeting. Shamal's parents were nothing like the other women's parents. They bent over backwards *not* to fuss over me. They wanted to make sure I knew that they were progressive people who did not believe in the old ways.

Nor did I—but a sandwich would have been nice! I wound up staying there from lunchtime until late in the evening, and they offered me nothing but tea! They were probably waiting for me to leave before they had their dinner, but as long as the conversation continued I wasn't about to cut it off. I covered the growls of my stomach with louder questions, eager to learn as much as I could.

I was as open and honest as I could be, and I waited hopefully for Shamal to open up a bit more, too. She never did. She seemed as frank as her parents, and I sensed no game-playing, no coyness or dissembling. *That* was a relief. But she remained a bit guarded, and not entirely enthusiastic.

When it became obvious that for courtesy's sake I should draw my visit to a close, I made it clear that I was impressed with her and asked her what she thought of me.

"I like that you are self-made," she said quietly. "You are independent."

I exhaled, and only then did I realize how tense I'd been, half holding my breath as I waited for some sign of how she felt about me. She seemed just the kind of girl I was looking for—smart and ambitious but with simple tastes. I told her parents that. If they could come to Belgaum to meet my parents, I said, we could talk about a wedding.

"You do not need to tell me what you are thinking right now," I added quickly, "but will you please call me tomorrow morning, before I leave Mumbai?"

They agreed readily but without giving any sign of how they felt. I was too excited to care—in my mind, my marriage was all set! At least, it seemed to be … although I did not feel entirely certain yet.

Shamal's eyes hadn't shone as I'd hoped they might. She wasn't lit up with joy. But I sensed a deep seriousness in her, and I reminded myself that not everyone was exuberant. She'd been honest, and she'd liked in me the very traits I liked in her. Surely that was the best possible foundation for a marriage?

The next morning I quite literally sat by Tai's phone, packed and ready to leave, waiting. I didn't have to leave for the train station until 2 p.m., but I wanted to have plenty of time to settle all the details and relay the news to Inni and Kaka. I rehearsed everything that had been said the day before, everything I knew about Shamal. And the more I thought about her, the more I felt sure she would be the right wife for me. The thought sent a glow through my entire body.

And then a chill—how was *she* feeling? What if I'd annoyed or offended her and she'd skillfully hidden her contempt? Maybe I had seemed chauvinistic when I rose to help her with her chair. Maybe I had stayed too long, and her parents had decided that I was a rude pig.

Noon came, and they still had not called. My stomach was too queasy to eat lunch. "They could have at least called to tell me they were not interested," I muttered to myself, trying to brush off a disappointment that already felt heavier, more crushing, than any of the earlier dead ends.

I had talked with this girl for only a few hours, and she hadn't exactly fallen all over herself to flatter me. If she wasn't interested, why should I care?

But she was cultured, I answered myself. She ranked high in her studies, she seemed to have deep principles and a strong moral compass, and she had a lovely smile that lit up even her sad eyes. Yes, she was introverted—but I liked her thoughts.

I tried all the usual ways to console myself. Obviously, she wasn't the one. There would be others. I'd jumped, just because she was the last on my list.

And then it was time to go to the station. Tai walked me out to the taxi, and before I left, she patted me on the shoulder. "Do not worry about anything," she said. "Things are going to work out. It's just a matter of time."

Suddenly I felt a little silly, being so eager to get married when she had long ago renounced such worldly concerns. No wonder she was such a peaceful person! Yet she seemed to understand exactly what I was going through, and her words comforted me—as much as anything could have.

I got on the train. As it chugged along, the face of each girl I'd met swam into my vision. But by the time the train pulled into the central Mumbai station, the one closest to Shamal's house, I could only see her face. It was clear and sharp, not blurred like the others. I could see her dark eyes, the slight shadow beneath them, her sweet smile.

Why hadn't her family called? Wouldn't we have made a good couple?

The train ground to a stop, people got off, people got on. The rumbling started up again—and something came over me. I jumped up, grabbed my blue suitcase, ran to the door and leaped off the train, which by now was building up so much speed that I stumbled onto the platform.

I steadied myself and hailed a taxi, giving Shamal's address. I knew it, I realized, by heart.

Her mother answered the door.

"Oh, it's you!"

I used the customary word for "father": "Is Baba home?"

"He's eating. Come inside."

As I stepped into their home, I said, "You never called me, so I thought I'd just stop by to see why. I was beginning to wonder if you were really interested."

Baba had come out in time to hear this. He said, "It's not a question of interest. It just doesn't look like we can match your expectations."

"What are you talking about? I thought we agreed that everything was fine! Did I say something wrong?"

"No, no, but such a gentleman, from the USA, with all your success, I don't think we can afford to marry with your family."

Bewildered, I slipped into American slang and blurted, "I don't know where you are coming from!"

Baba said, "When the boy comes home from America, the family usually has a lot of expectations about the wedding and the dowry."

"I have *no* expectations about money! Actually, I don't have any money either! I'm going to borrow more money on my credit card for the wedding."

He said, "I only have 15,000 rupees set aside for this wedding."

I said, "We will put our resources together, I will borrow 15,000 rupees on my credit card, and we will make this happen." By now I was thoroughly relieved—but he wasn't finished.

"You are asking us to come to Belgaum," he said. "Shamal does not have much vacation, and we have to spend money to come there, and then your parents might say no."

"That's not how it's going to be," I said, trying to keep exasperation out of my voice. "If I like Shamal, they are not going to disapprove. And they wouldn't dream of asking for more money."

"That is what everybody says," he answered, his voice still tight. "The last time, it happened to us. We went to Bangalore, and the boy's family started demanding all kinds of things from us."

"I can assure you that's not how my family operates," I said, straightening my back. "All I want is for everyone to meet!"

He paused for a long minute. Then he nodded slowly. "We will come."

I caught another train home and raced inside to tell Inni and Kaka about Shamal. "I have selected one girl," I said. "She is a doctor and works in a big hospital in Mumbai. I like her, and she has also consented. But—"

"Why do you say 'but'?" Inni interrupted.

"I told Shamal's parents to come to Belgaum and meet you and Kaka before we made a final decision," I explained, "and her father objected. He said, 'If we come all the way to Belgaum, and then your parents say no, what should we do?'"

"He was absolutely right," Kaka said quietly.

I looked at him, surprised.

"Look, Shri, I am a father of six daughters, and I know what parents go through when they're getting their daughters married," he said. "Did you like the girl? If you liked her, we will definitely support your decision. So why ask them to come all the way to Belgaum for our consent? You should have told them straightaway that it was fine.

"Call them now," he continued, "and tell them we have already agreed, and they should come for a wedding."

I shot a look at Inni, but she was nodding and smiling. Kaka, normally so quiet, actually pushed me: "Shri, call them up right now! Tell them, 'My parents have consented. Start immediately to Belgaum, and be prepared for marriage.'"

This was a new side of Kaka, and the force was all the more impressive because it was so rare. My heart swelled with pride in him—and with my own excitement, too. I called and gave Shamal's parents the good news.

My future life was about to unfold.

Shamal and her family arrived in Belgaum in mid-May. I was supposed to start my new job June 1! I managed a long-distance call to my boss to explain the situation, and he gave me a two-week extension without hesitating.

We would marry in the last week of May and even have time for a quick honeymoon.

Inni was a little nervous about meeting Shamal, who came from the big city of Mumbai and therefore, in Inni's opinion, would probably be arrogant, one of those modern girls who scorn tradition. But Shamal was nothing like that. She was so soft-spoken, and so kind and polite, that Inni liked her immediately. Kaka did, too. I knew he was smitten when I saw him showing her his radio. Even Rajani drew me aside and said, "She is lovely, Shri. You've chosen well."

Shamal's parents were another story. They seemed tense and anxious, and I had no idea why. Not even Inni's charms could warm them. They held themselves aloof throughout the wedding preparations, leaving everything to us and inviting only five relatives. That made five guests on Shamal's side and 295 family and good friends on mine!

Inni pulled me aside the morning after they arrived; their strangeness was already obvious. "Are we making them uncomfortable in some way?" she asked me. "Is there something we should do differently?"

I shrugged. I had no idea. And we were too busy to dwell on it.

To save money, we were going to do everything from scratch, as we had for my sisters. We rented the hall of a local temple and hired cooks, and once again, I negotiated the shopping. I bought all the ingredients, rented the utensils, and delivered everything to the cooks. My sisters and mother rushed around planning the music and parties and gifts. The wedding was to be May 24, so we had only a week to plan everything.

Shamal stayed in Belgaum that week before our marriage. I longed to get to know her better. I wanted to have long, deep conversations with her; I wanted to know everything about her. But with my whole family flying around making preparations, the mood was not conducive. So one day I suggested that we walk to the Ganesha temple outside the village.

I wanted Shamal to see the place, because I used to walk there with my friends when I was a teenager. I had happy memories of our adventures, and I wanted to at least share that small bit of my past with her.

The temple was far outside the village, and the road was pretty deserted. It had been a fine hike for me and my buddies, but it was not really so safe for a woman. I decided we should cut through the military compound.

Halfway through, a guard stopped us and snapped, "What are you doing here?" He had a weird look in his eye, and he seemed a little power-mad. I talked fast and managed to win the battle of words and get us out of there. I was relieved, but instead of being impressed, Shamal was upset with me.

"Why do you do these kinds of things?" she burst. "You should be more careful! We shouldn't have gone there in the first place."

It was the first of many occasions that would reveal her cautious nature, her constant anxiety and pessimism. I should have paid closer attention, but I was just so happy to finally be alone with her. We finished our long, hot walk, and as we came back to the village, I saw a nice restaurant that served delicate snacks. "Shall we stop and have something to eat?" I asked.

Shamal nodded, but when I asked what she would like, she said she was not hungry. "Are you sure?" I asked; I was famished. "I am sure," she said, "but you go ahead." So I ordered a *masala dosa,* a sort of South Indian crepe with a spicy potato stuffing, and spread it liberally with coconut chutney, and she sat with me as I ate it. We talked about the wedding, which made me happy. I liked talking about those tiny, practical details: They were the first things in the world that affected both of us equally and bound us to each other.

As we began the serious wedding preparations, we performed a *puja* (a ritual prayer and offering) to Lord Ganesh, the remover of obstacles, asking him to make this huge event problem free. Then, the night before the wedding, we had another *puja* and some gift-giving, so the families could get to know each other better. My father or mother would say, "This is Shri's sister," and then Shamal's parents would say, "This is Shamal's sister," and the two sisters would hug or touch their heads together, and the priest would hold a holy bowl by its handles and bless their union.

An Indian wedding, you see, is not just a marriage between a man and a woman. It is a marriage between the two families.

Usually there are lots of relatives on both sides, but so few had come from Shamal's side that in these rituals we used the same people over and over again to meet different members of my family. Gifts were saris or jewelry or fine fabric to sew or money in an envelope. Most came from Shamal's family to mine, as a way of honoring us.

Afterward, there was a feast, all vegetarian, with the emphasis on my favorite part: the desserts. We had *aam rus,* mango juice with cardamom and sugar and cream; *puran poli,* a sweetened bread stuffed with a paste of lentils and sweet spices; and *jalebi,* a syrupy spiral sweet made from chickpea flour and sweetened with jaggery, the coarse, dark sugar.

That night, Shamal's sisters hid my shoes and demanded money before they gave them back. This is a ritual way of exerting a little power over the groom, who must be nice to his bride's sisters before he can take her home and away from them.

When I woke at dawn on May 24, the air was already shining with heat. I dressed in a decorated *kurta*, and Kaka tied strings of pearls on my forehead and a blue silk cloth around my head, its ends hanging down my back. When everyone in my family was ready, I was to go outside and mount a pure white horse that had been decorated with ribbons and flower garlands.

I patted his side first, as much to soothe my own nerves as his. Then I pressed my heels gently into his sides and rode the mile or so from our house to the temple. A band was playing popular music, with trumpets and clarinets soaring high and a young man from our village singing. Our family formed a procession behind me, and soon the kids in the front were dancing, and so were a few older people. Neighbors lined the streets to watch and wave as we passed.

When we reached the temple, Vandana, my youngest sister, fed the horse sweetened grain. Shamal's mother fed *me*, putting a small piece of *pedha*, a creamy sweet delicacy, in my mouth and giving me sweetened milk to drink. She also placed a *tilak*, a mark of auspiciousness, on my forehead, using a dab of *kumkum*, a red powder. Then I took my shoes off, and she washed my feet, purifying me. For the wedding I would wear a *dhoti*, a long cotton loincloth, with the sacred thread across my shoulder and a large loosely woven cotton cloth covering my upper body. I removed my *kurta* and prepared, my heart racing.

Then, finally, I saw Shamal.

Her eyes were dark and serious, her skin glowed, and she had a slight, formal smile. She wore a silk sari, the most beautiful I'd ever seen, embellished with flowers and brilliantly colored borders. Our priest, Balu Guraji, tied the end of that cloth to the end of my cloth in a large knot, and then I took her hand.

It was warm and a little damp, just as mine was. I gave hers a little squeeze, and I thought I saw her smile widen just a bit. The ceremony began.

Seven times we circled the sacred fire, making promises for our future together. From time to time, we added ghee to the fire to make it burn even brighter. Balu Guraji — we used to call him simply Balu when we were growing up—was an interesting fellow. He lived four houses away, and he'd been a wild kid with terrible morals. Then he suddenly took up religion and became very devoted. His timing was perfect: Hindu priests were in short supply because there was no glamour or money in the profession and the priests' children did not want to live so traditionally.

I'd always liked Balu. He understood service. So many priests say, "Oh, I can't do that" or "I won't come there" or "You must have this or that; otherwise we cannot perform the ceremony." He was easygoing and more interested in the spirit than the rule. If we didn't have honey to offer, he'd say, "Just put a flower petal in there, and it will represent honey." Now that he was a priest, we had to be more respectful, so we called him Balu Guraji. I was glad that he was marrying us.

As he recited the vows in Sanskrit, he told us what each promise meant, urging us to stay faithful to each other. The hall was very crowded, and the smoke from the fire burned our eyes. For days we'd been running around trying to get things done, and neither of us had slept much. As we stood on the little wooden stage, poems were recited, Balu Guraji said Sanskrit mantras, and there was a lot of chanting. Every time it stopped, people threw rice at us. After the third time, we exchanged garlands.

Until that moment, a thin piece of cloth had been stretched between us. It is not considered a good idea to look at each other directly before you are officially married. But of course I'd sneaked a peek at Shamal, and our eyes had met through the gauze.

At the end of the ceremony, it was time for Shamal to bid farewell to her family. That is always a tearful moment, for the bride is leaving their home and making her way to her husband's. For Shamal it was especially hard, because she knew that she'd be going so far away.

I knew she was sad, but I was so thrilled just to be able to touch her, hold her hand, look at her and know that she was my wife. "Everything will be fine," I whispered to her as the guests lined up to shake hands and give us gifts. I kept telling her little things about the US, about what our life would be like together. "It's a new beginning."

We started our honeymoon at the beach in Goa, the smallest state in India, along the southwest coast. We'd lie on white sand, watching the warm seawater lap ever closer, fathomless, changing color with the light. Behind us was a thick, impenetrable fringe of palm trees. We'd nap in the afternoons, and at dinner we would eat fish and I would drink *feni*, a liquor made only in Goa. It's distilled from either coconuts or cashews, and it's very strong. Shamal actually dared a taste of it, even though she was raised, as I was, to avoid liquor.

"Whoa!" she said, laughing. "Too strong!"

We dozed at Goa for several days, then went south to Mysore, where the famed Brindavan Gardens are. I'd checked us into a cheap hotel, but as we walked through the terraced gardens that evening, past lit water fountains and topiary sculptures and a crystal greenhouse, I saw what looked like a palace in the distance. I asked a local man about the palace.

"That's the Royal Orchid Hotel," he told me. "It used to be a palace of the king; now it's a historic hotel. They call it heaven on earth."

The building was pure white, lit from the outside. I grabbed Shamal by the hand, and we went into the lobby. Gathering all my new-husband dignity, I inquired about a room. There were only 24, all filled with antiques, and the price of one night's stay nearly floored me. "Do you take American Express?" I asked, making my voice very casual.

"Yes, of course," the room clerk said.

"We'll take it."

I figured that Shamal would be thrilled. Instead, she seemed more and more uncomfortable. Her eyes were wide, which gave her a little-girlish, overwhelmed look.

"She's just not used to all this luxury," I told myself, elated that I could give her a real treat.

We checked out of the cheap hotel and carried our bags into an elegant room, and I ordered us a four-course dinner. Soon our room was filled with waiters in black tie pushing carts and setting a table on the balcony overlooking the gardens. One whipped off a silver domed lid with a flourish, and I grinned at Shamal—but she wasn't smiling. Finally, when all the waiters had left, softly closing the door behind them, I asked her what was the matter. She wouldn't answer until we were in bed.

Then she burst, "Why are we doing all this?" At first, she sounded like she was almost in tears. Then her voice got very slow and deliberate and angry, and she spat out each word one by one: "You ... are ... spending ... my ... father's ... money."

"No, I'm *not!*" I protested. "I'm spending *our* money, on a credit card we'll pay off as soon as I begin my new job. This is for us! I wanted us to have a beautiful start to our marriage!"

Our wedding night hadn't been exactly spectacular. Because there was no privacy in my parents' home, my sister Veena had lent us her apartment in town. But when we turned off the lights, cockroaches came out and started climbing all over the walls. It's not unusual—but the whole night we were never really at peace.

Still, it was better than this night. Nothing I said calmed her.

"Why did you have to take money from my father for our wedding?" she kept asking. She seemed to have this inordinate feeling of obligation to her father, and I didn't understand it. Every father pays for his daughter's wedding, and I had not even asked him to do that. Refusing to take what he did offer would surely have stung his pride and sense of honor.

I stole a look at Shamal's face. Her eyes were black, the tears shining like sleet caught in your headlights on a dark road. "What do you want to do?" I asked.

"Let's just go home," she said. And so we took the bus home, on day four of our weeklong honeymoon.

I had a lot to learn. Women, I knew, were supposed to be complicated. But my sisters had always been pretty clear about what they wanted from me, and so had Inni. Now I was a grown man with a wife—and I didn't have the slightest idea what thoughts were running through her head.

CHAPTER 5

Meet Me in St. Louis

I SPENT THE first year of our marriage trying to figure Shamal out—but there was, quite literally, an ocean between us. To get a visa to come to the United States as my wife, she had to wait a whole year. It seemed terribly anticlimactic: I finally had a wife, but we could not be together. I thought of her constantly, and everything I experienced came through that filter. If I ate fettuccine Alfredo, I wondered, as I twirled my first forkful through the creamy sauce, whether Shamal would like Italian food as much as I did. What would she think of the Gateway Arch monument on the Mississippi River in St. Louis—would she find it stunning, or silly? She'd hate the sprawling shopping malls, I suspected, with all their fluorescent glitz. What kind of apartment should I rent for us—would she prefer something modern in a glass-and-metal high-rise, or would she rather live in an older brick building with hardwood floors and stained-glass windows?

All told, I wrote her 73 letters—I numbered them to help her keep them straight!—and asked all sorts of questions, trying to prepare her for America and learn her tastes at the same time. I also wrote the kind of news you'd tell a spouse at the dinner table, making dramatic stories of tiny crises and triumphs at my Petrolite lab bench. My job was to make waxy molecules so people could have their paint and chewing gum, I explained. I told her about the Indian community in St. Louis;

about how August was a lot like our May, right before the monsoons start; about the lousy cold I'd caught.

Shamal wrote back maybe 15 times. Whenever I saw the familiar Indian stamps and her handwriting on the envelope in my mailbox, my heart leaped. I dropped all the bills and circulars and tore the envelope open. I slid it out and skimmed it fast, checked the ending to see whether she'd signed it "with love," then carried it to my favorite (and only) comfy chair to read and reread.

Rarely did she answer my questions; in fact, she voiced very few preferences or opinions about anything. She was warmest when she was worried (was I drinking enough fluids?) or confiding concerns about one of her patients or some problem one of her sisters was having. As a rule, though, she was reserved and matter-of-fact, telling me about her work at the hospital and keeping me posted on my parents. She had gone to live with them for several months, which moved me deeply. She felt it her duty as their daughter-in-law, and because my father was starting to have health problems she was keeping a close eye on his blood pressure and helping him learn how to manage his diabetes.

Inni and Kaka had already come to love her as one of their own daughters. As for me, I was grateful to her for caring for Kaka, but I felt even lonelier now than before. They were all together at home, and I was all alone across the oceans, waiting.

In December, I couldn't stand it anymore. *I want to be with my wife!* I said out loud one evening, driving home in a cold drizzle after working late. I stepped into my empty apartment, flicked on a light, and picked up the phone.

"What's the first round-trip ticket you have to Bombay?" I demanded, forgetting to use the city's new "Mumbai" name. I charged another plane ticket (yes, I'd paid off the other one) and flew back to see her.

But I missed my plane from Bombay to Belgaum. I'd forgotten the Indian system, in which a bus came to take you from the international terminal to your next plane at the domestic flights terminal. There was only one flight a day to Belgaum, so I was stuck. Frantic, I tried to call our neighbors, as my family still did not have a phone, but they did not answer. Shamal and my family would be waiting at the airport for me, and they'd arrive early and wait for hours, and then the plane from Bombay would finally land, and everyone else would get off, and I wouldn't be there.

I had no way of contacting them to explain. I knew Inni would assume the worst; she had never trusted air travel. Would Shamal figure it out and calm the rest of the family? Or would she fret, too? I suspected the latter; I could already tell that she worried about everything. I paced, thinking through every possible scenario. I had to *do* something.

Finally I found a flight to Goa, which left me with a five-hour taxi ride to Belgaum. It was very dark, and when it started raining I realized that the driver's wipers weren't working. He didn't seem fazed, just kept speeding down the narrow road through deserted countryside.

"Er ... if someone has an accident out here, how long does it take to get help?" I asked him.

"Oh, it takes hours," he told me, relishing my nervousness. I wondered whether I'd made a mistake and should have stayed the night and caught the next day's flight to Belgaum.

But he got me home safe. When I walked inside, Inni took me aside and told me quietly that they'd all come home very disappointed from the airport, and then Shamal had bolted. She didn't tell anyone, just left, and she'd been walking all over town, crazy upset. My family had been as worried about her as they were about me. She'd just returned shortly before I arrived.

I couldn't put my arms around her because even between husbands and wives such public signs of affection were not deemed proper. I pulled out the big bag of gifts I'd brought for everyone, and as they opened packages and exclaimed over them, my eyes kept straying to my wife. Her eyes were red and swollen, and she was very solemn and quiet. She wouldn't meet my eyes.

Was she furious with me for screwing up and missing my plane? I'd never seen any signs of a fierce temper, but maybe dumb mistakes triggered some extreme reaction in her. Still, anger wouldn't have left her eyes looking like that. Had she been upset because our reunion had not begun as planned? Maybe she was the kind of woman who had to have things go according to schedule.

If she wasn't angry *or* pouting, why was she being so distant with me? Obviously I didn't know my wife very well yet.

After dinner, I invited her to come with me for a walk. She nodded, and when she finally met my eyes, hers were soft, defenseless. Encouraged by that glance, I waited until we were far from the house, then took her hand. After months without any contact at all, just that slight touch sent an electrical charge between us.

"Why didn't you call?" she asked me, her voice so low, I had to strain to hear it.

"I tried! The neighbors must have been gone."

"I thought something very bad must have happened to you," she said. "Don't ever do that to me again."

I breathed out a long sigh. Temper or pouting would have come as a surprise; worry was almost reassuring. The intensity of her emotions had certainly taken me aback, but I was too flattered—she really *did* care!—to analyze any further. By the time we returned home, we were laughing and joking with each other.

The 10 days that followed were probably the most intimate days of our lives together. We spent all our time together. One of the two people renting the second, divided house (the one I'd insisted Kaka buy for the income) had just left. I begged my mother not to rent it to anyone until I'd gone back to America. At night Shamal and I went there to sleep, so we had a private space. We couldn't make any noise, of course, because the other renting family was right next to us, on the other side of a connecting door. We whispered to each other all night long, and we learned each other's hearts and memorized each other's bodies.

130

During the days, we'd walk, go to movies, eat. Sometimes we'd go back to our room in the afternoon and lock the door, which was completely unacceptable in our culture. A husband and wife may be together only at night! The woman in the family next door to us commented to my mother about our reprehensible behavior: "I have my *children* here!" she said. "They shouldn't be locking themselves up in the middle of the day."

With her usual diplomacy, Inni agreed heartily with the neighbor, then said nothing to stop me. She knew that I would be leaving soon— and she could see how happy we were.

Going back to St. Louis alone was even harder after those 10 days. But finally, on June 18, 1985, Shamal flew to the United States. She'd waited the requisite year, and as my wife, her green card status was now automatic.

I flew to New York to meet her, because I knew how confusing JFK Airport would be for Shamal. At JFK, I learned that her flight was four hours late, so I simply waited at the Customs line. As it got closer to her arrival time, I'd race to the bathroom and race back, terrified that I would miss her. Just as I was beginning to despair—had she decided not to come?—I caught sight of her in the line. She had a faint smile on her face, but she looked tired and worried. I'd been planning for four hours what I would say to her, but when she finally stood before me, all I could say was, "Oh, God, I'm so glad to see you. Finally you are in America!" I tried to hug her, but she smiled and gently pushed me back, reluctant to hug in a public place.

As was becoming a pattern, the flight delay forced us to miss our flight to St. Louis. Pan Am gave us a hotel room, though, and I thought, "This might be even better. It will break Shamal's long journey, and we can enjoy our first night together in America."

But Shamal was in no mood to enjoy anything. She sat stiffly upright in the taxi and didn't even look out the windows. She showed absolutely no interest in her new country. I kept telling her things: This is how they drive here, on this side of the road; I've taken a couple days off so I can be with you; you have to be careful about this ... but I felt no enthusiasm or interest in her response, just a vague sense of melancholy.

Jet lag, I decided. And intercontinental fatigue.

The next day, as we made our way back to St. Louis, Shamal warmed up a bit. At home I'd arranged all kinds of things, bought a satin bedspread and some silk flowers and some paintings at a garage sale. I'd even stocked the kitchen with lentils, vegetables, wheat flour, and spices, and I'd made a few dishes the day before and had them waiting for her. I put the satin bedspread on the bed and a soft comforter beneath it. I watched her face eagerly, as I showed her around her new home, but she didn't say much. She still looked exhausted. When I showed her where she could bathe and put her things, she rummaged through her suitcase for her toothbrush and nightgown. My compulsively tidy wife left the rest of her things packed and, now, swirled and rumpled. When I looked in on her about 10 minutes later, she was fast asleep.

"Coming to a new country is difficult," I thought, "and everybody reacts differently." I slid into bed beside her and tried to sleep.

I'd thought that marriage would be the simple, comfortable arrangement I'd watched my parents forge over the decades. Instead, I was beginning to realize just how complicated it could be. Many lessons followed.

Once, for example, Shamal and I were discussing something and she brought up the events of the day before our wedding, when we walked to the temple. "I was so hungry and thirsty!" she said.

"But I asked whether you wanted anything, and you said no!"

"When I say no, it doesn't necessarily mean no," she said—in a voice far firmer than the one she'd used to deny any food or drink. "If you had insisted, I would have eaten something."

Marriage, I decided, is a walk on a very high tightrope.

Still, Shamal was the kindest person I'd ever met, and perhaps the most intelligent. We would go out for dinner, or to a concert, and talk for hours. She was a little bit insecure—she always wanted us to go everywhere together, even to the grocery store—but I didn't mind.

What did make me sad was that she never seemed truly joyful about anything. She was either normal or down, never up. And when she was sitting quietly and didn't realize that anyone was watching, her eyes were sad.

I didn't know why.

The issue of our taking money from Shamal's father didn't go away. I could see that it was eating at her, so one of the first things I did, as soon as I had some money, was return the 15,000 rupees, hoping to put an end to that issue.

It didn't seem to make her feel any better, so next I returned the gold jewelry they had given Shamal. She cared nothing for jewelry, so I could explain very tactfully that she was not wearing it and suggest that they give it to one of their other daughters.

That didn't help, either. Shamal kept saying, "It's just the fact that you took the money!"

I stopped even trying to understand.

Then, a few months later, we were having a cozy Friday night at home. It was snowing, so we'd turned off all the lights and pulled the drapes open to watch the world turn white. Shamal was sitting on the sofa, and I was stretched out with my head in her lap.

"When we have kids, they'll have to teach *us* how to build a snowman," I remarked.

"I'll heat the chocolate afterward," Shamal promised. "You're supposed to put marshmallows in it."

We started talking about our childhoods, and suddenly I felt the need to tell her my deepest secret. I sat bolt upright.

"Shamal," I said. Her eyes, sleepy as a cat's, flew open. "I have to tell you something," I said. "I have false front teeth."

"*What?*" she said, and burst out laughing.

"You're already making fun of me?"

"No, no, Shri, of course not." She giggled again. "I'm just relieved."

"Well, it was very difficult to say," I informed her. "When I was a kid, my teeth protruded, and it made me look ridiculous. But you know how it was back home: Nobody even went to the dentist for checkups, let alone something like braces. I'm not even sure they *had* orthodontists in Belgaum!"

Now she was listening with her usual solemn attention.

"Anyway, when I was 20, I actually went and asked a doctor to pull those front teeth out and give me a bridge," I said. "And it made a huge difference. I had more confidence, because it made me look a lot better."

"It certainly did," she said, kissing me. We sat quietly for a few minutes, her head on my shoulder.

"Shri?" she said, and her voice was different. Trembling.

"Yes?"

"I want to tell *you* something."

"Anything," I said, holding her closer. She started her next sentence several times, but each time stumbled or broke it off.

Finally, she blurted, "The father you met at the wedding is not my biological father."

I pulled away just far enough to watch her eyes, which looked dark and scared. I stroked her cheek with my thumb and waited for more. I was desperate to understand that particular relationship, because it had caused so much tension in our own marriage.

"My biological father was an engineer, and he died in an accident crossing a bridge," she told me. "Baba is my stepfather."

She said, her words tumbling out rapidly now, that she'd only learned this a few months before we married, when she was applying for a residency and needed her birth certificate. She said it upset her so much that she walked all over Mumbai, crying hysterically and thinking about killing herself.

I tried not to look startled. First, I couldn't see why such news would have been so traumatic for her. I mean, yes, it must have been sad and confusing, but the father she'd lost was the father she'd never known. *Killing* herself over it? I couldn't even see why it had been such a dark secret.

Then I remembered her reaction when I'd missed my plane to Belgaum. She'd done something similar then, walking all over town and crying hysterically. I didn't know what to make of this, other than to realize she was more fragile than I'd thought. And that she needed to wander by herself when she was upset.

We talked for an hour or so, Shamal with relief. But I could still detect a huge sense of loss and remorse inside her. And she had regrets; she felt she would have treated him differently had she known he was her stepfather.

"I always teased him, especially for quitting his job and staying home smoking so much," she said slowly, staring at the snowflakes as they swirled in the pool of light under the streetlight. "I was mean."

Gradually I began to see: She felt guilty because she had taken their relationship for granted and treated it casually and because she had judged him and made his life perhaps a little difficult. Then, shortly before we met, she'd learned the truth. He had rescued her mother from widowhood and taken on the financial and emotional burden of his new wife's daughter.

He'd never made a big deal of it, but Shamal knew that paying for her wedding was a sacrifice. Now that she knew about all the previous sacrifices she'd never recognized, she wished we had not asked it of him.

By this time, I wished that too. After that night, I tried even harder to lighten her mind, but very rarely did Shamal loosen up enough to be comfortable and playful.

When she did relax, we had a wonderful time. Often just a glass of wine would be enough, and suddenly life would seem good, and we'd be having fun together. But she didn't *celebrate* things. Even when something good happened, she could only worry about what might happen next. I was just the opposite: ready to celebrate each triumph and unconcerned about what would follow.

135

"Problems just have to be solved," I told her. And every time I said it, she'd shake her head, as though to warn me that it was never that simple.

Only one thing brought Shamal pure joy. I saw the difference the day I took her to the gynecologist because she'd missed her second period. I was in the room with her when he came back in and said, "Yes! You are pregnant!"

We went straight home and called our families and friends. "Do you want a boy or a girl?" everyone asked, but we didn't care about gender. We were just so happy.

The next evening I came home from work to find her humming, a lavish dinner almost ready, candles lit on the dining room table.

"Very soon," she told me, smiling softly, "I will be a mother of a child, and you will be a father."

The first challenge was picking out the right name.

"Our child is going to grow up in America," I said, "so we should not have a very complicated Indian name."

"No," Shamal agreed, "but it must have some Indian meaning."

By the time she had an ultrasound and we learned that we were having a son, we'd settled on his name: Neel, if you spelled it the Indian way, but we would spell it Neil to make it American. In Marathi, the word means blue, and Lord Krishna is always depicted as blue, which gives the name powerful significance. What's more, all of Neil's friends at preschool would be able to pronounce it!

Getting ready for the baby was great fun, but even then Shamal couldn't relax and enjoy the experience. She was worried sick about the entrance exam for physicians from abroad. She was terrified that either she'd fail and be unable to practice in the United States or would do badly and have to go to some small town to practice. "I don't want us to be separated," she told me.

I'd bought her every preparation book I could find. Twice the scheduled date for the exam had arrived. Twice she'd choked and refused to go.

Then I had an idea. "Aren't there classes you can take?" I asked her. "Just to help review and prepare, so you have some confidence? Why don't you look around and see?"

She said nothing more about it. Finally I asked again, and she said, reluctantly, "There is a class, but it is too expensive."

"*Take* it," I urged her. "The cost means nothing."

She registered the next morning. I'd drop her off at her coaching class before I went to work, and after class, she would study in the library until I picked her up.

Then came the third exam date. "We are not doing this again," I told her, trying to put just the right ratio of firmness and gentleness into my voice. "Go to the test center and write whatever you can. I don't want you to just miss it."

So she went.

When the results arrived in the mail, I was out of town. When I called home, she told me the envelope had come.

"Open it!" I urged.

"Noooo! I can't face it. I'm waiting until you come home."

I got home the next evening, dropped my suitcase and headed straight for the mail pile.

"It's here," she said, coming out of the kitchen with the envelope in her hand. "You open it!"

I tore it open, scanned the flimsy computerized sheet, and grinned. She'd gotten an 85 percent! I whooped and hugged her. She refused to believe me, so I showed her the letter.

She sighed, gave a small smile, and said, "Okay."

I said, eagerly, "What are you thinking?"

"Oh, I'm thinking that when I start my residency, it's going to be very hard for you and the baby," she said, her brow already furrowed with her next worry.

She said she couldn't imagine how she would manage to be both mother and doctor. "I will be working day and night during my pregnancy. And how can I pay attention to my work after the child's birth?"

I promised her we would manage. "I will help you out. I will look after the baby."

We took Lamaze classes, and we practiced the breathing exercises and got ourselves ready for the baby in every imaginable way. Shamal received invitations from six or seven universities but accepted a residency in neurology at Saint Louis University Hospital.

Everything went along smoothly until the end of her sixth month.

I took her for a routine test, and the doctor called us into his office afterward and informed her that she was already starting to dilate. If she continued working the way she was, with long hours on her feet and constant stress, she'd go into labor too soon, and Neil wouldn't survive. She had to go on bedrest until she reached the point in her pregnancy where it would be safe for him to be delivered into the world.

I was nodding my head when I heard Shamal say, "Oh, no. I can't possibly take bedrest. Our hospital is understaffed."

Now, I'd often watched Shamal's medical colleagues shoot each other down, but it was even more amusing to see my own wife try to discount the advice of her physician. He leaned forward and said, very deliberately, "Madam, there are still two months in which your baby needs to continue to grow before delivery. If you do not rest, you might give birth to a premature baby, and you will be solely responsible for the consequences."

We came home from the clinic in silence. I was waiting for Shamal to concede his wisdom. But that evening, she was still sticking to her point of view. "I am working in the emergency ward at the moment, so I must continue working for at least one more month."

Now it was my responsibility to make her understand. "Look, Shamal, I don't want either you or our baby to be in danger because you overexert yourself at the hospital. Call the dean immediately, tell him what's happening, and ask for leave. *Please* do this, for God's sake!"

The conversation went on for another hour—Shamal was so conscientious that it could make her terribly stubborn. But I put my foot down and kept it down, and, finally, she asked for the leave.

Those next weeks went by quickly, and at last, we reached week 32. Shamal and our baby were both out of danger! Now there was nothing to worry about even if she went into labor at any moment. We were free to lead our normal lives.

I went right out and bought a big cradle—which, typical of American home furniture, was in pieces in a box—and cursed for hours as I tried to put it together. I'm okay with test tubes, not so much so with hammer and nails and screws. It was, in my opinion, a very complicated cradle, with a special door you could lower to pick up the baby. I struggled through the whole weekend, but I finally had it together. And the drop-down special door worked.

The following weekend, Shamal and I decided to go boating at Creve Coeur Lake, a large lake in the suburbs west of St. Louis, which was one of our favorite things to do. It was one of those perfect spring days: The sun was very warm, the grass the brightest green you could imagine, and the breeze gentle enough to ripple the lake. "This will be one of our last carefree days," I teased Shamal as I pumped air into the plastic inflatable rowboat I'd bought for $20 the previous year. As always, I played the role of oarsman and rowed us all around the lake. We had a blissful time—Shamal's eyes were clear, her brow smooth, her laugh easy. We came home at sundown, all giggly and sleepy.

The minute we walked into the house, Shamal's face changed. "Call the hospital," she said. "The pain has started."

Her bag was already packed, so there was no tension. "Don't worry, darling, we'll be fine," I said confidently, and I called the doctor and then helped her into the car. The hospital was about 20 miles away. I was going just as fast as I dared when I glanced down at the fuel indicator and realized I was about to run out of gas. I cursed myself for not checking sooner. We'd spent the whole day boating, and I'd had so much fun, I'd forgotten to look as we drove home.

Within seconds, I spotted a service station and skidded in. I filled up gas, fumbling with the pump, and then continued on to the hospital. The doctor was waiting for us—"What took you so long?"—and, without waiting for an answer, he took Shamal into the delivery room.

"Wait, I'm coming, too!" I called, eager to be present after all our Lamaze lessons. He glanced back and nodded permission.

I was in the delivery room the whole time, holding Shamal's hand, counting with her to help her focus on her breathing, and wincing as she screamed. Neil was indeed a few weeks premature—but he was perfect. When I saw him, I was so excited that I could hardly think straight. The creation of a new human being! He looked very fair, almost pinkish, with very bright eyes. As he slid into the world, I held my breath—even after all those hours counting Shamal's breaths! Taking pictures with tears in my eyes, I watched the nurses clean him up, cut the cord, weigh him, and wrap him in a blanket.

First they gave him to Shamal, and she held him close. Then, exhausted and beaming, she handed him to me. For once, she was as happy as I was.

Hours later, the nurses made me go home to get some sleep. The joy carried me through the long fluorescent halls and out into the parking lot, until I could no longer feel my feet hitting the ground. Now I knew what people meant when they talked about being so happy that they were walking on air.

I'd been alone for so long in my life. I'd left home at 18, which is very unusual for an Indian kid, and all those years I'd been alone in a strange country. When I found Shamal, I suddenly had a partner, someone to share the rest of my life with—and I couldn't even be with her for a year. Then, when she joined me, there was still such a separateness about her that I sometimes felt lonely even in her presence.

Now we'd grown used to each other's very different rhythms, and having a baby had drawn us close. I was beginning to feel that deep sense of peace that comes with a good marriage. I looked forward to coming home at night, because Shamal would always be there. Maybe not literally—she might be on duty at the hospital—but she'd be home soon, and her presence filled the rooms. Never again would my house be dark and cold and empty.

And now, with Neil, we were more than a couple. We were truly a family.

After Neil's birth, Shamal had a lot of pain. She'd thrown her back out during the delivery, so she had muscle spasms. Worse than that, she also had the emotional pain of postpartum depression.

At first I didn't know what it was. All I knew was that she seemed especially sad and anxious, despite the joy of Neil, and I couldn't imagine why.

"Just enjoy the time off," I urged her. "Don't worry. I have no problem helping feed and clean the baby. Just be yourself."

I thought with a pang of what it would have been like for her back home. In India, the woman would often go to her parents' home in the eighth or ninth month of her pregnancy. Then, after the delivery, she would stay in the hospital almost 10 days. When she and the baby returned to her parents' home, someone would come to massage her and bathe the baby. Their room would be kept dark for three weeks or so, and she would do very little except rest and nurse him. Her husband would be informed when the baby was born, and he would show up on the second or third day, visit for a while, then go home and return for them in a month or so.

I couldn't give Shamal that, but I did whatever I could. My parents were coming to be with us for the first six months, and hers for the next six months. She'd be back at work soon, but I'd be sharing Neil's care. Bathing him, for example, was my job.

When it was time, I took him into my arms and headed for the bathroom. Then I stood there, staring down at the tub. He'd drown if I put him in there! Or, if I made it very shallow, he might wriggle around and bang his head on the porcelain.

Then I figured it out—I'd shower with him in my arms! I hurried back and laid him in his crib while I stripped off my clothes. He was wailing at being left, and I was rushing, fumbling with a stuck zipper on my jeans and trying, because somehow it seemed faster to pull my jeans off before taking off my shoes. I raced back, ignoring the drawn curtains, and grabbed him out of his cradle. But at the shower door, I stopped.

"The minute we both get wet, he'll get slippery," I reminded myself. "He wriggles like an eel—how are you going to soap him and regulate the tap and keep from dropping him?"

I sat down on the closed toilet seat, Neil in my arms, and thought hard.

"You are a scientist, Shri," I said aloud. "Solve the problem."

I had it! I got dressed and went to the store.

I came home carrying a small rubber tub I could set inside the sink. That way, I could keep both hands free for the bathing and keep my son safe.

I felt very strong and capable in those weeks after our son's birth. I was taking pictures all the time, inviting people to come and see the baby. Every day presented some new little problem, and every day I found a way to solve it.

It was good that I was feeling strong, because Shamal had had to go back to her residency, and she was working 60 hours a week, sometimes on the evening shift. I'd pack up Neil and we'd bring her dinner, because I knew she wouldn't take time otherwise.

Meanwhile, as our parents arrived, we waged the giant battle of child-rearing styles. Sometimes the battle was fought between generations, sometimes between the sexes.

I had thought a lot about being a father, and I had compared Indian and American ways in my mind, deciding how to blend them. The American methods were often more logical, I thought. I liked the idea of the baby having his own room, for example, and I saw no need to go and pick him up every time he cried.

Shamal and Inni had their own ideas. Inni was especially fierce; she believed in having the baby in the same room, holding him constantly, massaging him with oil. "It's all right if you keep the child in a separate room," she finally said. "Let him sleep there alone. I don't mind. But I expect at least one of you to attend to him when he wakes up crying." But of course she raced to do that whenever we didn't.

"Oh, Inni, you don't have to go running to pick up Neil whenever he cries," I told her. "If he has eaten properly, his diaper is clean, and he has no other ailment, then let him cry, and after some time he will quiet himself."

This made Inni furious. "Shri, you don't tell me how to bring up a child! A baby communicates with his parents by way of touch. He can't speak and explain if something is wrong. The only way he can attract your attention is by crying. He needs the warmth of your touch."

"Yes, I agree, a child yearns for touch," I said. "But let him finish his crying first, and then you can cuddle him. Otherwise he will develop the habit of crying just to get your attention. You have come here to stay for six months. You will pay immediate attention to him every time he cries, and not only will this habit affect him, but it will be difficult for us to break when you leave."

I won the argument. Inni was very strong willed, but I was even stronger willed! I did allow her to massage Neil with oil, though, because she so loved doing it and I saw no harm in it. She also used to chat with him for hours. I still don't know how she managed to talk to a month-old baby. She used to show him things around the house, play with toys, sing a lullaby. She even laughed with him, and in general, she kept him in the pink of health.

I had to give her credit. Still, I did not want to mix Indian superstitions and bizarre traditions into our parenting. I was amazed when Shamal consented to the touch of lamp-black you smudge on the child's cheek to keep away evil—a ritual devised because if the baby looks too pretty someone might be envious and cast an evil spell. I thought it was hogwash.

We all compromised a bit—but on one subject I would not compromise.

Neil had been born on May 18, 1988, just six days before our fourth anniversary. "We will celebrate at home this year," Shamal said, but I shook my head. Too often I had seen our friends stop being lovers when they became parents. I did not want our marriage to suffer, and I saw no reason that it should. "We'll go to a nice romantic restaurant," I told her, "and we'll bring him with us."

So we found a very soft blanket and tucked Neil into his car seat, and he slept right through our candlelit dinner of steak and lobster. The next night we went to a concert, and again he was quiet and happy. Shamal was so relieved, she began to relax a bit.

At the end of that first year with Neil, I was finally eligible to become a US citizen. Excited, I studied for the silly little exam and breezed through it. The interview made me more nervous—my visa experiences still haunted me—but this time everything went fine. Before I knew it, I had my hand over my heart and I was reciting the Pledge of Allegiance to the flag of the United States of America.

Many of my friends in the Indian community had no intention of ever becoming citizens. Most were in the States to work, and when their children grew up they intended to return "home." Some even went earlier, when their daughters reached adolescence, to avoid exposing them to American-style dating.

"If you're going to make a life in America, you have to accept your new country for all of its strengths and weaknesses," I once told someone who was preparing to leave. "You can't just pick and choose, any more than you can do that with another human being."

My love for America was unconditional. Its freedom meant more to me than its advertising, saturated with sex, or its casualness about marital and family obligations. I could ignore the ads, and Shamal and I could create our own family rules.

But we couldn't force India's rigid, traditional society to give us freedom.

Because I was a "resident alien"—a phrase that made me feel like a Martian—I'd been required to wait years before I could apply for citizenship. But I think I'd known since my first semester in Akron that I was going to make my life in the United States.

Miss Virginia had been right after all.

The door to our first house was painted bright red, and I loved it. We bought the house in 1988, soon after Neil was born. It was brick, white with black and gray speckles, and it sat on a tree-lined little street in the old-fashioned suburb of Webster Groves. It cost $99,000 and had a split-level design, three bedrooms, a two-car garage, and a long back yard with big trees.

A lot of good things happened while we lived in that house. Our parents came to visit us for the first time. Our second son was born. We named him Samir, telling each other that he could shorten it to Sam later if he wanted to sound more American.

We made friends that soon became a close-knit group of 10, all of us Maharashtrian immigrants. We went to each other's homes for dinner, celebrated holidays together like a family.

The boys grew out of babyhood. In the summer we got a little plastic kiddie pool for them and splashed around. At Christmastime we bundled them into the car and drove around looking at all the icicle lights and prancing reindeer and life-size Nativity scenes. It was not unlike the Lord Ganesha festival, I murmured to Shamal, amused at the full circle our lives had drawn.

Our best friends were a couple named Guru and Kalpana, both bright and funny and kind. We went on camping and float trips together, cooked meals with each other or went out to restaurants, stayed up late at night watching movies. Guru and I had mock-fierce table tennis and tennis competitions.

Of course, Shamal was really the competitive one, especially if we were playing cards or solving some kind of puzzle. We used to divide into sides, the women on one and the men on the other, and then we'd sing songs and try to end them on a difficult letter. Wherever you stopped, the other side had to start singing a song that began with that letter. Shamal's eyes would glow, and she'd plot hard to make sure that her team won.

I liked seeing her carefree and absorbed in play. The other times I saw her pulled away from her worries were the times she spent with the children. She'd laugh aloud when she played with one of the boys, carrying him on her shoulders or back, making him giggle. At the park, she'd play and run. Even with a board game or throwing dice, she'd tease: "If I get a 7, I'll be able to knock your piece out!"

I wasn't the least bit competitive in those small things, only in the big picture. But I loved watching Shamal throw herself into a game. Those were the only times I really saw her out of her shell, free of all worries.

There were other good times, though. They came when we went out to a good restaurant and she drank a glass of wine, or when we took a cruise and she was too far from home to do anything about her worries.

Shamal was so unfailingly kind, I don't think anybody ever realized how much she fretted, or how dark her moods could be. Children adored her because she was so loving and playful with them, and older people loved her because she was so caring. There was nobody who did not like her.

But there was nobody who really understood her, either.

CHAPTER 6

Evolution of an Enterprise

WHEN WE BOUGHT our house, I was still working at Petrolite, and it should have been enough. But I was one of 250 research chemists in a company of nearly 2,000 people. There were plenty of challenges—we made all sorts of specialty chemicals and additives used to manufacture everything from chewing gum to carpeting to paint. I specialized in synthesizing new molecules.

One day the chairman of our company, Mr. William Nasser, visited my lab. I was totally engrossed in my work, setting up an experiment to make new molecules. My eyes were covered in goggles, my body in a loose lab coat, and I had an array of instruments and materials scattered around my bench.

"Hi, Shri!" he said, startling me. "Congratulations!"

I had no idea what had prompted this—and, clearly, neither did my boss, Mike Naiman, who hadn't been alerted to the visit. Mr. Nasser pulled up an old lab stool and started chatting, clearly euphoric. All I could think about was whether his brand-new, very expensive suit would get stained with my chemicals.

"Shri, can you imagine?" he said, oblivious to the mess. "We struggled for two years to find the right adhesive for a client who makes carpets. He is extremely happy with the quality of adhesive you prepared, and he just placed a very big order with us. Congratulations and keep it up!"

Before I could even thank him, he was gone. I was thrilled; my immediate boss was less so, though, because Mr. Nasser had gone around him and approached me directly. Even worse, four days later, Mr. Nasser returned and invited me to accompany him to the next meeting of all Petrolite managers. "I want you to present a paper on the discovery of your new adhesive," he told me.

Again I was tickled, and I couldn't wait to tell Shamal. I flew to Tulsa, where these quarterly meetings were held, in the company's private jet with Mr. Nasser and four other people. I was on the bottom rung of the ladder, a mere chemist; above me were our group leader, a general manager, a vice president, and, last, Mr. Nasser. Yet he was interested in my work and treated me with great respect, and we became friends in spite of the difference in age and status. He invited me to all of the quarterly meetings in Tulsa, which for me were like going to picnics, except, of course, that I got to wear a coat and tie instead of my loose and clumsy chemist's lab coat. Different scientists made presentations, nearly always interesting, and dinner was always a lavish spread, the typical American banquet.

But when I got back to work, all was not well, it seemed. Mr. Naiman treated me a little suspiciously. "Shri," he told me, "if you discover something new during your lab experiments, let me know about it first. *I* will convey the information to the company."

I thought I knew what he was doing; he wanted to take the credit for my breakthroughs. So I ignored his request and continued to provide all the information about my experiments to my senior bosses directly. But he and the manager of the manufacturing unit joined forces and started harassing me. They said that if I didn't tell them about my research experiments first, they would make sure that the products I was researching never got manufactured.

Over the next year, they pressured me constantly, and the experience was intimidating. I felt less creative every day. As I drove to and from work, I'd be asking myself, "Is this the American dream?" It had bought us a two-bedroom house with a two-car garage, but I wanted something different. Sometimes my work was appreciated, sometimes not. Now, my supervisor was trying to stifle—or steal—my results.

I continued to ignore his schemes and focus on my work. One day, Mr. Nasser came back to my lab, but this time he was not happy or relaxed. "Look, Shri, we have encountered a serious problem in one of the reactors," he said urgently. "We have noticed a certain variety of high molecular weight polymer during a chemical reaction, and some of the pipelines of the reactor have been blocked. Can you do something about it?"

I was glad to know he trusted me, but terrified to take up this challenge. "Give me the samples," I said, "and I will try my best." I had no confidence I could solve this one, but I started studying the polymerization process.

While I was trying to solve the problem of the blocked pipeline, a different—and dangerous—incident took place. I was overseeing an important but difficult experiment in a pilot plant, which is a small-scale version of a manufacturing process. There was one small reactor, essentially a miniature version of the actual reactor in the real plant; it looked like a giant pressure cooker and measured about 6 feet wide and 8 feet high.

We wanted to try manufacturing a new type of additive by using hydrogen bromide, a gas that can be poisonous. We took the special precaution of replacing all metal pipes in the reactor with a special grade of glass pipes. The plant engineers checked all the glass pipes, the required chemicals were poured into the reactor, and then the hydrogen bromide was released. The chemical reaction would begin when the temperature reached 120 degrees Celsius.

We stood back to watch. Suddenly I noticed a boiling chemical solution oozing from the reactor—and with it fumes of poisonous hydrogen bromide. There was clearly some leakage somewhere in the reactor. We had to close the main valve.

"Run away! Move! Now!" I yelled, and everybody ran toward the laboratory door. I ran toward the reactor instead and, without bothering about the poisonous fumes, I shut off the main valve. Anything could have happened: The gas could have been fatal, or the reactor could have exploded. As it was, the only casualty was my nose.

Inhaling those fumes permanently damaged one of the sensory centers in my brain. I would never again smell the velvety spice of sandalwood, the rough sweetness of coconut, the delicacy of *chapha*, a white flower with a long, narrow leaf and the deepest fragrance you can imagine.

But I was proud of myself for taking the risk to shut off the valve. Otherwise, things could have turned out far worse.

I was still trying to solve the other problem with the blocked pipeline in the reactor, the one Mr. Nasser had asked me to study. There was no solution in sight. The chemical reactions sometimes were completed, sometimes stopped halfway through. Whole batches might go to waste.

One day, when I was testing various solutions and solvents, I realized that when a few drops of tetrahydrofuran was added to the solvent, the reactor functioned very well. Tetrahydrofuran didn't allow any residues to accumulate near the reactor mesh or inside the pipes. This meant that the reactor could continue functioning smoothly.

My discovery was extremely profitable to Petrolite, and I was promoted to group leader. But I still didn't have the freedom or the power to make my own decisions.

The other reason for my discontent at Petrolite was that I could see no real way to give myself new challenges. I'd realized early on that, when you're working as a scientist, you are stereotyped into doing only technical work. Everyone assumes that if you can invent molecules, you can't possibly be a people person or an idea person.

Initially I'd decided to break that stereotype by getting an MBA, and I'd finished it in 1988, just before Neil was born. That had gotten me a middling sort of supervisory position, but I still felt restless. "What *would* I want?" I asked myself. "What would make me happy now?"

The answer came immediately: "There are 10 managers, and I'm at the bottom. I want to have my own company, my own business, even if it's very small. I want to *shape* a company and watch it grow and improve."

By now I knew the unwritten rule in most American corporations: A highly educated Indian can become a good technician or even an eminent scientist, but it is very difficult for him to climb to the very top. He will never be the chairman of the company, because that title is often reserved for white Americans.

If I wanted to be the head of a company, I would have to buy my own company.

I kept scratching my head, thinking about all this. I didn't have a big product idea, a new invention, something innovative like a new mousetrap. I couldn't afford to start a company from scratch; it would be easier to buy one that was already running. But I didn't even have the capital or the experience to do *that* much.

I decided that I would go and work for a small entrepreneurial company first, with an eye to owning it in the long run. I grabbed the St. Louis Yellow Pages and found a section called "Testing Laboratories." I made a list of the small ones and started sending them my résumé.

Most of these companies' owners didn't understand why someone with a PhD and an MBA, already working at a $300 million company, would want to come work for them. Then I came across a potential employer: Alan Siegel, the 74-year-old owner of Industrial Testing Laboratories. He was a grandfatherly man, and he took a liking to me. He had 30 employees and sales of about $3 million, and I could see right away that those sales could be increased.

"Look, I want to work for you," I told him.

"Ah, but Shri, I don't have a position!"

I told him the truth: "I want to work so I can someday take over your company."

That's when he told me to call Clara Craver.

Dr. Craver's company was even smaller than Alan Siegel's, just four people: a secretary, a chemist, Clara, and her husband, Ken, who'd retired from Monsanto. He kept urging her to sell the business so they could travel, but she was a workaholic. Tough, brilliant, and impatient with idiots, she'd formed her small chemical testing company on her own back in 1959. She'd made up the name by combining "chemistry" with "infrared spectroscopy," a technique was used to fingerprint molecules so you could identify unknown substances. That was her specialty: identification, along with deformulation, or taking things apart.

The company solved problems. Maybe someone had made a batch of contact lens solution that was causing eye irritation, and they need to know what's gone wrong. Or a ballpoint pen manufacturer finds that a new ballpoint made a competitor in Japan has brilliant shimmery ink that dries very quickly. Dr. Craver's company would find out what that ink's ingredients were by taking it apart and fingerprinting its various components. "Look," Clara would say, "the Japanese company is using a different material as a catalyst." It was all perfectly legal, because the company had obtained the knowledge on its own, not through industrial espionage! If their ingredient was patented, the client was out of luck. But sometimes it's just a trade secret.

My brain raced with all the problems her chemical testing lab could solve for various companies. I slowed myself down and broached the topic of a position with Clara Craver.

"I have no money to pay you," she told me crisply.

I replied that the money didn't matter. "You may have a PhD, but you don't know how to do this," she said, glaring at me. The things Clara Craver did, solving industrial problems, weren't things schools teach you.

"No, I don't," I agreed. "I'm a synthetic chemist; I make molecules."

"So why should I talk to you?"

I was frank with her; I explained that eventually I wanted to buy her business. I got the response I'd come to expect: "But you don't have any money. Why should we bother?"

Finally, though, I persuaded her to hire me part-time.

I'd go to the lab on my lunch hours, sometimes after work and always on weekends and vacations. But I still wanted my own business, and as I got to know Clara better we talked often about it. She was the brain behind all the work the lab did, so she'd have a hard time selling it to anyone else. But by then I had learned her techniques. Besides, I *knew* I could have better client relations than she had! Clara was not an easy person. She was so straightforward that she blurted out whatever was on her mind. She'd send a client packing if she didn't like what he said to her.

She tried to send me packing, too. "You don't have enough money!" she regularly reminded me. But by then she was beginning to like me, in spite of herself. I was starting to learn the business. She didn't charge enough, I decided. She didn't vary her services; she tried to solve every problem with her single tool, the infrared spectroscope. And she was entirely inflexible: A client would call with an emergency and she'd say, "My daughter Susie is coming from out of town with the grandchildren, so I can't take on any work for a week."

I'd listen and wince. I kept coming there on lunch hours and weekends—by now it had been at least a year—and I kept reminding her that I wanted to buy her business.

She wanted $75,000. I could raise $65,000, which was my offer.

To make matters worse, I suddenly had a rival. An older guy named Fred Firestone, about 6-foot-3 with silver hair, showed up. One day I saw him walk into the lab with Clara, his arm around her shoulders as he told her what an amazing company she had built. She was flattered off her feet. He was around all the time after that; he'd put his arm around Clara and say, "How's my girlfriend today?" I wanted to throw up.

I watched Fred carefully, and one day I heard him telling Clara that $75,000 was a bargain. "This is a gold mine," he said. "I'll give you

$85,000, if you will consult with me." I stood there at my lab counter, frozen and seething at the same time. Surely she wouldn't overlook me and sell it to him? By now I was running all the research; I knew more about the business at that point of time than she did!

The next day, Fred walked into the lab beaming. "I have just reached an agreement with Clara," he said very loudly, "and I'm the new owner!"

He shook everybody's hand and talked about what a great company we were going to build together. I shot Clara a hurt look; I felt utterly betrayed. On the other hand, I really couldn't blame her. Fred had tendered a better offer.

I went home and thought very hard. I wasn't ready to throw in the towel just yet. The next morning, I went to see Clara at her home. I had a plan; a long shot, but it just might work. I was beginning to sense that this guy Fred was not for real.

"Clara, what if Fred *doesn't* buy the company?" I said very carefully.

"That won't happen," she said, sounding more gay and carefree than I'd ever heard her.

"But if it does? Will you sell it to me for $75,000?" I had no idea where I'd find that much money, but I knew I had to increase my original offer of $65,000.

"You're wasting your time," she told me.

"That's fine," I said, "but can we have a backup agreement, just in case Fred doesn't come through? Then you will have a fallback position."

Even in her current giddy state, Clara was still Clara—shrewd enough to like the idea of a backup plan. She agreed. I had the papers drawn up immediately and took them back to her house for her to sign.

The next week Fred came to Clara and said, "My investors can't free up the money quite yet. Will you take a loan from me?" I'm sure he expected her to smile and agree—but we had signed the agreement. Besides, I think his charm was starting to wear off. Clara didn't like people who failed to live up to their side of an agreement—period.

So there it was: I had my company—but only if I could find the $75,000! It would have been more convenient—and perhaps wiser—for me to wait another two or three years before finalizing this deal. But I wasn't going to let this opportunity go.

The first three banks I approached said, "You have never done business before!" But, as usual, adversity motivated me. I'd thought about this a lot, realizing that not only did I manage to try harder when somebody threw an obstacle in my path, I also slowed down when everything was fine, and then I actually became *less* efficient. Overcoming a challenge gave me energy.

I kept at it, and finally I put together the structure: I borrowed a huge sum from the Bank of America, and I found out that Petrolite was trying to get rid of people and asked them to put my name on the list. That gave me six months' salary and severance pay. But I was still short $25,000.

I went to Dr. Craver. "My loan has been sanctioned by the bank, and I have withdrawn money on my credit card, but still I am short $25,000," I said. "I have put all my cards in front of you. You tell me: How shall we go about this contract?"

She looked at me closely. "All right," she said, nodding briskly. "I will give you a loan of $25,000. You may repay this within a year."

And so, in October 1990, I bought my own business.

I walked through my new company, climbing wobbly stairs from the lab in the basement up to the lab on the first floor. That was it, the entire business. I walked through with my briefcase still in my hand, and suddenly I remembered my first job, as dental assistant, and how I had to carry the dentist's bag upstairs. I grinned and looked around. There was nobody around to carry *my* briefcase.

The young chemist stayed to work with me, but I had no other staff. Clara and her 70-year-old secretary had both retired. There was a clause in the contract, though, stipulating that Clara continue to guide the new owner by providing 40 hours of counsel. To fulfill this clause, I used to call her for guidance, and of course she would insist that I continue to do things just as she had done them. She gave me some good advice, but she also used to interrupt my decisions or contradict my plans. I didn't like her interfering, and I was relieved when the 40 hours were over. Now the responsibility for the lab was entirely on my shoulders.

We had no fax, no copy machine. To make copies, I had to go to the grocery store across the street. I would do the chemistry work, go to the typewriter and type up the report, call the client, and, finally, put up a sign reading, "The owner is out for some urgent work. Kindly return in 15 minutes." I'd rush across the street to make a copy of the report, then come back and remove the sign. Or I'd go to court and serve as an expert witness, then come back and sweep up the lab. I would answer the phones, work in the lab to solve client's problems, type the report on the computer, and take the packages to the post office to be mailed.

The adrenaline surged all year; I told Shamal it was like working in an emergency room, always a crisis. But I loved it. Some clients wanted to meet me urgently, and they'd offer to come to my office. And I would panic because I knew if they walked in there, it would not be impressive.

"Sir, it's my pleasure to come to you; don't take the trouble to come all the way to my office," I would say. When they did insist, I'd put the meeting off, telling them that I was busy that day—perhaps the next day? "Hmmm ... let me check my schedule." And the next day I would carry in the vacuum cleaner from home and clean the entire office before putting on my suit and tie to look like the CEO of the company.

I had developed an unwritten code of conduct for myself. Rule No. 1: "I will not continue to run this business as a hobby." My second rule, therefore, was to never say no: "Let the customer come up with any problem. We will strive to sort it out for him."

Clara had used only one method of chemical analysis: infrared spectroscopy, at which she was brilliant. But she declined any job that required a different type of analysis. So my third rule was never to use only one technique. I used nuclear magnetic resonance spectroscopy, mass spectroscopy, gas chromatography, high-pressure liquid chromatography, and more. Each method had its own uses, and my clients were glad that I could call on the full array.

That first year we made only $150,000, and I couldn't afford to give myself a salary. The following year, though, we added a big new client: a US naval laboratory in Maryland. Labels had fallen off hundreds of old bottles, and they wanted to know what chemicals were contained in them. I bid $50,000, but later I learned that nobody else had even bid, because it was a warfare center and those chemicals were very explosive. Some hadn't been opened in 20 or 30 years.

I ended up analyzing about 300 chemicals. *Very* carefully.

New clients came. A pharmaceutical manufacturer brought me green tablets spotted yellow and white for no apparent reason. They did not want to get in trouble with the Food and Drug Administration, which would mean a product recall, a hefty fine, or both. They had to figure out what was causing the odd spots on the tablets.

"Show me the samples of both tablets, the good ones and the spotted ones," I said. I took their formula and collected all related information. "When did you notice this problem? When do the spots appear? Is it worse in summer than in winter? Have you changed anything about your method of formulation recently? Is there any change, however slight, in the active ingredients?" Once they'd answered these questions, I began my chemical analysis and immediately identified the problem. The company was using a particular type of starch to bind the ingredients, and a solvent in the starch, which was not necessary to the binding process, reacted with the green coloration of the tablets. The spotted tablets were harmless. I wrote my report, and they were able to avoid any fines or compensation by noting, "Our lab has certified the tablets as safe." Of course, they still had to throw away the spotted tablets and change the type of starch they'd used, but the damage to their company was minimal, and they were so relieved that they referred many new clients to me. I had solved the Case of the Polka-Dotted Pills.

On another occasion, a beer company president called me on a Friday and said, "There's this slimy material inside our beer bottles, and we don't know where it's coming from, and we need to know by Monday morning."

I said, "Of course." I'd do whatever it took, always.

Shamal's work was a little more demanding then, because she had to go whenever her patients needed her. We traded off the child care, and often I'd take Neil with me to work. Letting him crawl around the lab was impossible—there were too many instruments, chemicals, and tool-boxes—so I brought his toys and set up a playpen in a vacant part of the lab, making sure he was always within eyesight.

One day I unfolded the playpen and plopped Neil inside—and then it struck me that I'd forgotten to bring his toys. Nothing in the lab was safe enough to substitute, so I thought for a while and then handed him the telephone. A few minutes later, I glanced over and he was engrossed, pressing different keys. I returned to my work.

Fifteen minutes later, a police officer was at my office. "Sir, whose house is this? Is there a child here in danger?"

Test tube in hand, I looked at him, bewildered. "This is not a house. It is my place of business, and I am working in my office."

He pushed me aside and said, "We want to search the premises. We have reason to suspect that a young child is trapped here and he is in trouble."

Then I looked down at Neil, his chubby fingers wrapped around the keypad of my phone as he waved it in the air. The police officer followed my gaze, and we both burst out laughing. Somehow Neil had managed to punch 911, and the operator had heard him babbling.

After that, I was more careful about mixing home with work.

In our first year, we outgrew the original lab facility. I started searching for a new place. When I talked to my bankers, they mentioned that they had an old building for sale. The mortgage payments would have been pretty high, so I went for the same strategy I had used to help my dad buy the house in Belgaum: Buy the property, rent out part of it, and use that income to make the mortgage. So I bought the building from the bank and converted its basement, which was 1,800 square feet, into a laboratory. On the first floor I used one 900-square-foot block for offices for the lab and rented the other three, using the rent I collected to make payments on my bank loan. I now had three times as much space, and I didn't need to make my loan payments out of pocket.

Most of my clients were companies, but one day a middle-aged woman walked in and said in a trembling voice, "I have a problem. Will you solve it for me?"

"May I know your problem, please?" I asked.

She opened a huge purse and pulled out a man's white dress shirt. She pointed toward red and pink stains and announced, her voice firmer: "I want to know what these stains are from. This is my husband's shirt, and he says these are ink stains. I want you to find out whether that's true. But I don't want you to destroy the shirt, and I don't want him to notice any difference."

"Okay," I said. "I will try my best to find out." I quoted her our usual fee for that sort of analysis, and she agreed readily.

"How fast can you do it?" she asked, and I told her to come back in three hours.

"Did you find out?" she asked.

"Yes, we did," I said. "The stains are makeup and lipstick."

"Oh my God!" Her eyes were full of tears, and she sat down. Nobody said a word. The story was obvious: Her husband had lied to her about an affair.

That day I didn't feel so good about finding the answer. For weeks afterward, I couldn't forget the look on her face.

There were other domestic cases, including one that really shocked me.

A woman came in, looking terribly worried. She pushed a bag of all-purpose flour toward me. "Will you test this flour?"

"Yes, of course," I said, "but what's the problem?"

"One of my friends visited today. I made gravy from this flour, and after the meal we both had stomachaches and diarrhea. We couldn't figure out why. My husband said, 'This must have happened because of the gravy,' and he even suggested that someone had mixed poison into it. I was terrified. How could someone do that? *Why* would someone do that? I think he must have told me deliberately, to upset me. We haven't been getting along well—oh, never mind. I just wanted you to test this flour and let me know that nothing's mixed into it, so I can relax."

I did the analysis myself, and I was shocked to find traces of a poison used for killing rats. When I handed her my report, she looked very nervous. She thanked me, but after she left, so many questions remained. Had her husband poisoned the flour? And if he had, why would he alert her? The woman got her answer, but there was no lab out there to answer *my* questions.

Another, less disturbing story involved bumpers. Our client manufactured them for Ford Motor Co., his only client. But Ford had stamped one of his batches "Rejected" and sent them back. The reason given was "Paint sprayed on these bumpers is not able to stick for a long time and is peeling off the bumpers."

The manufacturer could not afford the dissatisfaction of his only client. He had to find out why this problem had occurred. Someone recommended my company to him. When he approached me, I asked to see his rejected bumpers. This time I used Clara's beloved infrared spectroscopy, and after several runs I solved the mystery. In the manufacturing process, two different types of polymers were mixed, and the mixture was heated to a certain temperature to melt these polymers together. That formed the tough plastic used for the bumpers. In the rejected bumpers, however, the polymers had not melted properly, and therefore they had not blended properly. Also missing was the "compatibilizer" that was supposed to hold the polymers together.

160

Now I had to find out why, so it wouldn't happen again. When I experimented further, I got to the root of the problem. The temperature scale installed in the factory was faulty, and it showed an erroneously high temperature before the desired temperature was actually reached, resulting in the mixing of the two polymers before they were actually hot enough to melt. The scale was repaired immediately and the bumpers' quality restored.

This client was extremely happy, and my cost estimates left us with a comfortable profit margin. Sometimes, though, my estimates went haywire.

Take the case of the foul-smelling tablets. A pharmaceutical company asked me to analyze tablets containing calcium carbonate and other chemicals. When the tablets were made, they were odorless. Later, though, they began to smell foul, and the company could not figure out why.

I decided that the problem must not be too complicated, so I gave them a very modest estimate, then started my gas chromatography analysis, sure I'd find the solution in four or five hours.

Four days later, I still hadn't found the root cause of the problem. We used every method we could think of to analyze those tablets, but each time there was no difference in the chemical makeups of the normal ones and the ones that smelled obnoxious.

Four *weeks* passed. By now, I'd decided, the problem wasn't chemical, so it must be biological. I had to get the tablets tested at a biological lab. I took samples and went to a biological lab as a customer. I had guessed right: The bad-smelling tablets were hosting microorganisms that were giving off the odor.

I paid my bill and chalked it up to experience.

Four years after Neil was born, in 1992, we had Samir. My father was ill by then, and my whole family was adamant that he should not travel to the United States. I insisted. We brought him to visit us, and he was fine. He spent some time with Samir, and we had some of our last, best conversations.

A month after he returned to India, he died of heart failure.

With my father gone, I missed the rest of my family even more, and I wanted Neil and Samir to be with the rest of my family and understand the Indian culture. Now that we could afford it, I wanted to go to India more often than once a year. I missed my family, the music, and especially the street vendors—on every corner there's the *paan* guy who wraps a betel nut leaf around sweet spices, dried fruit, betel nuts, and grated coconut. The red betel juice stains your lips and mouth. He has different kinds of leaves and fillers, so you can just ask for Kalkatta paan or Banarasi paan (*paan* means leaf).

And then there's the *pani-puri* vendor with his big huge clay pot of spiced water (*pani*). He fries *puri*, thin-walled puffballs of flour the size of a golf ball, punches a hole in the wall of the ball and fills the ball with a spicy blend of tomatoes and chickpeas, and then dips the ball with his hand into the big pot of spiced brown liquid and fills it up. You pop it into your mouth fast, because it's not leakproof. It just has this huge interesting taste. Chickpeas, potatoes, sprouted beans, spicy juice, crispy cover—in that little ball you have 100 different taste sensations. It's all about the art of making it.

Shamal didn't long for those sensations, though; she felt uncomfortable traveling in India if I was not by her side. And I think the tension with her family made everything else tense, too. She wanted to help them more, but even though she was now making a good salary she somehow did not feel able to send them money herself. She would say to me, "I envy you when you are so helpful to your family." We sent the same amount of money to both families every month, but she was bothered, I think, by being a woman and not feeling that she could use her money in the same way a man could. Her mother had talked so often and so resentfully about women's inequality and society's unfairness that, I think, Shamal felt inhibited even when there was no reason. Here she was, a respected neurologist making a six-figure salary in America and living in complete freedom. She spoke about limits that, to me, were nonexistent.

One day, back when I was working at Petrolite, Shamal's mother had sent a letter saying, "We are all fed up with life in Mumbai. Your sister's in-laws are treating her badly; they are not progressive. And your other sister is unhappy because she cannot bear a child, and we feel so sad for her. And your dad can't find a job, so life is miserable here for all of us. This is our plan: Baba and I will come to the US, then your sister will get divorced and come with her daughter, then your other sister will come, and then her husband will come, and they will adopt a child. You don't have to pay for us; just find us an apartment and put us up until Baba finds a job."

Shamal didn't show that letter to me for a couple of weeks. Then she handed it to me. We were living in a three-bedroom house then, just starting to be able to save some money, and suddenly I saw us trying to support five more people for who knew how long.

"We really can't afford to put them up like that," I told her. "The visa laws are such that your father couldn't come and work; for him to get a green card will take five years. The same will be true for your sisters." Shamal was very naïve about things like that, and so was the rest of her family. I don't think any of them had any idea about the green card rules. So Shamal called her mom on the speaker phone and asked me to explain.

When I did, her mother said, very tersely, "Okay, that is fine," and ended the conversation. She never brought up the plan again, and Shamal didn't speak of it until years later.

My business continued to grow—partly because I was working 24/7. I wasn't necessarily in the office, but I was always connected by phone. My secretary would connect all calls to my cell phone, and she was under instructions to never tell anyone, "Dr. Thanedar is not in the office" or

"He is in a meeting" or even "He will call you later." I always answered the phone, even when I was very busy. If I was out of the office, my secretary would pretend that I was there. "To whom would you like to speak, sir? Dr. Thanedar? Kindly hold on a second, and I'll connect you to him." Presto! The call was diverted to my cell phone. The customer thought I was leaning back in my office chair when in reality I might be slicing a banana for Neil's cereal, or pulled over at the side of the road, or dripping wet from a shower. I'd just wrap a towel around my waist, come out, and talk to the customer for as long as he wished.

Once we were taking a weekend road trip and we were in a restroom. It was time to change Samir's diaper. Just as I was unpinning it, the phone rang.

"Hello? Am I speaking to Dr. Thanedar? I am a research director, and we have a very serious problem in our company that we'd like you to solve."

I talked to this research director about his very complicated problem for the next 10 minutes—and solved my son's diaper problem at the same time.

Having sons made me especially sensitive to one of our clients: the Gerber Co., which made baby food and packaged it in airtight glass bottles. Gerber was thinking of changing to plastic bottles, which would reduce packaging costs and eliminate the danger of breakage. To make such a huge shift, they'd need packaging so reliably pure and safe, it would win an instant stamp of approval from the Food and Drug Administration.

I analyzed plastic jars from four companies over six weeks, running every test I could think of. The jar I recommended won FDA approval without reservation. Gerber was as happy as the babies who model for its labels, and the company paid me $150,000 for this project. When I deposited the check, I had to smile: The year I bought the company from Dr. Craver, $150,000 was the total revenue.

As the company grew, all sorts of things shifted. Now Siegel wanted to sell me *his* business, which was barely breaking even. The prospect appealed to me, and we came to a very informal verbal agreement. However, before I could purchase the company, a British firm called Bodycote offered him twice as much money as I had. He took it, of course; I would have done the same.

In 1994 Shamal finished her residency and started practicing as a neurologist, on staff at St. John's Mercy Medical Center. We celebrated our 10th anniversary that year, and Guru and Kalpana threw us a big party. Then, as soon as Shamal could take a break, we went on a cruise. All 1,700 passengers were Indian, and the cruise had been organized by the husband of a big Indian movie star, so there were many well-known actors and actresses on board. It was all very glamorous. We left the boys with a babysitter and, for the first time, just the two of us went.

At first, Shamal fretted. "Why are we doing this one?" she asked me. "It's more expensive than a normal cruise."

"Yes," I said, "but it's special." She worried, too, about leaving the children—but once we were on board she relaxed, and we had an amazing trip. Dinners, dancing, standing together on the deck, looking at the stars with no little sticky hands tugging at her sari … it was heaven. I remembered that disastrous honeymoon night at the Royal Orchid Palace Hotel, which was supposed to have been heaven on earth. This was more like it.

Now we had two good salaries, and life was starting to be what we wanted it to be—or, at least, what I wanted it to be. Not having money was easy for Shamal; it was familiar. Having money was a little disturbing to her; she felt as if it got in the way. Maybe it was her upbringing, or her innate modesty. Maybe it was a fear that the higher you go, the further you might fall.

At any rate, she couldn't shake her worries. I found that out full force earlier that year, when I bought my first Mercedes. Owning one of those cars had been my dream since I got my first real job, at Petrolite. I bought the cheapest Mercedes I could find, but Shamal was furious; she thought it was wasteful and obnoxious, and she cried hysterically. I kept trying to reassure her that we could afford it, that it didn't cost too much, but she just sobbed harder, talking again about the 15,000 rupees her stepfather had given us for the wedding. In matters of money, logic had no power to sway her.

She did eventually agree to move to a new house in a somewhat ritzy suburb called Town & Country, though. It cost $550,000 and was set on a terraced hill overlooking a clear bluish-green swimming pool. We all loved to swim, and Shamal turned very playful when we were outside. We'd splash around in the pool or race the kids up and down the hill or push them on the swings next to the pool. Then Shamal would bring out lemonade for everybody, and she'd settle into one of the lounge chairs to work the crossword puzzles she loved.

We were very, very comfortable—I saw now why people used that word to talk about having enough money to live as you desired. No more crowded, cramped rooms, no more loans or scrimping or working two jobs at once. Over the next two years, our life as a family would get easier and easier, filled with every possible sign of contentment and success.

CHAPTER 7

"Nobody Needs Me."

AUGUST 31, 1996, was Neil's thread ceremony. It was a celebration of his age, a rite of passage. For me, it also felt like a celebration of our life as a family. After so many years of work, look where we had arrived!

We finished furnishing the rooms we'd use and strung them with festive lights. (The new house was so big, we still had several rooms empty for future uses, so we just kept those doors closed.) Shamal left all of the decisions to me. She didn't care about décor; she saw interior design as irrelevant, just surface display. You bought some sturdy furniture and decided whether a room was worth painting or not, and that was the end of it.

So here I was, buying modern art and big mirrors and adding a gold surround to the very ordinary fireplace. Shamal humored me, offering opinions when I asked, but her focus was on the kids: making sure they went to good schools, learned about religion, and took extra math classes. She rolled her eyes when I offered her paint swatches. She couldn't care less.

I cared more about the kids' education, too, of course, but somehow I was confident that the kids would do fine. Decorating the house was like a hobby, and I already knew exactly what colors I wanted on the walls, what kind of paintings. Why did I care so much, after coming from a background just as down to earth as hers? We'd both grown up in houses where the furnishings were very basic.

I think my hunger for beauty started back in Mumbai, when I would go to Prabodh's apartment and page through his books and stare at his paintings. That was when my appreciation for color and shape, symmetry and movement, took root. I read endlessly about art in those years, and I longed to surround myself with canvases and sculpture.

That craving had never left me. I wanted to live among things that stopped my eye and made me feel a certain way—or, better yet, made me think in a new way. And now that we could afford it, I was eager to fill our home with thought-provoking beauty.

Of course, I also loved throwing parties, and our first son's eighth year, his coming of age, was a huge milestone. I hired the best caterers and sent out specially designed invitations to the entire Marathi community in St. Louis. All this seemed too much fuss to Shamal, I could tell. My exuberance often irritated her; she felt that we shouldn't really celebrate things so much. But I liked the splash a party made, the way it let your happiness spill over onto everyone around you.

Guru showed up at 7 a.m. the day of the ceremony, long before our other guests, because he was as much family as friend to us. Shamal had no brothers, so it was Guru who acted as our sons' uncle at ritual times. About 150 people came to Neil's ceremony. As they arrived, a clarion (*shehnai*) played light melodies. We gave our guests flowers and sweets and perfume. A Hindu priest from Chicago, Mr. Karandikar, flew in for the occasion because he specializes in thread ceremonies.

Neil looked truly handsome in his small *dhoti*. A magician performed for the children, and musicians played all night. Shamal looked gorgeous. She wore an emerald green nine-yard sari, instead of the usual six-yard sari, and its graceful folds were so complicated that friends came to help her put it on. She even wore jewelry, which she usually avoided. She wore my grandmother's golden *nath*, a special nose ring. And she wore a special *bindi* on her forehead, a crescent with a star in the middle.

That night, we sat listening to the musicians playing Indian music. First I looked around us, smiling at the sight of all our friends, the bright colors of their festive clothes glowing in the lamplight. Then I looked through the window to the garden, which we'd lit with thousands of twinkling lights. Everything looked beautiful. "We'll sleep in tomorrow morning," I thought, leaning back in one of the comfortable chairs we'd bought.

I sighed happily when I felt the leather warm to my skin and settle into the curve of the back of my neck. Now I was thinking back to all those early days when we were getting up in the middle of the night, taking care of first Neil, then Samir, both of us working long hours, passing the babies back and forth, saving money…

After the music stopped, people drifted off through the garden, and Shamal and I went to sit together by the pool, watching the floating candles. The moonlight played across on her face, and she was very quiet, deep in thought. I was tired but still elated.

"Don't you think we've come a long way?" I asked her, trying to share the feeling of triumph and contentment that had spread in me earlier that evening. She smiled sadly, looked out at the pool and said nothing.

I told myself she was just exhausted.

Around the middle of September I heard from my little brother, Ravi. When I'd left for the States, he'd still been a little boy, 10 years younger than me. But now that we were both grown up, that distance had closed. The better I came to know my little brother, the more I respected and liked him.

He was very smart, a professor in Pune, but was stuck at his university, with tenured professors above him and no room for advancement. For months I'd been trying to talk him into coming to the US.

Now he'd been invited to a conference and was coming here. He'd be the first sibling to visit me. I was thrilled. My mind raced ahead, planning what I would show him and thinking about all the fun we would have.

Then an idea came, and I called and asked Ravi: "Inni has been wanting to come, too, but she is getting frail. Will you bring her with you?"

Shamal was listening to my end of the conversation, and every time I glanced up at her, she looked more tense. Suddenly she tapped me on my shirt and said she wanted to talk to me. "Tell him not to come," she said, her voice low but urgent.

I covered the phone. "How do I do that? *Why* would I do that?" I was completely confused.

She burst into tears and said, "You don't understand."

I hung up and quizzed her, but all she would do is repeat her request and brush aside my questions. All that night, I tossed and turned, my brain coming up with one scenario after another. Not even my wildest speculations could account for the intensity in my wife's voice.

The next day, I called Ravi and said, "I don't know why, but Shamal doesn't feel comfortable with you coming."

There was a long silence. "I can't back out of this conference; it was a big honor," he said slowly. "How about this: I'll only come and visit, I won't stay in your house. But why doesn't she want me to come?"

All I could say was, "I don't understand it myself—and she's not very clear about it."

By the time Ravi and Inni arrived in the US, Shamal's mood seemed to have lifted. "Of course they must stay with us," she told me, dismissing their plans for a hotel. She embraced them warmly, treated them with her usual kindness, and cooked wonderful dinners.

But I couldn't let it rest there. I went through the motions of entertaining them, all the while keeping one eye on Shamal and still trying to puzzle out her initial reaction.

Then, a few days into their visit, Ravi said impulsively, "Show me your office." The two of us drove there. Once we were inside my private office, he took a letter from his pocket and handed it to me.

The envelope was postmarked from Mumbai, but the stationery was American—much thicker and heavier than the flimsy, pulpy paper Indians use. And I recognized the handwriting on the envelope.

I unfolded the letter and started to read it. The writer, who purported to be an elderly man, was saying that he had come across Ravi's horoscope and felt obliged to write and warn Ravi. The message was crystal clear: Ravi should most definitely never go to America. If he stayed in India, he would be a success, but if he came to America his life would fall apart.

I read the few lines again and again. Then I slowly refolded the note and handed it back to him. I didn't know what to say.

"It was Shamal, wasn't it?" Ravi asked me gently.

"Yes. That is her handwriting."

We looked at each other, speechless.

That Saturday, Shamal picked Neil up from soccer practice. I got home shortly after they did. I was surprised to see the garden door open. "Where's your mom?" I asked Neil.

"She just left," he said, shrugging.

Suddenly nervous—she'd been so strange lately—I called her cell phone. "Oh, I'm just driving around," she said, but her voice sounded blurred, distant.

"Where are you?" I asked, again and again. She wouldn't tell me.

A couple of hours later, she came home.

The minute the door opened, I jumped up and hurried to the door.

"It's all right," she said, touching my cheek. "I'm fine now."

She would say no more.

The next morning we went to the Missouri Botanical Garden for a leisurely walk. Still rattled from the day before, I accidentally drove the car into a post in the parking lot. It was just a bump, but the fender was dented. Normally something like that would have made Shamal frantic about the cost, but today she acted as if it didn't matter.

We walked around the garden, and she seemed pensive. A little sad, perhaps, but it was the kind of mood that often overtook her.

Monday, she was fine. Everything felt normal again, and I breathed a sigh of relief.

Tuesday afternoon we were waiting for her to come home from the hospital so we could all have tea together. I'd taken off that day, and Ravi and I were sitting by the pool. At first we talked with great passion about our work. We compared our lives, teasing each other lightly. Then we ran out of conversation, and we started saying, "When Shamal gets here..." As the sun sank lower in the sky, we fell silent. The feeling of dread washed over me again, and I shivered. Unable to wait any longer, I called her cell.

She said she was driving to Kentucky Lake.

"Why are you doing that?" I burst. "That's three hours away! We've been waiting for you, so we could all have tea together ..."

"I left the hospital on time, but I wanted to take a long drive," she said. Her voice sounded strange. "I am not feeling well."

"Then come *home*!" I said.

She blurted out something disjointed about how she was creating all the problems and not making anybody happy and she was going to jump in the lake.

"What are you talking about?" I asked, trying to keep my voice calm and slow. I was alarmed, but not as much as I should have been. Shamal had always gone for drives when she was upset. She loved to drive even when she was happy; we'd drive almost five hours to Chicago sometimes just to get good Indian food, and she would drive halfway just for the fun of it.

Usually about twice a year she would get very moody and upset. She'd reach for the car keys and start to leave home. Almost always I was able to stop her, saying, "You're not in a mood to drive."

But never before, when she was upset and reached for the keys, had she talked about killing herself. She'd only said something about suicide one time, back when she told me she'd wanted to kill herself after learning that her stepfather was not her biological father.

Now, for some reason, she was again desperately unhappy. I had to get her back home so we could figure out what was wrong and fix it. I kept her on the phone, kept talking, trying to remember how I used to get teenagers to open up back when I volunteered at the Ozone House hotline.

None of the old tricks came back. "Please, Shamal, just come home," I finally begged.

She was silent for a long minute. "All right," she said. "I will come soon."

Half an hour later, she hadn't arrived, and I got really scared. I called her cell phone again.

"Shamal, where are you?" I asked. My voice was sharper than I intended, because I was so scared. "We're all quite worried! Please, come back!"

"I am still driving toward the lake," she said, and now she sounded grim and calm, not hysterical. "I am going to jump in the lake and commit suicide."

"Don't be stupid," I blurted, my own emotions going haywire. "Tell me what's bothering you. Clear it from your mind. Be frank. And before anything, turn your car around and come home!"

"Nobody needs me," she said. "I am a burden."

We kept talking, and she kept going back to that statement, no matter how I protested. I don't even remember everything I said, but finally, around 9:30 that night—six hours after she'd left work and started driving—she said she would come home, and I believed her.

I hung up and just sat there for a long time with a million thoughts running through my head. I felt helpless. Hands shaking, I called her mother in India.

"Shamal is terribly upset," I said, "and I can't even find out what's really wrong. Please, will you talk to her and see if you can find out?"

"I cannot do that," her mother said, without even taking a minute to think about it or ask for more information. "I don't want to get in the middle between the two of you."

This didn't come as a surprise; Indian families hold everything very tightly within the walls of the home. I had never before asked Shamal's mother to intervene in any way. But this time, I didn't know what else to do.

"Look, she's unhappy, and I'm scared. We've got to do something," I said urgently. "She's talking about ending her life!"

Just as I said that, Shamal's car pulled in the driveway. "Wait," I told her mother. "Here she is!"

When Shamal came in, I handed her the phone and said, "Here, talk to your mother!" She gave me an angry look and said into the receiver, "Oh, don't worry, *Aai*," the Marathi word for Mom.

"Everything is fine," she went on. "He just worries for no reason."

She hung up and told me, very emphatically, "Don't worry. Everything is okay. I'm fine now."

That night in bed, she surprised me with her eagerness to be intimate. It took me a minute to shift gears, but she was unusually passionate and insistent. Relieved, I tried to match her intensity, and afterward we lay entwined for a long time. She fell asleep, but I didn't want to let go. As I held her, I kept hoping that everything really was okay now, hoping it so hard and repeating it so often that it was essentially a prayer. I didn't know what else to do.

Wednesday morning was so tranquil, it was hard for me to believe that the night before she'd been heading for a lake. Shamal looked absolutely composed. When I opened my mouth to talk about the night before, she said, "I'm truly all right now. I have no problems. It has all been sorted out."

I'd taken the day off, and she was off that day as well. I made us some tea. Ravi was there, and I said to both of them, "Let's go out in the back yard." I felt strongly that I wanted Ravi with us. Except for the weirdness about this particular trip, Shamal had always liked him. He is a calm, steady person, very wise, with a strong moral character and absolutely no interest in material things. I trusted his judgment—and I needed his perspective.

It was a gorgeous, sunny day, and we climbed to the top of the gentle hill behind our house. Sitting up there, holding our tea in the cool fall air, I said to Shamal, "I really want to understand. You have been so unhappy. Help me understand; I'm lost here. And I'm worried about you."

She wouldn't open up for the longest time, kept insisting everything was fine. Even Ravi's gentle questions, she met with silence. Then, abruptly, she started talking, and once she did, her words came in a rush.

She talked about a woman's life and how men and women are not equal. She talked about people who had taken up women's causes in India and how women have been oppressed for ages. As she spoke, I could hear her mother's angry voice; many of these things had burned in Shamal since childhood.

She also talked about her family. "I don't feel as comfortable helping my family as you feel helping yours," she said, her voice accusing. She said they'd wanted to come to the US and I hadn't let them.

I said, "What do you mean? They came in 1991 and 1994!"

But no, she was talking about that time they wanted to move here permanently, along with both her sisters, and I'd tried to explain how unrealistic that was. "The whole society is this way," she said. "A man can do what he wants to do; a woman cannot."

She seemed to have her life and societal injustice tangled up together. If she had been so fiercely angry all these years, I thought, why had she remained so passive? I wasn't stopping her from doing anything! I'd paid that wedding money back to her father years ago, and we sent the same amount of money home to both families every month.

Ravi said, "If what Shri sends is not enough, don't you feel that you earn your own money, and you can help them as much as you want?"

She said, "But he does it so naturally! I can't do that! Society is male dominated."

Ravi and I looked at each other, bewildered. Shamal scrambled up from the ground and went down the hill without looking back.

Then she went inside the house and helped my mother cook lunch for all of us, refusing our nervous offers to help.

I wondered how trapped she felt by the traditional roles. Was being female the problem, or just something to blame? We had plenty of help around the house, and, by its very nature, her career always came first. When she was needed at the hospital, she had to go. I'd always thought we had a good balance: Both of us cared deeply about both work and home, and we juggled the responsibilities together. She was just a better cook than I was! Certain things we'd fallen into naturally, by habit, I suppose. But was it a *problem* that she did the cooking and I did the yardwork?

No, no. I was overreading this. It was really about her parents. The root of her angst over gender inequity seemed to be her inability to help her parents. In all these years, I had never known that she felt constrained. I'd always figured that if she wanted to do more for them, she would have done so, or urged me to do so. Surely this wasn't all because I'd found it too impractical to bring her entire family over to this country and support them for years?

Maybe she'd never voiced what she really wanted—or she'd voiced it so quietly, I hadn't paid enough attention.

Shamal had *always* been quiet and a bit sad—even when I first met her, in her parents' home. She was deeply sensitive, and she saw far more darkness than light. I'd long ago accepted that as simply her nature.

All day I thought about this, my mind unable to leave her words. That afternoon, she said again, "I'm fine now." This time, I was smart enough not to take her words at face value.

In the evening my brother and I went out for a drive and stopped at a McDonald's, acting like it was a fun outing for us so that Shamal wouldn't have to worry about fixing dinner. From there, I called Savita, a friend who is a psychiatrist.

She was very abrupt: "I'm feeding my kids; I can't talk now." Disappointed, I hung up without giving her any details.

Half an hour later, Savita called our home, contrite, and told Shamal, "I have time to talk to Shri now."

We came in just after Shamal hung up the phone. Her eyes were still clouded. She relayed the message, then studied her tightly interlaced fingers. Without looking up, she said, "Why did you call Savita?"

"I had a question for her," I said quickly, trying to keep my voice light and normal. We left it at that.

That night at bedtime, Shamal was again eager to be intimate. Afterward, as I held her, she said, "I was wrong. I accused you unfairly."

Thursday morning, she went to work as usual.

Around 10 a.m. that day, October 17, panic rose up in me. I don't know what triggered it. By then, I was feeling anxious pretty much constantly, but this was different. It came without words, and it filled me, drowning all common sense. I called Shamal at the hospital.

"How are you feeling now?"

"Fine," she said.

"Do you have a little bit of time to talk?"

We had a long conversation. As we talked, I felt calmer. I took my usual role, emphasizing what a good life we had, with good kids and good careers. "Whatever problems we have," I ventured—still not even sure what they were—"could we not overcome them and make a new beginning? Let's get past this, Shamal!"

"You're right," she said quietly. "Let's work on it."

At 2:30 that afternoon, I called again and told her I'd decided to take Ravi and the boys to see Meramec Caverns, a system of ancient caves in the Ozarks. I'd never been there, and I thought that it might be fascinating enough to get everybody's mind off the last few days. I was feeling bad that I'd neglected Ravi's trip, focusing all his time and attention on my problems. I also hoped that Shamal, with her scientific curiosity, might be intrigued enough to join us.

"Do you want to come home early so we can all go together?" I asked, trying not to sound too eager.

"No," she said, answering instantly. "It's going to be very hectic today. I won't be able to make it. But you all go, and have a good time. Just don't forget that you have to take Samir to swim practice later."

I promised, and we said goodbye.

The caves were chilly and dark, with spotlights every so often to illuminate dramatic rock formations. Huge stalactites hung from the ceiling, looking like ornamented pillars from one of the Hindu temples back home. We walked through a dark, narrow passage that opened onto a big pond. As we stepped out of the passageway, we caught our breath: A crown of stalagmites and stalactites was reflected on the water's black surface. Then we walked again through the darkness and came to a wall where, all of a sudden, the US flag was projected, rippling across the stalactites as though flying in a breeze. Samir was so excited, he started jumping up and down as they played the national anthem.

My cell phone didn't work inside the caves. I remember feeling grateful for the respite. I'd been tied to a phone 24/7 for so many years, doing business wherever I was. Any chance to be out of contact felt like a little burst of freedom.

When we came out, just as I was unlocking the car, my phone rang.

"Mr. Thanedar?" a man's voice said urgently. "Where have you been? I've been trying to reach you for the past hour." He identified himself as a doctor and spoke over my confused questions: "Listen carefully: I am calling from St. John's Mercy Hospital."

"I am so sorry," I said, assuming this was one of Shamal's colleagues. "We were inside Meramec Caverns and—"

Before I could finish apologizing, he cut me off. "Your wife has been admitted here, and she is in serious condition."

My knees buckled. I somehow managed to get into the car and sit down, but I couldn't answer for a second, couldn't even think. Finally I mustered, "What happened? Tell me exactly. She was fine this morning!"

He said, "Your wife fell out of her car, and she is unconscious. Hurry to the hospital, please," and hung up.

A storm was brewing, and I stared through the windshield at the dark clouds. Then I felt adrenaline stream into my system, firing me with energy. I started the car, my hand trembling, and floored it. The kids were in the back seat.

"Put your seat belts on," I said. Ravi was studying my face worriedly. Nobody spoke.

I drove as fast as I could without losing control of the car on the slippery roads. As I steered through what was now a downpour, my phone rang again. It was the hospital chaplain. He asked me, in a low voice, if there was anyone I want to inform about Shamal.

"No," I said instinctively, and hung up. I was completely thrown by the question. What did he mean? Inform them of what?

I drove faster.

Thunder crashed above us. One hand on the steering wheel, I called Guru's house and asked his wife, Kalpana, to stay with my mother and the kids. "Shamal is in the hospital," I said in a rush, and Kalpana, who'd been as close to my wife as anyone ever managed to get, agreed immediately. She was outside waiting for us when we pulled up, and she took the boys by the hand and went inside.

She must have called Guru straight away, because by the time my brother and I ran through the hospital doors, he was already there. And he already knew what the doctor was drawing me aside to tell me.

My wife was dead.

Guru saw me with the doctor and joined us: "How could this happen? Was it an accident? Was she taking some kind of medication?"

I shook my head helplessly. All I could think in that moment was that this was a horrible, shocking family secret I had to guard, even from him. Indian society can be so judgmental. I had my sons to protect.

The doctor had assumed that we were all family, and he was starting to answer. I asked him whether there was a place we could go to sit and

179

talk privately, and we stepped away, leaving Guru and another friend behind with my brother.

The doctor told me that Shamal had taken an overdose of antidepressants. I barely heard him.

"May I see her?" I asked.

He took me to her room. She was covered, and I pulled the sheet back to see her face. I was startled by how calm she looked. The lines had smoothed from her forehead, and she looked more at peace than I'd ever seen her.

I stayed there for a long time. I touched her cheek, tentatively. She was still warm. "Why?" I kept asking her. "Why? Why? *Why?*" No answer came. She was gone.

I would never talk to Shamal again. When that finally got through to me, I sat and sobbed, my forehead against the mattress. Then, with a jolt, I sat up. *What about the children? I've got to take care of them!* I left in almost a panic, rushing past Guru and the others as they hurried up to talk to me. "I've got to go," I said urgently.

With every passing minute, they were becoming more convinced that I was hiding something about Shamal's death. I only realized that later.

At the time, I was too stunned. All I knew was that I couldn't face anybody. I walked past them and found my way to my car alone.

By the time I came home from the hospital, there were about 30 people gathered at our house. In our community, word of mouth moved faster than an Internet posting.

I took the boys aside and drew them both together into my arms. "Samir, Neil, your mom is no more!" Neil understood immediately, and he burst into tears. Samir, who was just 4, kept saying, "Where's my mom? Where has she gone?" Sobbing, I told him, "She has gone far away, to God!"

The boys and I cried for a long time. Finally, I took their shoes off and urged them to lie down in their beds and rest. I covered them and went back out to the living room to face the friends who had gathered.

"I can't tell you anything now," I said. "I will give you the details as soon as I understand what happened."

When they all left, I forced myself to pick up the phone and call Shamal's mother.

I expected hysterics, but she was almost eerily calm. "What time did it happen?" she asked.

"About three hours ago."

"Okay," she said. "How are the children?"

"*Okay?*" I repeated to myself, stunned by her casualness. There was nothing okay about this.

I tried to tell her everything I knew, but she asked no questions. "When did you last talk to her?" I asked. "Did she say *anything* that would have suggested—"

"No, no. The last time I talked to her was when you asked me to, on Tuesday."

"Do you want to come for the funeral? We will wait …"

"No," she said. "She is no more."

I hung up and stared at the phone. It was almost as if she'd known, as if she'd been waiting for the call.

The morning after Shamal's death, I woke to a sick remembering of everything that had happened. The shock numbed me at first, but then adrenaline took over and I threw myself into investigative mode.

I had to know more.

At the hospital, the doctor had told me that Shamal had taken an overdose of amitriptyline, an antidepressant. They also found needle marks on her stomach and both phenobarbital and lidocaine in her bloodstream, so they assumed that she had numbed the skin of her stomach with lidocaine, then injected the phenobarbital. People in our subdivision had called the ambulance, because she'd driven into a cul-de-sac at the other end of the subdivision and parked her car there. Some kids were outside playing, and they said they saw a woman open her car door and fall out of the car, collapsing on the ground. They ran to help her, and when they saw that she was unconscious they ran back inside and one of their mothers called 911.

The police told me they'd found an empty bottle of amitriptyline pills in her car. They'd also found a bottle of lidocaine. On the front seat of the car was a folder in which she'd left two notes. The first was very neatly written, in very formal English. In it she said that no one was responsible for what she'd done but herself; her language was so precise, it was almost a legal document, and she'd signed and dated it. The second note was written in Marathi and addressed to me.

Dear Pra, she wrote, using a nickname she'd used for me when she was feeling romantic or very warm. It was her short version of Prasad, my nickname at home in India. *I tried my best to keep you happy, but I failed in my efforts. I am ending my life because I don't want to trouble people around me. I never thought I would say goodbye to you this way. If you get my insurance money, help my parents. If you don't, use our stock portfolio. I've always loved you and always will. I never could make you happy. Always yours, Shamal.*

When had she made up her mind? Back when she'd driven toward Kentucky Lake? Or had something happened Thursday that pushed her over the edge?

I questioned Inni about what she knew. "Tell me again the exact sequence, everything she said and did," I begged Inni. At least 20 times poor Inni recited the same details for me: "Shamal came home at 4:30, as usual. She made me a cup of tea, and she gave me those Marathi books I'd been wanting to read. She apologized that it had taken her so long to find them." That part always caught her, and tears would come to her eyes. "Then she picked up her keys and purse. She just said she was just going to go buy some vegetables for dinner."

She'd taken off her wedding band and wristwatch first. I'd found them on top of her dresser. I couldn't tell Inni that, though; I couldn't bring myself to tell her that her death had been a suicide. Without knowing how deliberate Shamal's actions had been, they could still imagine that she had taken too much medicine accidentally.

I went out to the garage. The police had told me that Shamal's little red Mitsubishi was still parked in the cul-de-sac. I'd gone and driven it home when I got back from the hospital, too numb to even register what I was doing. Now I looked down at the door and saw the scratches. I ran my finger over them, and suddenly I could see her kneeling there, trying to get the key into the lock. I closed my eyes, trying to blot out the image of my wife scrabbling so desperately at a locked door. Had she changed her mind? If not, why was she fighting so hard to get back into the car?

One of our neighbors, a colleague of Shamal's at St. John's Mercy, came to talk to me that afternoon. He told me that around 5 p.m. Thursday he had passed her as she was pulling out of our subdivision and waved. She met his eyes but did not smile or return his wave, which he found odd.

"She had already cut herself off," I thought, remembering with a chill how distant her voice was when we talked about the caves.

Slowly I was reconstructing Thursday afternoon. She'd driven someplace for about 15 minutes before coming back into the subdivision. At the T where she would have made a left to come home, she made a right. She stopped the car in the cul-de-sac. And that's when she injected the phenobarbital.

It took me too long to realize something very simple: I had to deal with everybody else's grief as well as my own. And because I'd been secretive and private, our friends were making sense of an inexplicable tragedy by blaming me.

Three days after Shamal's death, they came over in a huge group. "Shri, we have come here to know the truth of Shamal's death," Guru said, almost coldly.

They threw question after question at me: "What was wrong?" "Why didn't she go to a doctor?" "Why didn't you take her to the hospital?" "Is it true you wouldn't let her family come here?"

They were accusing me of withholding information about her death—as though because I wasn't telling them everything I must be somehow complicit.

Finally I said, "Look, you are my best friends. Ask me anything, and I will tell you everything I know. The only reason I have kept silent until now is that I don't know what to tell my children."

That didn't stop them. They kept asking questions, and, as I heard the suspicion in their voices, all sorts of things came back, like the time I had said to our friends, "Help me understand why she cannot go twice a year to India?" I wanted to go more than once and we could afford it, yet she refused, and I was at my wits' end to understand why. She would just say, "Because I don't want to." I'm a very rational person; I need reasons. At the time, I saw nothing wrong in sharing that disagreement with our friends.

They also knew that early in our marriage, when Shamal wanted her parents and sisters to come to America, I discouraged her. Now they seized upon that: "You didn't allow her family to come; that's why she killed herself."

In the middle of all this, the doorbell rang: It was two officers from the Town & Country police force. The sergeant asked to see Shamal's car, so I excused myself from my friends, who were looking at me strangely, and took him out to the garage. Ravi came with me; by now I was feeling that he was the only one I could trust.

I unlocked the car, and when I opened the door I saw all kinds of things inside: a big water cooler, two or three kitchen knives, even some sharp gardening tools. A fallback if the drugs didn't work? A shudder passed over me. Folded loosely on the back seat was a blanket—maybe she'd used it to cover herself when giving the injections.

That night I barely slept. The next morning I dug out the piece of paper on which I'd scribbled what the doctor told me, especially the names of the drugs she'd taken. Slowly I went down the stairs to the little storage room in our basement. Shamal kept her medical texts there, and a little desk. On top I found her fat pharmaceutical reference book. I turned to the page for amitriptyline and froze.

She had underlined information about its dosage and effects in blue ink.

She used to come down here when she was upset, I remembered. I'd just assumed that studying and research soothed her. Now I reached for one of the psychiatry books stacked on the corner of the desk. Flipping through, I found highlighting—some orange, some pink, some blue, as though she'd done it on different days. One highlighted section was on depression. The second was on suicidal impulses. The same topics were highlighted in another psychiatry book.

She'd thought about suicide before we married, when she learned that her stepfather was not her biological father. She'd thought about suicide the weekend before she died. How many other times had she considered it?

I put the book down and turned back to the pharmaceutical book, reading about antidepressants and how it can take weeks for them to start making a difference.

I read about their side effects, which included dry mouth and insomnia. In a flash I remembered the icewater—she'd never drunk much water at all, but in the last month or so she'd started carrying a bottle of cold water everywhere she went. I'd noticed—without registering the significance. She'd also had trouble sleeping—and now I learned that this was another side effect of some antidepressants.

So she'd been trying, all alone, to feel better. If she hadn't wanted to confide in me, why hadn't she at least told one of our friends? I asked myself the question but knew the answer instantly: Our community was still a century behind the times when it came to mental illness. She would have been afraid that people would think less of her, think she was crazy. They'd get awkward in her presence, stop trusting her opinion, hover a bit too much—or, worse, ignore her words altogether and pretend that she'd never spoken.

I didn't know what to feel. Anger at society, and at Shamal herself, shot like jolts of lightning through a heavy, black grief that never left. I knew that if I stopped for even a minute, the sadness and rage would overwhelm me.

So I kept moving.

I went to the hospital and talked to the doctors and nurses there about Shamal's last day. They reported that she had been almost normal; only one of the nurses remembered her being a little short about something that hadn't been done—but the rebuke was still delivered in her soft-spoken way.

I came home to silence. No calls from our friends, no gathering round of our small community. Automatically I'd stopped at the mailbox and grabbed the day's mail. Absentmindedly I rifled through bills and charge-card offers as I walked into the living room. At a plain white envelope, I stopped short: It had my best friend's return address sticker in the upper left-hand corner. "How strange," I thought. "Why would Guru write to me instead of calling?"

I opened the envelope and pulled out a letter, typed so formally it looked like business correspondence. It was signed by three of our closest friends, with Guru's name first. "You are free to follow your path," it said. "We shall go on our own way. We are not concerned with you at all."

My whole body went cold. This was something I'd never dreamed possible. I'd cheerfully criticized my Indian community in St. Louis from time to time—but only the way you shake your head over your family's eccentricities. I'd never stopped loving them. And their presence had anchored every major event in our lives.

Granted, there had been tension in some of the friendships even before Shamal's death. As my business became more and more successful and I bought nice cars and a big house, even Guru had started to resent me a bit. He'd tease that he wanted my friendship more than

I wanted his, and he was always grilling me about my business: "Why are you so secretive?" he once asked me. I laughed and said, "Look, it's a competitive world." And he said, "You are not helping others learn from you."

Guru had also kept urging me to socialize more with the community. 'I don't need the community all the time,'" I would say.

Now, perhaps, he wanted me to feel how much I really did need them.

After the initial shock of Shamal's death wore off, I made myself a sober promise: "I am going to get my family back on track." I stopped going to work; instead, I spent my days at bookstores and public libraries, buying books, reading everything I could find on depression, on suicide, on how to help children after a parent commits suicide.

It took me 10 days of reading to accept the fact that I had to tell the children the truth.

It's not easy, telling a 4-year-old this kind of truth. But everything I'd read said that if a child is to recover from a parent's death, he needs to be able to count on his other parent. How could the boys count on me if I lied to them?

I sat down with each one in turn and explained, very slowly, and as gently as I could, what had happened.

A dam broke open.

Samir told me, through sobs, "Daddy, when she dropped me off at school"—he floundered for a minute, trying to figure out which day it had been, and we finally decided it would have been Tuesday morning, two days before she died. "She kissed me, and then she said, 'Mommy is going to go far, far away.'" He gulped, then started sobbing even harder. Ever since she died, he'd been feeling awful, because he thought if he'd told me right away I could have stopped her.

Neil just kept asking me, "Why did she do that? *Why?* What did I do wrong?" When I told him he'd done nothing wrong, he shook his head violently and started to recite all the things his mother had begged him to do that he'd screwed up. "I forgot to put the garbage out," he said solemnly, "and I used to whine about drying the dishes, and I talked back to her when she said I couldn't go for the sleepover, and—"

I took him by the shoulders. "Neil! Those are just normal little-boy things. They had *nothing to do* with what your mother did. It was her own mind not being well. She never would have chosen to leave you otherwise!"

He nodded, but I wasn't sure the words had reached him.

As for me, I started seeing a therapist, someone the minister at the funeral home had recommended. He was open, easygoing, and conversational, very matter-of-fact. I poured out all the agonized questions I couldn't bring myself to share with anybody else.

Above all was one question: Could I have gotten her admitted to the hospital—involuntarily committed—before her depression turned suicidal?

"That would have been very hard," he pointed out, "especially with Shamal's being a doctor. She would have known exactly what to say to get out of it."

What if they had given her some electrical shock—maybe that would have jolted her out of that mindset? "She was a *doctor*," he reminded me again. "If she'd wanted help, she could have walked into a psychiatrist's office on her lunch break at the hospital, or confided in a colleague."

He kept coming back to the thoughts that made me feel guilty: I should have not gone to Meramec Caverns that day. I should not have trusted that she was okay.

"How long does it take to pop 50 pills?" he asked me. "She could have gone to the bathroom and done it, even if you were with her all day long."

How could I not know she was mentally ill? I managed a suicide hotline in Ann Arbor, for God's sake. Why wasn't I paying attention? "There are *psychiatrists* whose wives or husbands are depressed, and they don't know it," he pointed out.

He wasn't the passive sort of psychologist who just sits there and strokes his beard, and I was grateful for that. He'd challenge me, challenge my thoughts. He'd say, "Maybe, yeah, you were responsible" for this or that, "but, you know, we make mistakes."

I found a counselor for the boys, too, but after a few visits they didn't want to go anymore.

"I will let you stop on one condition," I told them, "and that is that whenever you have thoughts or dreams about what happened, you come and talk to me."

Luckily, Samir was young enough to say, "Why did Mom tell me she was going far away?" and then, after I soothed him, ask for a peanut butter sandwich. He would have bad dreams and tell me every detail. Neil was just 8, but he was extraordinarily self contained. He missed his mother desperately, but he kept most of his sorrow to himself, as though if he let any of it out, it would overwhelm him.

I understood the feeling.

Weeks went by in a blur. I was still investigating; the part of my mind that needed answers was not yet satisfied. I just needed to know everything about her in the weeks and months before her death so I could try and understand more clearly what led up to it.

I got the records for Shamal's cell phone and our land line. She had called the Cincinnati immigration office, and when I reread that line a chill ran through me. Cincinnati was where Ravi was supposed to land. I moved to the next line: She had also faxed something there. Then she'd had two long conversations with her mother in the days before her death: one on Wednesday and one the next morning, the day she died.

She'd also sent something by way of FedEx to Mumbai. Whatever she sent had arrived two days before Ravi received the letter warning him not to come.

I set the matter aside and focused on healing myself and being there for the children. When I read about single parents and bereavement, I learned that the most important thing for the boys was to know I was still there, that I loved them with all my heart, and that I would never leave. So I tried to prove that in every way I could think of.

Of course, I also had my own tangle of emotions to unravel. There was a lot of guilt: What could I have done differently? My reading helped me understand what Shamal must have been feeling, and the therapist helped me realize that there was nothing I could have done that would have lifted the burden from her.

By now, our closest friends had stopped calling altogether. It was my American friends who were standing by me. They brought me casseroles, books on coping with a loved one's death, even a Bible!

But no one was more helpful than Shamal's cousin in Chicago—although he had no idea what a bombshell he was dropping.

He called me in November, after learning of Shamal's death. "Just like her father," he said sadly.

"*What?*" I was not sure of what I'd heard.

"Didn't you know? Her father jumped into the well in their yard," he said. "No one ever wanted to talk about it. He was an engineer, and he used to have hallucinations. He'd get up in the middle of the night crying or shouting. And then, when Shamal was a year old, he jumped in the well.

"Before she met you, Shamal was engaged to a young man from her subcaste," he added, "but somehow he found out about her father's suicide and told her he couldn't go through with the marriage."

I thought back to our wedding, and how tense Shamal's parents—and Shamal herself—had been in the days of preparation. Was it because they were hiding the truth about her biological father? It would never have made a difference to me.

But I might have taken Shamal's comments about suicide, those last few days, more seriously.

She'd talked on and off for years about studying genetics, maybe even specializing in it. I encouraged her without ever really understanding what that might have entailed. Then several years went by without her even mentioning it. She was absorbed in her neurology practice, so I assumed that she'd made her choice.

Was the interest in genetics because of her father? Was she trying to figure out whether he'd suffered from an illness and, if so, whether she might have the same predisposition?

That Wednesday before her death, when I'd called our psychiatrist friend, the thought had just barely touched my mind that Shamal was ill—perhaps ill enough for me to have her hospitalized, even if she refused. At first when she'd talked about jumping in the lake I'd written it off as one of her moods, perhaps connected to her father again. But the depression had not lifted.

Still, she was living life normally enough that week: going to work, eating, going to sleep—going through all the motions. Was that one comment enough for me to force her into a hospital? I set aside the idea as soon as it entered my mind.

Had I known about her father, I wouldn't have taken the chance.

In December, I flew to India and went to see Shamal's parents. I didn't call first; I was afraid they'd find some excuse not to see me. The visit was too important to me to chance that.

Instead, Shamal's mother greeted me warmly and brought tea, and Baba went out to get some food. Then I started telling them, all over again, every detail of their daughter's death. They hadn't even asked me for these details. But they were the only other people on earth who had loved her as I had, and I felt that they should know everything.

My mother-in-law's strange calm when I told her that Shamal was dead had unnerved me. If she'd known how desperately unhappy her daughter was, why hadn't she told me and urged me to do something?

I talked and talked, retelling every detail. They kept silent, nodding occasionally. Finally I gathered my courage and asked her mother again, "When did you last talk to Shamal?"

"When you told me to," she said. I pressed harder. When she wouldn't budge, I pulled out the phone records.

"Oh, yes," she said, "but those were just quick calls. They were nothing."

"One lasted 48 minutes," I pointed out, keeping my voice as quiet as I could. "The other was nearly an hour."

"It was nothing," she said again, very firmly.

Then she told me that there had been another call, very short, around 5 p.m. St. Louis time. "Shamal told me, 'I'm putting some coins in, and I don't have enough coins, so we might get cut off, but don't worry.'" *That* was the 15 minutes, I realized. She'd driven to a pay phone to call her mother one last time.

"What did she *say*?" I asked, grabbing my mother-in-law's arm.

She just shrugged. "It was nothing."

At that point her husband went into the other room and returned with an envelope they'd received by FedEx, dated the Tuesday before Shamal's death. Inside was a check for $8,000—they had not cashed it— and a letter written in Marathi. She'd written the same words she wrote to me: "I never thought I would say goodbye to you this way.

"Imagine that a crazy child was born," she continued, using a Marathi word that could mean either insane or crazy wild, "and she died, and everybody is relieved." She told them she would have told me to give our sons to her childless sister, but she knew that I'd never stand for it. She said that she'd asked me to give them money and knew that I would. Then she ended: "At least be happy now. Enjoy the money."

Her father slowly refolded the letter. They were still very calm, very reserved, very polite. The only time they ever fought me was when I mentioned mental illness. Then they flashed back, "You are so worldly and so wise—how could you not console her and be a little more under-standing of her?"

"It was an *illness*," I said. "I did not know."

Then I asked if it was true that Shamal's biological father had com-mitted suicide.

192

"Yes," her mother said, her voice squeezed tight. She said she'd explained everything to Shamal after she found her birth certificate. But Shamal had told *me* only the lie about an accident on a bridge.

It dawned on me that after Shamal's father's suicide, her mother had isolated herself and her daughters, avoiding any confrontation with the rest of the community. After my own recent experiences, I could understand the impulse.

"Why did you never tell anyone?" I asked gently. She didn't answer. But now her silence no longer bothered me. I was beginning to understand.

If I'd been living in India when Shamal killed herself, I would have been arrested for inducing someone to commit suicide. So would a parent or any other close relative. There were so many abuses and stresses—women tortured, for example, to bring more dowry—that laws were made to discourage any behavior that might prompt a woman to kill herself in despair.

Even in St. Louis, a good friend had come to me and said, "I really care about you, Shri, so I am going to tell you this: This town will never accept you again. You should leave St. Louis."

Her words stung, but I knew that there was truth in them. The Indian community, whether at home or abroad, does not easily forgive even a divorce, let alone a suicide. That was why Shamal's mother never told anyone the truth about her first husband. And that was why my friend had urged me to leave town.

It would have been the easy way. But the more I tried to hide, the more people would point fingers at me. I wanted my friendships restored. I wanted everyone to know the truth, whatever it was.

I was wary of secrets.

CHAPTER 8

Living and Loving Again

BACK IN THE States, away from the crowd of family and friends that had surrounded me so warmly in India, I felt more alone than ever. Our closest friends in the States were no longer sticking by me.

It was odd, though. As these huge holes opened in my life, they were filled in unexpected ways. Strangers and casual friends gave me great kindness, with no judgment. And of course Inni's support, my entire family's support, was unconditional. I'd never in my life felt more grateful for my family.

I also had more answers. I'd learned a lot more about my wife on this last trip back. The more I learned, the less guilt I felt. Knowing why and how was making a difference. I still didn't know all the answers, but I had a sense of her state of mind in those last days. The phone calls, the letter she'd written to her parents, the circumstances of her father's death—it was all fitting together with a chilling finality. I no longer had the frantic sense that, with one word or gesture, I could have changed the outcome.

As for my business, which until recently had been the driving force of my life, I was completely neglecting it. That changed after a fateful business conference I attended in Florida.

Early in 1996, months before Shamal's death, I was at an *Inc.* magazine conference in Florida, where I attended a session in which a business consultant named Dan Sullivan delivered a presentation. He began with the usual sort of warmup, and I settled in for another mildly interesting session. He gave a general introduction about the burdens of running a company. Then he said abruptly, "Your business cannot grow if you are running it like a one-man show."

I lowered the conference agenda I'd been scanning to my lap. He now had my full attention.

"Each of us has certain unique abilities," Sullivan was saying, "activities we are passionate about, that *give* us energy. Everybody can pay bills and vacuum the floor." Now I was listening closely, with a strong, slightly creepy feeling that he was speaking directly to me. His point was simple: The business owner must engage only those activities he's passionate about—and delegate the rest, perhaps to someone who has a passion for *those* activities.

He'd hit my problem head on. I was a damned good chemist, I reflected wryly, but I had a bit to learn about running a company. I'd stretched myself far too thin, trying to do everything at once.

His voice faded again, and my own thoughts took over. What *was* I really passionate about? Buying companies, I answered myself instantly. Buying *underperforming* companies and then turning them around into profitable ones.

I walked out of the session in a daze, my brain whirring.

And when I got home, I started assigning away everything else I did— the marketing, the customer relations, the media relations...

Until that epiphany, in early 1996, I'd worked day and night, doing all kinds of things to keep the company going. Now I took a deep breath and cut myself loose from all the day-to-day operations of my business, delegating the work and trusting my employees to handle everything. Then I started analyzing acquisition opportunities in the market.

Sullivan had said that productivity and growth depended not on how many hours you worked but instead on how much time you carved out to think about your business. He suggested keeping some days entirely free for brainstorming; some days as "buffers," with a mix of work and recreation; and some days focused on nothing but the details of running the business.

I did this faithfully and, sure enough, my life began to smooth out. Now everything started to fall into place, with just the right rhythm to keep me creative *and* keep the business in tune.

Unfortunately, there was one thing I hadn't considered: human relations. When I tried my new method with my existing staff, it led to disaster.

I'd always wanted the employees who handled client relations and business development to be scientists like me, you see. So when it came time to delegate, I found three reliable scientists within my company who were eager to take on the additional responsibility. I suspect they thought that putting on nice suits and meeting with people would be easier than standing in a lab all day in a baggy white coat, brewing chemicals.

It wasn't. One by one, they grew frustrated and left the company. Instead of smoothly passing off some of my responsibilities, I'd lost three good scientists from my lab.

"Don't lose patience," I told myself, muttering the phrase daily as I went around looking for people who'd be more naturally oriented to the task but still have PhDs in science. After meeting with a long succession of science nerds who were sadly devoid of people skills and also meeting jovial chemists who had no clue about our scientific processes, I found two—Vance Lyon and Fred Willard—who had both sharp minds and excellent communication skills. I made them directors of business development, and soon they were handling client relations far better than I had. Now I could relax and start brainstorming and focusing on my vision for the company.

My first priority was clear to me: It was time to expand the business, take over another chemical analysis company like ours. Just as I started making plans, I heard about the perfect company: Betec, in St. Paul,

Minnesota. Its owner, Steve Morrison, was 65 and had suffered a heart attack. The company was most definitely for sale.

I called Morrison and told him I wanted to buy his company. It would be our first acquisition. I decided not to use consultants; I didn't use anybody, really. I did it all on my own to save money. At that point we had revenues of just over $1 million, and Betec had revenues of about $400,000.

I had seen their ads in the paper, side by side with mine. I'd always liked that company because they specialized in plastics testing—which was a service I knew how to provide, although we didn't have a strong presence in that area. I wanted to add that capacity. So I went to Mr. Morrison. As it happened, his business wasn't doing so well. He'd lost a key employee, he had health issues, and he was extremely motivated to sell. I toured the lab and looked at the projects Betec had completed for its clients. I looked at his QuickBooks accounting records, noting the yearly expenses. I asked Mr. Morrison what his expectation was of the valuation of the company.

I also talked to a couple of Betec's major clients to see what impression they'd formed of the company. Mainly I spent a lot of time studying the company's technology and figuring out why clients valued its services.

I liked what I learned, so I asked my attorney to draft a two-page letter of intent. The price I'd come up with was a little lower than what Mr. Morrison had told me he expected, which was around $300,000. We started negotiating. His point was that he'd gotten an offer for $300,000 a few years back, which he had not expected. I countered by pointing out that not only were the trends moving downward but he'd also lost a key employee who was now running her own business competing with him, and she possessed a lot of sensitive information.

We went back and forth, made some adjustments, and settled on $215,000. Within a few days we'd closed the deal, and I was the owner of another company.

I met with his employees and told them I'd be moving operations to St. Louis within the year. Just as I'd expected, some quit and others agreed to make the move. The surprise was that not a single customer objected; it just didn't matter to them where the company was based. Reassured, I started planning the transition.

Then Shamal died, and all my plans ground to a halt. Forget buffers, forget productivity—I forced myself into the office for an hour or two each day, maximum, and I spent the rest of the time taking care of the boys and reading, learning, trying to understand. At night, I wept. During the day I'd have flashbacks of the happiest times in our lives together—the trip we took to Washington, DC, to celebrate the Fourth of July in the capital; the time we took the boys to Disney World; the visits to India; how Shamal finally relaxed when we sailed off on a cruise and left our everyday cares behind us...

I tried to shake the thoughts and get on with practical things. My sons were sad, but they were still hungry. I cooked as much as I could: hamburgers, pancakes, French toast. Most often I made *phodniche pohe*, because Shamal used to make it all the time. I'd wet the flattened rice, cook it with spices and onion and boiled potatoes and turmeric powder and cumin, then garnish it with grated coconut and coriander leaves. Then there were clothes to wash, uniforms to iron, hobbies, homework, doctor's visits ... How had Shamal done it all?

Samir had worn eyeglasses since he was 4, and he kept falling asleep with his specs on. Trying to systematize, I built in a last-minute bedside check once his light went out. He also demanded a new and exciting story every night, a fantasy full of fun with a cheerful ending. It became harder and harder for me to muster the energy, especially when it came time to frame that cheerful ending.

Luckily, Inni was around to help me manage the boys' lives. My own life narrowed to domestic routine and private sadness. I couldn't sleep; I'd get the boys to bed, then throw myself on what I still thought of as our bed, lying there half the night exhausted but wide awake.

About six painfully slow months went by. Our old friends were still keeping their distance, but even casual neighbors started saying, "What about you? What about the rest of your life? Aren't you going to get married again?"

At first I was startled—and a little put off—that they would even suggest it. Too much had happened, too much shock and pain, guilt and wondering. Besides, Shamal was irreplaceable. As angry as I felt toward her, on my darkest days, for leaving me, I felt that I could never recapture our marriage with another woman.

I brushed the suggestions aside, but they wouldn't leave me altogether; I was lonely, and the thoughts of another marriage kept drifting back into my mind.

One Saturday morning I tied on my apron and started mixing pancake batter. Inni came into the kitchen and stood quietly for a moment in the corner, watching me.

"Prasad?" she said. "What have you decided?"

"Pancakes," I said over my shoulder.

"I am talking about you, not breakfast," she countered.

"About me?"

"Yes. Have you decided anything about remarriage?"

I looked at her in amazement. This wasn't like my return home to India after grad school, when she brought up marriage as I'd expected and I feigned disinterest. This time, I really *was* surprised.

She persisted: "Prasad, I feel that this is the right time for you to get married again."

"O-kay," I said, mixing faster. "Let me see."

"Don't take this casually, Prasad," she warned. "I will not be able to stay with you forever. Your children need a loving mother, you need a companion, and your home is starving for a prudent housewife. How long will you continue as a lone parent? Children need the love and care of both a father and a mother!"

She left the kitchen, and I ladled the batter absentmindedly, making the first pancake so big and lopsided, I couldn't even flip it.

I thought about what Inni said for weeks, and slowly something opened up in my heart: a willingness, even an eagerness, to try again.

That summer, I took the boys to Paris. We found a lot to enjoy. At the Louvre, Neil had a list of works he wanted to see, and he gave us lectures about what he'd learned in school. Samir listened, wide-eyed. He was wowed by his big brother, who knew so much and explained it so well. Neil had read a book on the plane and knew what we should see and why it mattered, so he led the way the entire trip.

The coolest thing was the Eiffel Tower, and we were staying nearby. We walked there, the boys goofing off along the way. We went all the way to the top, and we had lunch in the restaurant at the top—hot chicken vegetable soup and a sandwich filled with vegetables and decorated almost like art.

The boys liked the tower so much, they wanted to go back that night to see how it looked all lit up. We took lots of pictures, many of them silly, with a perspective that made it look like we were patting the top of the Eiffel Tower. Away from the tensions and grief in our home, the boys and I really relaxed for the first time since Shamal's death.

But whenever we went to a café, we'd be seated at a table for four, and I'd find myself staring at that empty fourth chair.

After that trip, very tentatively, I mentioned the idea of remarriage to the boys.

It was at night, after we'd finished watching a movie with just a bit of romance in it. "Would you guys like me to find somebody to take care of us?" I asked. I was stammering a bit; this was even harder than I'd expected. "Not another mom," I added quickly. "Nobody will ever replace your mom. But somebody else?"

Samir, who was four-and-a-half, had heard the grownups urging me to remarry, and he echoed their words with feverish enthusiasm. "Yes, Dad! We don't want to be alone forever!" Too young to really grasp the significance of loss, he knew only that he wanted to have a mother again.

But Neil, at eight-and-a-half, was far more mature, and he had been both emotionally and intellectually attached to his mother. "How can you even think about another marriage?" he asked me, his eyes flashing.

"I could never call a strange woman 'Mom'! We are *fine*, Dad.

"If you think cooking is a big problem," he added, his sarcasm scathing, "*I* can cook for us!"

And he did. He learned to cook. He was so intense, so fiercely determined to keep any other woman out of our lives, that I dropped the thought immediately.

Inni, meanwhile, had stayed with me all this time to help cook and take care of the boys. I began to worry about her. She was not strong enough to work this way, and I knew she missed her own home. Finally, she brought up the subject again.

She didn't have to say much—just a firm "Shri? It's time."

I nodded. I'd already decided that I would at least try. I'd keep an open mind, meet a few women, and see how it went.

To be honest, I doubted that I'd find someone I liked enough to marry. Meeting the right woman now would be even harder than it had been when I was young, with no history of my own. I needed someone the boys could love, someone who would treat them as her own children. On that point I would not compromise.

As soon as my St. Louis friends sensed my change of mind, they started mentioning unattached women. I was 41, and the women people began introducing me to were in their late 30s and early 40s. They, too, had history. Trying to sort through all that to find the right partner was as hard as I'd feared.

Besides, many of the women were trying too hard to impress me. Friends back in India had women to suggest, too, but when I flew home to meet these women my defenses rose. They all wanted to show me their knowledge of America and how easily they'd be able to adjust, and I could feel their eagerness to come here, strong as a heartbeat. Many were more interested in my wealth than in me; none had Shamal's simplicity of heart.

I began to think that Neil was right, that we were fine on our own.

But loneliness swept over me again, a huge tide of loneliness. Some of it, I think, was left over even from my marriage, from the days when

Shamal went behind that wall of quiet and refused to open her heart to me. Yes, I should have realized how sad she was and dug deep until I understood the tangle of her thoughts. But she also should have trusted me.

I put an ad in *The Times of India*. History was repeating itself.

This time, my ad read: "Businessperson with two children wanting to meet someone caring and loving and willing to move to America." I received 400 responses, and I read through each one carefully. I was spending an inordinate amount of time on this project—it had essentially become my full-time job—because I didn't want to just marry anyone. "If I don't meet the right person," I warned myself, "my life will be far worse than it is now, when I'm alone."

Every time the children had vacation, I would take them with me to India. Spring break, Christmas, summer, Thanksgiving. I would run the ad again, stay a few weeks, gather the responses, and, when I came home, write or email them. If they seemed at all promising, I would place an overseas call.

But I soon realized that I should have worded the ad differently, said less about the "successful businessman," because some of the women it was drawing were not very honorable. I saw only a handful of them more than once, and of that handful only one struck me as someone I could be happy with for the rest of our lives.

This woman was intelligent, she was fun to be with, and she talked warmly about my sons, saying how charming they were and how she loved them already. She had a daughter herself.

I met her in Mumbai, and I saw her several times, taking her to lunches and dinners. I wanted to spend time with anyone I might marry, not reach the sort of snap judgment so common in Indian marriage-making. She took my interest seriously and started coming on a bit stronger.

When I told her I wouldn't be back again until summer, she called to tell me that she had taken her daughter out of school and was coming to the US. The call surprised me, but she had a sister in Cincinnati, and she said she was just visiting. We ended up going together to Disneyland, almost like family. She got very involved—she helped the boys learn to swim, and she taught us all fine table manners and helped me pick out a new wardrobe. She told me she would help me live well, using my money. I didn't mind the implied insult; I knew I'd come from a different background and didn't have that kind of class.

This, I thought, was the right woman. I was ready to ask her to marry me when she said she wanted to come and see my home. I was having a party for Neil's birthday, with a concert and a religious ceremony, and she invited herself.

She showed up, and the whole town knew there was a new woman in my house. The gossip started instantly. She stayed with us for a couple of weeks, and luckily, Inni was there at the time. She told me that when I was gone, she behaved very differently. Inni was as watchful as a hawk, and she noticed the woman treating the boys harshly.

With that, everything she'd said started to unravel. The boys had never liked her, and I'd been trying to tell myself they would change their minds. Now I began to realize that she'd lied about many things. She'd told me how rich she was, dropped the names of movie personalities, done everything possible to impress me. It was all a façade, I realized. All she really wanted was to make sure her daughter had a good future in America.

I was crushed. After gearing up, braving Neil's disapproval, and doing all that research, I'd found a woman who turned out not to be real. I decided to give up on everybody else I'd met, stop searching, and let fate decide.

Then one day I remembered a letter I hadn't answered. A man had written me about a young woman he knew who'd been widowed just two weeks before my wife died. Her name was Shashi, and she was not very educated, which was probably why I hadn't put her among the top prospects. Still, she took care of her family, especially her mother, who was completely blind, and worked two jobs. An older man she worked with, a man she was fond of and called uncle, had written on her behalf.

(Later she told me that he'd asked her, "How long are you going to do this? Your parents are not going to be there forever. Where is *your* life?" He showed her my ad, but she brushed it aside, saying, "I'm not going to do that." She was determined not to remarry. So he said, "Fine. If you won't write, I will. Just give me the details." Seeing how tense she looked, he told her breezily, "Think of it as a lottery ticket. You are not the only one who is going to apply, you know." Feeling a little silly, she agreed— but she refused to give him a photograph of herself. "If he is interested," she said, "he can meet me.")

When I reread the letter her uncle sent, which described her kindness and integrity—and provided no photograph—I just picked up the phone and called her. She happened to be in her office, at a small private financial institution in Mumbai.

I said, "Your uncle sent me a letter about six months ago? In May? I am now here in India, and I would like to meet you."

She was startled, but she agreed. She sounded warm, if not entirely enthusiastic. She lived in a suburb of Mumbai and rarely came downtown. But she agreed to come and meet me at the Pritam Hotel, where I was staying.

She walked in wearing a lovely aqua sari with a gold border, with her eyes trained downward. She had on no bindi, no bangles, no cosmetics. In the hotel's luxe environment, she seemed a little bit unsure of herself.

I always met women in the lobby first, and then, if they felt comfortable, we talked in my room. By now I was a pretty shrewd judge of character—there's no training like a bride search—and Shashi impressed me as simple, generous, caring, and sincere. We chatted longer than we should have, about both of our families and also about how hard it is to get over a relationship. I was struck by how genuine she was, how matter-of-fact. I felt like I'd known her for years.

"I wish I had more time," I told her, and meant it. "I enjoyed meeting you. But I have to get ready to go to the airport." I escorted her home, and although she didn't say much, I could sense that she liked me, and that the time had been special for her, too.

When I dropped her off, she took a few steps away, and then turned back to look at me. I was, of course, watching her, and our eyes met.

That's when I knew that I was coming back to see her again as soon as possible.

On the plane home, I started worrying that she was too good to be true. Money didn't mean a thing to Shashi, I could tell, despite the hard work she'd done to keep her family going. She was gentle, but she stood on her own two feet; she seemed to always have helped others, rather than demanded help from anyone. I really liked that about her.

Back home, I called Ravi and told him about meeting her. He was worried that she didn't have enough education.

"She's perfect," I told him. Her lack of sophistication didn't bother me at all. My country placed far too much emphasis, in my opinion, on educational credentials and finances.

"But don't worry," I added. "I'm going to keep looking." That puzzled him, too. If she was so perfect, why keep looking? "I know," I said, answering his unspoken question. "I should just end my search here. But I am *trying* to be *systematic*. I don't want to rush into anything. I want to follow my brain, not my heart."

The next time I met Shashi, we talked longer. We were at the hotel again, the Pritam—whose name, ironically enough, means lover. We went out to a great restaurant, and along the way we passed a street vendor selling dresses. I insisted that we stop, and I bought her a black dress with yellow flowers. It wasn't very expensive, but she was thrilled. At the restaurant, she ate shrimp for the first time. Afterward we walked on the beach and held hands. Then we sat down on the sand, looking out at the water, and talked about our pasts.

She said, very calmly, that her husband had been an alcoholic. When he drank, he hit her. They'd had no children. I was amazed by her easy acceptance. "I suffered a lot," she said with a shrug, "but I still loved him. He was important to me. And he only hit me when he drank."

I talked about Shamal, then, and how her life had ended, and how hard it had been for the boys, and how the community had shunned us. I'd decided to bare all and not hide anything from her. Shashi wasn't shocked by the word "suicide"; she didn't recoil, and I sensed nothing artificial or forced in her response. She stayed warm.

I saw her every day on that trip, and before I left I'd planned my next trip back. I wanted to keep getting to know her, and I also wanted to go slowly for the boys' sake. Samir was growing more and more impatient for a new mother, but Neil was still saying, "Why are we doing this?" Several months went by. We'd been dating since September, and now it was March of 1998, and I was back in India for the boys' spring break. I was still taking my time, thinking everything was going along really well …

Toward the end of my visit, Shashi put her foot down. "I am not going to see you again," she told me. "I am getting too involved with you, and it will make it too hard on me to end this." She was speaking very firmly—but her eyes were sparkling with tears. "It is easy for you," she blurted. "You are seeing other people. You keep telling me you have a few more names on the list. Well, for me you are the only one, and it will make it too hard on me when this ends."

I protested, trying every way I could think of to calm her and reassure her without committing myself entirely. I babbled in this fashion for a long time, but Shashi had made up her mind. "This," she announced, "is our last meeting."

I went away feeling like my heart had just fallen out of my chest and landed in the road.

On the plane back home, every time my thoughts drifted, her face was before me. I wanted to slip her sari down and stroke the soft, golden skin of her shoulder. I wanted to hold her against me until we fell asleep together.

By the time the plane landed, I knew what I had to do. I drove home, I hugged the boys, then went into my office, picked up the phone, and punched in India's country code.

"Shashi, I want to marry you," I said when she answered, "but first I want you to come to America, because right now you don't know anything about life here. And I want you to meet the children again."

She'd met the boys once, but they'd spent most of the time talking about hockey, baseball, Nintendo—all things that were foreign to her—and the conversation had been disjointed and awkward for everybody.

She agreed to come, and my heart soared. Then her visitor visa was denied by the US consulate in Mumbai.

"Here we go again with the visas," I thought.

Then I learned that there was a fiancée visa that would allow her three months in the United States. In April of 1999, she flew to St. Louis.

By then, Inni was tired. I could see it in her eyes, in the stiff way she moved when she stood after sitting for a while. She had done too much for us already. Also, I thought it would be good for Shashi to be alone with the children, instead of being under the supervision of my mother, who was a strong, take-charge sort of person. So I flew Inni home right before Shashi arrived.

Before she left, though, Inni helped me host, in her inimitable style, a fundraising party for a cause dear to one of my friends' hearts: Saint Louis University's hospital auxiliary services. I'd come to share his dedication, because the auxiliary helped fund health care for those who could not afford it. Inni urged me to play host, and she assured me that she would help.

I thought perhaps she would be shy, speaking so little English, but no. Not Inni. She wore her best sari, put on all her jewelry, stood at the door and welcomed each guest, most of whom were my American business acquaintances. Somehow she must have managed to make small conversation, too—I have no idea how—because people would come up to me and say, "Oh, your mom is so charming, and she's so proud of you, and

I understand she's going back to India next week?"

My mother had spirit and style. I told her there were no words strong enough to thank her for all she'd done. She'd kept me sane, she'd kept my sons on course, and she'd held our family together.

The year we'd had to wait for the fiancée visa for Shashi was probably lucky, because enough time passed that even my stubborn, fiercely loyal Neil was missing having a mom. He'd begun having nightmares in which there was a bad person chasing him, and then the person took the mask off, and it was his mother. He was so afraid to have that dream, he would not go to sleep. Black circles showed through the thin skin under his eyes.

"What does it mean? Is she evil or loving?" he asked me urgently.

"Your mother was a good person, but she hurt you," I told him as gently as I could. "You don't know why, and we cannot always find reasons for everything. So in your dream, she is both." I emphasized over and over again that it wasn't his fault, and that she loved him very, very much. Then I said, "Of course you are angry at her." I took a deep breath. "I am too, but only because she left us."

The suffering and sleeplessness turned him around on the idea of me marrying again, I think.

In April of 1999, I took my mom home, then picked Shashi up in India. We went to get her visa at the American consulate, and she was so excited when she actually got it. We hugged each other and went right away to buy tickets to the US.

When the plane landed in St. Louis, we drove home in my Mercedes, which I'd parked at the airport garage. She was amazed at the ease, at how new and quiet my car was. As I drove her to my house, she kept saying, "I can never live like this. I'll never even be able to drive a car!" She was overwhelmed—but not in a negative way. She was bubbling with excitement, even as she blurted out all her misgivings.

"In four quick months, you will be able to do all those things," I informed her.

When I opened the garage door with the remote, she gasped again. She squeezed my hand as we walked through the garage door into the kitchen. The boys were waiting for us. Samir came and hugged her right away. Neil was hanging back, his eyes unreadable behind his big thick black glasses. Then he picked something up and held it out to her: a vanilla cake mix cake, displayed on one of our good gold-rimmed china plates. He'd baked it for her, frosted it in chocolate icing, and, with one of those icing tubes, written in slightly shaky white letters, "Welcome to America!"

He looked up, meeting her eyes for just a second. "I have baked this cake to welcome Mom!" he said in a rush. She went to him and took the cake, setting it down carefully and murmuring how beautiful it was. Then she gave him a long, grateful hug. They both had tears in their eyes, and so did I. Samir, meanwhile, was bouncing up and down, asking when we could eat the cake.

That night, Shashi told me that her last fears had dissolved. She hadn't been worried about Samir, who'd thrown himself into her arms the second she walked through the door and stuck to her like Velcro all night. But Neil's cake ... When we went to bed, she told me what went through her mind in that instant: "Oh my gosh! This is what's been so lacking in my life. This is what I needed. My family is complete now."

I think what Shashi and I liked best in each other was that strong sense of family, as well as our candor; we were both very frank and went straight to the point, and that made all the newness and strangeness very easy to navigate.

Things didn't go as smoothly with the Indian community, though. Their mistrust of me had not yet dissolved, so they tried to talk to Shashi. They kept finding ways to bring up Shamal's suicide, as though they thought I wouldn't have told Shashi what really happened.

Shashi and I married on August 7, 1999. We had a small wedding at home. We decorated our indoor pool and floated candles, and we covered the little stage at the corner of the pool with bright flowers. The silk of Shashi's sari was yellow, a color that symbolizes a long and happy married life. I wore a kurta, the long-sleeved shirt, in a gold linen-weave silk, with pants to match. A Hindu priest read the sacred text, and we made the circles.

The next day, we had a reception. I invited the entire Indian community, but barely a fourth of them came. All of my old "close" friends declined my invitation.

A few years after the wedding, Inni returned. She met Shashi, and they spoke easily together. When Inni blessed me, I could see in her eyes that she was content with my decision.

"Now forget whatever has happened in the past," she told me. "All is well that ends well. I am truly delighted to see you all happy here."

As soon as I'd realized Shashi was going to come and join me and we were going to start a new life, I'd sold our house. We had to make a new beginning, I knew. I bought a house in a nearby neighborhood, Topping Meadow. It was almost twice as big, about 8,000 square feet, and I hoped that Shashi would have fun decorating it with me.

She'd grown up watching CNN and American TV in India, but she'd been raised very conservatively and had not traveled much or lived very independently. She and I did not even speak the same native language, and her English was only a few words. Every day I asked myself, "How can I make this easier for her?"

I prepared Shashi; I prepared the boys. I put a lot of thought into every step. She won't feel independent, I realized, unless she drives, so we signed her up for driving lessons. She insisted that she would not take a new car, so I gave her my Mercedes. This was not the huge sacrifice she thought it was; it meant that I got to buy myself a new one!

After Shashi's first few driving lessons, I taught her myself. One morning I surprised her by saying, "Drive to the boys' school by yourself."

"I can't!" she said. "I need someone with me! It is too soon!"

"You can! You drive beautifully. You'll be fine. Take the cell phone, and call me when you get there and tell me everything you've seen along the way."

And so she did, and she was so proud of herself!

We went together to the grocery store, and then I told her to go alone one day and just buy one thing. "And swipe the card?" she asked, a mischievous gleam in her eyes. She was figuring things out.

The boys and I shopped for her at first, because American clothes were so different. We really had fun. They would stop at a mannequin and say, "*That* dress would look *great* on Mom!" For our very first outing, a picnic at their school, I had bought her some Nike tennis shoes, a pair of white shorts—she had never worn shorts, and her eyes flew open—and a top. It was okay if the top fit a little snugly, I told her.

"Will it be okay if I wear a bindi?" she would ask me when we went out. "How do I dress to go to a movie?"

"This is America," I reminded her. "You do whatever you want to do. Nobody will care."

Very soon, she relaxed. The only time I saw her really panic was when she bought her first two-piece bathing suit. She came downstairs to our pool completely covered in a giant bath towel. I reminded her that the boys were children still, and we were in our own home. She still wore the towel until she slid into the water! But the next time, the towel was smaller, and soon it lay beside her on the lounge chair, forgotten.

Shashi is an amazingly adaptable person. I had sensed that when I first met her, but now it hit home, as I watched her gracefully adjust to an entirely new culture. She liked just about everything about America. Other than missing her parents, she was exuberant.

Still, she had plenty to learn, and I worried about her and made sure to come home for lunch every day to eat so she wouldn't be by herself. I called her several times a day, and I kept checking in, to make sure she wasn't overwhelmed.

"But these are happy changes," she told me, pointing out that in her new life, she wasn't struggling financially, she wasn't trying to cope with an alcoholic husband, and she was free of the constant niggling worry about what everyone else in town was saying about her. Her Mumbai suburb had rows and rows of houses, and everybody knew everything that was going on in someone else's house. As a widow, she could never wear a red or gold sari, because those were auspicious colors, and she was not supposed to wear jewelry or live gaily or even observe the festival rituals. Now she cut her hair, which fell all the way down her back, to an easy-to-manage shoulder length, and she started wearing the fingernail polish and jewelry that would have been frowned upon back home.

The boys, to my huge relief, adjusted as easily to Shashi as she adjusted to America. Again, it wasn't hard; she was doing good things for them, cooking for them, doing their laundry. We were going out for dinner again, the four of us, as a family.

Her interactions with the boys were entirely genuine, I noticed, and she's such a selfless person that her presence didn't feel like a Band-Aid. She truly became a second mother. Our family felt whole again.

Neil was fine now. He later told me that he realized from the way she treated him that she loved him just as much as she would if he were her own biological child. "Once I knew she could love me that much, for no good reason," he said, "I had no choice but to love her back!"

The other turning point, I think, was the night we learned about Shashi's father. It was July 1, 1999. She'd only been in the States for a few months—we weren't even married yet. Late that evening, the phone rang. It was her cousin, but he quickly passed the phone to another relative, who passed it to her brother. No one could bring themselves to tell her that her father, to whom she was extraordinarily close, had died suddenly, a heart attack in his sleep. He'd gone to the hospital earlier in the day complaining of stomachache, and apparently he'd been talking about Shashi and how much he missed her. Then he went to sleep—and never woke up.

When her brother managed to tell her, she screamed and handed me the phone, too upset to answer. Samir heard her scream and came running downstairs from his room. He stayed by her all that night as she wept, and at one point, I overheard him say, as he tried to comfort her: "See, Mom, you are big enough, and you lost your dad. Think of me when I lost my mom." She sobbed and held him even closer.

As life steadied itself again, I found that I wanted to buy another company, and I discovered one that specialized in metallurgy and environmental chemicals. We didn't have those skills, but, on the other hand, they weren't doing as good a job as we were. The owner was going to close the firm.

Alan Siegel's company had been bought by Bodycote, the British firm, three years earlier after they made a higher offer than I'd made—and every year since, they'd lost money. It made me sad: Before Shamal died, I'd spent so much time trying to figure out what would make that company profitable. Siegel would ask *me* questions about his company because I'd come to know so much about it. Bodycote's manager now came to me, said he was going to close the lab and lay off all the employees, and asked whether I wanted to buy the equipment.

"Not only the equipment," I told him. "I'd like to buy the entire company, as a running business, and keep all the employees." So he sold it to me—at a fraction of the cost I would have paid three years earlier. And several of the scientists I kept would become key employees in my company.

Because of that acquisition, my company's sales grew to $6.1 million in 2001, and I started to receive all kinds of business awards.

Awards no longer meant much to me. My first big award had come in 1997, when my company had been named one of the 50 fastest-growing companies in the region—but I'd missed Shamal so much, I hadn't enjoyed the dinner. All those conversations we'd had over the years, all the times I'd talked to her about my dreams ... I took Inni to the dinner, and she wore a beautiful sari and didn't understand a word anyone said. We were the only Indians present. And all I could think about was Shamal, and how I longed to have her at my side. If only I could have just one more conversation with her. If only I could have stopped her from brooding, or at the very least, realized the brooding was part of an illness.

Next I was named a 1999 Ernst & Young Entrepreneur of the Year. I was in black tie—American clothes are very stiff and uncomfortable, I still think—and we had cocktails and dinner in a huge ballroom at the Ritz-Carlton. When they called me up to receive the award—which I genuinely had not expected to receive—I was not prepared. It was a long walk from our table to the stage, and it felt like everything was happening in slow motion. People were clapping. When I reached the stage, I had no idea what to say, so I blurted out what had happened after Shamal's death: how my employees had helped me, so that I didn't even have to be in the office, and how I'd realized not only the need to delegate but the power of delegation. Afterward, people jumped to their feet, applauding.

Once Shashi was with me, though, life started to regain some of its joy. In 2003, we took the boys on a Royal Caribbean cruise. I was relaxing on deck, idly watching the seagulls, when my cell phone rang. I'd told my staff not to contact me unless it was an emergency, so I answered. I was surprised to hear the courteous voice with an Indian accent.

"Good morning, Dr. Shri Thanedar, and hearty congratulations!" he said.

"Good morning," I said, "and congratulations for what?"

"Sir, I am calling from Delhi. You have been selected as an outstanding overseas entrepreneur by the government of India, and your award will be presented in Washington, DC, by the former prime minister, Mr. P. V. Narasimha Rao. We wrote to you, but did not receive a reply. Will you be present at the ceremony, sir?"

"I'm very honored," I said. "I will let you know. Can you give me more details about this award?" I gave him the fax number of the ship and hung up, wondering whether this was some kind of joke.

I called a friend in California who keeps in touch with the political establishment in India. "Congrats, Shri!" he said immediately. "Go ahead and accept it! It's a very prestigious award."

The fax came through minutes later, and I immediately confirmed my consent. The next day, my cell phone buzzed again. This time, it was polite voice with an American accent.

"Mr. Thanedar? Hi! I'm calling on behalf of the Indian-American Friendship Council. We have chosen you to receive our entrepreneurship award. It will be given at a business conference at the White House. Will you be able to attend?"

Was this April Fool's in July? I had two awards to collect in my adopted country's capital, one the day after the other.

"Shri, what's happening?" Shashi asked, gently touching my shoulder. I was holding the phone in front of me, staring at it blankly. Hurriedly I raised it to my mouth again. "Yes, I will accept the award, thank you very much!"

He told me about the security clearance they'd require for everyone who attended. Once again, I gave him the ship's fax number. Then I hung up and told my family. Once the screaming and yelling was over, we started making plans.

"Dad, are you going alone?" Samir asked.

"Is it okay by you if I go alone?" I asked, teasing him.

"No, Dad!"

I said, "We're all going. We'll be in Miami in five days, and then we'll board a plane immediately for DC."

Neil, our practical son, said, "What about clothes?"

I stopped short. He was right. Normally we would have bought new clothes for such an occasion, but there would be no time. Shashi saved the day: "We'll wear the formal clothes we brought for the cruise."

At the first ceremony, to my surprise, former Prime Minister P. V. Narasimha Rao spoke to me in Marathi. He also chatted with Samir, putting his arm around his shoulders and laughing with him as though there was no difference in age or status between them. The next morning we had breakfast with a group of US senators and representatives, and we spoke freely about business matters. I found myself asking questions about everything from public policy to taxation. It felt like my teenage days, when I wrote all those letters to the editor ...

Only far, far better.

The core business grew into an umbrella for several smaller acquisitions but still solves all sorts of problems, from contaminated apple slices burning people's mouths to corroding circuit boards on the space shuttle and bags of bird food exploding on the shelves. We suggested a natural extract to replace potentially toxic organic chemicals in a bandage remover, found a formula for a faster-acting diaper rash ointment, and identified toxins leaching from a frozen-food manufacturer's cook-in-the-bag packaging. When a contact lens cleaning solution was causing eye irritation and the company had to recall an entire batch, we conducted a comparative analysis and, using mass spectrometry, found an organic solvent that had not dried off completely. Problems solved.

We don't do things in a cookie-cutter way. At first we had all the usual titles—system scientist, director of technical services, vice president of technology, and so on. But some of these titles you can use without ever knowing what they mean. So I stepped back and thought about it.

"We are basically three types of people," I told my employees. "Our business is about solving people's problems, so the scientists are all solvers. When a young scientist joins us, we tell him or her, 'You are a solver,' and that will make it clear how important they are.

"Owners are owners of a project," I continued. "They have to supervise the solvers, but I don't want to just call them supervisors. They *own* the project, which means that when a customer comes in and says, 'I have this problem,' they will take that project on their shoulders.

"And then there are quoters; 'Can you do this?' 'Yes, we can.' 'How much?' The job of the quoter is to quote a price." Simple as that. And it made sense to everyone.

I operated with transparency, what I call "open book management"; it comes very naturally to me. I give our employees all the details about our expenses, revenues, and finances. I treat every employee as a partner—I want them all to know what we're spending on office supplies or what we made working overtime on that last contract. Even the woman who cleans the bathrooms: I want her to know what the company's EBITDA —earnings before interest, taxes, depreciation, and amortization—is and how that will change her bonus next quarter. It is her company, too.

Our company is an interesting mix of cultures. Most of what we do is done in the American way, but I've brought a few differences. For instance, when I watched my employees buy expensive supplies in bulk and take the first price offered, I groaned. They did less bargaining than my mother did when she bought cauliflower at the market! Americans seem to feel that they are insulting someone if they question a price; it's like they take the person's word for it. I say you have got to at least ask for a discount! I use all my bargaining skills when I am buying a company. (I once went to a negotiating class, and my consultant said, "Why are you going? You could *teach* the class!")

I find that when you involve employees in running the business and treat them with respect, they treat clients better. And we are, in the end—whether dear Clara Craver wanted to admit it or not—a service business.

But my other motivation is that I see business as a game. If you tell someone to come and play the game but never teach him the rules, how will he know whether we are ahead or behind? If he doesn't know that, how can he play his best?

Every time I acquired a company, I met with each employee of that company face to face, just the two of us. "If you owned this business," I'd ask, "what three things would you change to make it better?" Often I could see a pattern in their answers, and that's what I paid attention to.

They might say, "When the clients come, we are dishonest and we tell them we can do more things than we are actually able to do." Or, "We say things like, 'Oh sure, we'll get working on your project next week,' when the truth is that the equipment we will need is going to be tied up for another three weeks. We don't always share that information, but when it delays the project it comes as a shock and makes the customer unhappy." Sometimes they confided that certain managers talked down to them, belittled them, or played favorites, resulting in morale issues.

People were honest with me about these things because I stressed, "This is your company. If you were to make it better, what would you do?" Right at the beginning, I told them, "You know more about the company than I do, so I am going to rely on your experience." That humility made them open up. It was the first time they'd been asked for their opinion and not just told what to do. I think they found it refreshing.

In 2003, after the space shuttle Columbia crashed, I realized how tender early grief had made Samir. He was in class at the Bal Vihar ("children's school"), which met weekly at the Mahatma Gandhi Center to teach Indian cultural heritage. His teacher asked the students to write to the families of the seven astronauts who died. Samir, 10 at the time, told a reporter that it was important to write to "take away some sadness, but you can't take it all away, because it will always be there as a memory." He added, "We wanted to show other people care, and everybody in the United States is mourning, too."

Shashi carefully clipped the article from the newspaper and put it up on the refrigerator. She and Samir had been close from the start, and she never once resented his love and grief for his first mother.

Just about that time I started to see some of the tensions with Neil that I'd dreaded years earlier. He was 14, and for the next four years, until he left for college, he and Shashi would be a bit wary of each other. As Samir grew into his teen years, similar tensions began to show.

I trusted Samir completely—he was a sensitive, conscientious kid—but Shashi had the strict, authoritative attitude with which she had been raised back in India. All the usual—at least, in America—teen behavior was magnified by the cultural difference. Samir hung on the phone with girls for hours, his palms sweaty as he experimented with flirting and eased into asking for a date. Shashi did not understand the need for such silliness. "Why does he make his computer go black the minute I walk into his room?" she would ask me. "Why does he talk back to me?"

"He is only speaking his mind, and politely," I'd point out. "He has the right to have an opinion."

"No," she contradicted me. "He is being disrespectful. Why are you supporting him?"

Shashi has a deep, pure respect for anyone older. If the mother of a friend comes to visit, Shashi will touch her feet. She wasn't expecting that of Samir, but she did interpret much of his behavior as disrespectful. "People in America don't grow up respecting age above all else," I tried to tell her. "That concept just is not here." Personally, I was sympathetic to the American way; I like it when people have to earn someone's respect. But in India age is automatic status, and it demands an immediate response. So if Shashi asked Samir to do the dishes and came home to find them stacked in the sink, she was furious, and she was even angrier if he tried to offer an excuse. She simply wanted him to keep his promise.

"No more TV!" I remember her saying one evening. She grabbed the remote—usually the property of the males in the house—and fumbled for a minute before zapping the TV off.

"But, Mom, it's the World Series!" both boys wailed.

"It's a weeknight," she said firmly, and that was that.

Harmony was restored between Neil and Shashi when he went off to college. He'd proved himself responsible and successful, and that was her big thing. He had good grades and good friends, played sports, pledged Sigma Phi Epsilon, treated adults politely, did volunteer work—was an all-around good kid. She relaxed.

He also relaxed a bit, learning to *listen* to her instead of instantly rebelling. He still went away and did as he chose, but she felt heard and respected, and as long as nothing bad came of his American decisions she only wanted him to be happy.

With our family life normal and my business growing, I found my restless mind pulling me back to a part of my life that I had long neglected: the arts. I'd been consumed by everyday life, ambition, grief, rebuilding. I hadn't been around people like Naushil and Prabodh in years—but they were where my journey had started.

Shashi and I started going to Marathi plays, and I found myself talking about them for days afterward. I was almost addicted to them, and to classical and popular Indian music. I started a website, Marathi USA, with a database of artists in both India and the United States. We promoted visiting Indian artists, and Shashi and I began hosting small performances. Artists from India would come and stay with us. When I was 19, Prabodh had taken me to a concert by renowned classical singer Prabha Atre, and now she'd performed in the small theater in our home and was sleeping in my guest room and eating breakfast with us!

In 2005 we had an even larger home built, almost 18,000 square feet. I designed it myself because I wanted to ensure that we included space on the lower level with a stage and seating for at least 120 people. I also wanted it to remind us of things that made us happy, so I put in a grand double staircase like a movie set, huge windows so light could fill the house, and the feel of a luxury cruise ship.

In 2006, the CEO of a multibillion-dollar company flew—in his private plane—to meet me at the St. Louis Ritz-Carlton. He presented me with a letter of intent to purchase my company at a price with many, many zeroes. I finally had my life settled and balanced, and now this? I tried to keep myself from counting the zeroes, but still I felt a warm, light-as-air happiness. I had built something worth this much money to a company as big as his?

But I looked again at all the zeroes, and suddenly I was not willing to sell my company. I was having too much fun.

Instead of selling, I spent several million dollars buying two more companies, both specializing in pharmaceuticals, which I'd decided was the new opportunity field.

In 2003, I found the first of the two pharmaceutical companies at a trade show. Everybody was selling their services, but at this one booth the guy was snoozing; quite literally, he was fast asleep, with his chin on his chest. I said to myself, "This may be the company I want to buy." It was called Guidelines Integrated Research. I glanced down at the guy's name on his badge.

"Mike!"

He started.

"Are you the owner of this business?"

"No," he said, "I'm the president." Two gentlemen, investors, owned it. I asked whether there was a way for me to meet them. He looked dubious; the company's performance had not exactly been stellar.

"This is exactly what I want," I told him. "I want to fix it. If it were running perfectly, I wouldn't want to buy it."

I renamed the company and expanded its value-added services so it could provide premium services at premium pricing instead of having to charge what everyone else charged because it did what everyone else did.

Next I bought Analytical Development Corp. of Colorado Springs and Coastal Medical Research of Daytona Beach, Florida. The Daytona company was running human clinical trials for new drugs; this Colorado Springs company analyzed drug and urine samples for potential adverse effects. There was a good synergy between them. I worked on improving processes and systems at both companies. Then, in the fourth quarter, I launched a new company of my own to provide management services for the clinical trials the Daytona Beach company's conducts.

The five-year plan I had come up with in 2003 was simple: become a one-stop shop for pharmaceutical companies that were developing new drugs. The shift meant controlling every variable and maintaining absolutely sterile conditions at all times, because we had to establish the purity of pharmaceutical products, analyze any impurities, determine the strength of active ingredients, and keep our pharmaceutical work segregated from any other work we did.

But the shift also meant a *lot* more revenue. It was plain to me that the pharmaceutical industry had a much higher growth trajectory than the chemical problem-solving we'd been doing. So to our old list of clients—an assortment that included FedEx, Emerson Electric, Dow Chemical, Ralston Purina, Pillsbury, Monsanto, Georgia-Pacific, Gillette, and BFGoodrich—we now added Pfizer, Merck, and Johnson & Johnson. Everybody wanted to develop a blockbuster drug, and they could only do so much in house.

As of 2008 we have about 350 people, 62 of them PhDs, doing pharmaceutical chemistry, with sales approaching $60 million. When a company president comes to us, writes a molecular structure on a piece of paper, and says, "Can you make that?" we work until we find the right recipe. Once we've worked out our method, we start testing the compound for safety and purity. We have expertise in both. Next we formulate the compound into pills, perhaps with a timed release, or an injectable liquid. Our goal is to help our clients be the first to bring a new drug to market, because being first means more money. To that end, we've developed what I call Phase I Express, a way to streamline the process to make it as fast and unencumbered as possible.

Am I the typical American executive, driven and workaholic? I've searched my heart to learn the answers. I've even made myself a checklist, grading myself each week on how much time and effort I put into the different parts of my life. Each week, I grade myself on important matters: health, relationship with Shashi and my sons, philanthropic and charitable activities, social commitment, and financial health.

Somehow, I don't think I'm typical—driven, yes, but not typical. In this phase of my life, it's not as important to earn money. If I worked harder, I could make my company twice as profitable. Instead, I hire smart people and let *them* do that, over time. I reward them with bonuses and incentives, and I keep a watchful eye on the work and manage the acquisitions. But my focus is no longer adding zeroes; that's no longer sufficient to make me happy.

Really, though, it never was.

I've bought about eight different small labs, most of which were struggling to survive. Every time I think about another acquisition, I look at the company and ask myself, "Why would I do better than the owners?" If I don't have a good answer, I don't buy it. If I *can* do something better, or meet a new challenge—say, improving its services and profitability—that's when I'm tempted.

Neil and Samir are drawn to business, too, so I've started posing scenarios to them, changing the company names for their anonymity. I'll take a decision I've already made, give them all the raw information, and ask what they would do. They love it; Samir says it's a chance to see what he could do. I think that's always been part of my motivation, too. Through our discussions and mere observation, Neil and Samir have learned a lot about business, and I am confident that someday they will be successful business owners, too.

So I've slowed down—but I have not changed. The dream is still, always, to do better. It's not that I'm not content; it's just that I have this curiosity, this urge to go to the next level and see what it's like. Obstacles push me to overcome them. Other people say, "Oh, I was destined to do something great, and then this happened, and now I can go no further," but in my case it's the opposite.

Maybe there is freedom in starting with nothing—no stature, no expectations.

Of course, Inni did have expectations; she was convinced that I would become a genius scientist. She was my biggest inspiration, long before the obstacles themselves began to motivate me. She showed me what it meant to be strong.

From the start I knew the debt I owed to Inni, but it took me years to realize that Kaka taught me just as much. He turned over such huge responsibilities to me. He trusted me enough when I was just 14 years old to hand over his life savings to me. He let me negotiate for the two houses. He let me negotiate my sisters' weddings.

So I don't know whether it was watching Inni handle adversity or hearing Kaka say, "Here, I trust you." Kaka was never a go-getter, never a fighter or a take-charge sort of person. He always appreciated anything I accomplished, but he didn't apply any pressure, which was unusual in our culture. Now that I am older, I cherish that peaceful acceptance as much as I cherish my mother's strength. I want to weave the two approaches together, just as I've interwoven the Indian and American ways of life.

I only saw my father cry once, and that was when I was walking with him through JFK, in New York, after his first trip to the US. His shoelace had come undone, and I knelt to retie it. He started crying. "What's wrong, Kaka?" I asked, alarmed. He simply patted my shoulder and told me that nothing was wrong at all. It was only that he had seen how successful I was, and still, here I was, bending to take care of his shoelaces.

I think by then he realized that I could never have created something like my business in India. For one thing, the need to offer bribes every step of the way would have driven me insane. I have no patience for winks, nods, and secret codes. In America, things get done if you make them happen; in India, nothing gets done unless money is paid under the table. I am not formally very religious, but Inni and Kaka raised me to think that those ways, even though they were accepted everywhere around us, are immoral.

Inni died in 2005, twelve years after my father and at the very same age. She was herself—vibrant and active and giving advice to everyone in Belgaum—until the very end.

Neil is just finishing college, at the University of Michigan–Ann Arbor, as I complete this book. He says he's grown to be more like me than like his mother, but I see Shamal in him every day. He has her gentle, serious smile, and he is dedicated and sincere, competitive and single-minded. I'm a little more playful; I'll find my way around something. I'm more of a people person—but Samir is more of a people person than any of us! He has a gift for relationship, for connection and fun and teamwork and advice. Neil and I wonder sometimes what path he'll take in life—politics, maybe? International relations? Certainly nothing dull. We figure he'll change majors a couple of times, try a couple of different careers, move very fluidly through a life that touches and changes everyone around him.

He reminds me, often, of Inni.

Neil, meanwhile, is as sure of what he wants to do as he was his freshman year, when he announced his major and handed his advisor a list of the courses he wanted to take and the order in which he wanted to take them. He and I had gone back and forth, me insisting he should get his science degree first, spend a few years doing research, and *then* get his MBA. He wanted to get a business degree immediately. Neil being Neil, he did both, double-majoring in molecular biology and business. Now he's working on helping doctors and engineers move medical inventions from a sketch to an actual product.

He has become my most trusted confidant, smart and idealistic and steady. He says that I think differently than anyone he's ever met, but he's learned to explain the difference, because he thinks that way, too. "It looks on the outside like you are moving very fast and it's all action, but the thinking takes place behind the scenes," he once told me, "and you always have the sense that good things will happen eventually. You don't see challenges as negatives, and you don't worry about something bad happening. If it does, you don't take it as final; the bottom is never the end. You say, 'And then what?'"

I just grinned, because I'm starting to see the same responses in him. Watching us survive whatever has come our way has, I think, made Neil much more of an optimist than he would have been by nature. He's never careless, though, and he's still as grave and practical as he was at 8, when he assured me that he could learn to cook. I've given him a

Visa card with a $5,000 limit on it, and most months he spends about $120—a few meals, maybe a doctor's appointment. He took forever flying home on his most recent trip because he booked a flight with two connections. He said it was half the price of the direct flight.

Yes, he and Samir know that we have enough money for direct flights, but I think wealth almost embarrasses them. Neil works for the Detroit Redwings, and he volunteers with the Detroit Partnership, helping clean up crack houses and hold food and clothing drives. Samir volunteers with cancer patients at a local hospital and works on political campaigns he believes in. I make sure they go to good schools, because that's my big regret: I wish I'd gone to Kellogg or Yale for my MBA, not a small liberal arts school, and I wish I'd gone into business sooner.

I take as much advice from my sons as I give, maybe more. But I do emphasize one thing that contradicts what their American friends hear from *their* parents: Don't focus on earning money. I want them to learn; I want them to do something creative, something important. I told Samir last summer, "I'd rather you go work for free for a political campaign than go to Waterway and wash cars to make money." Their American friends' parents instill more of a "You've got to get a job and make some money" attitude. I say, "If you can do something that will enhance your career later on and enhance your life, do more of that. You'll make money in the end. This is the time for you to acquire skills."

It's a little ironic, I know. The first half of my life was a press to make money, first for my family's sake and then to prove my success beyond all doubt. But as happy as it made me to buy an 18,000-square-foot house, I think I was even happier when I built myself that little study room in the attic back in Belgaum. Money isn't really the point. Freedom is.

Knowing what I now know about Shamal's biological father and her own death, I watch my boys like a hawk. Neil even asked me once, "Do you ever worry about me being like Mom?" The question took me aback—for years he's called Shashi "Mom," so for a minute I wasn't

226

sure what he meant. "I mean, getting depressed," he said, and I knew immediately.

"I pay attention," I said. "Does it bother you?"

"No," he answered, his voice lighter. "I'm glad you do. It's nice to know somebody's keeping watch."

I'd been honest with him all along; I'd told him that his mother saw huge intelligence in him even as a child but perhaps (this part she did not share with me) also worried that his sensitivity would make him vulnerable to moods as dark as her own. He said that the more he talks about it, the less it scares him. The worst he's ever felt, he said, was when he was scared to sleep after she died, because of the nightmares.

"You were just always there," he said. "What I remember of it is, I became very distant, kind of got lost in it. I didn't need you to drag me out, and you didn't. But you were right there the instant I came out of it. And you always made sure there was help if we needed it—with anything, counseling or tutoring, whatever."

Samir, I worried about less, because he's always been such an open, lighthearted kid. But when my business shifted and at least 80 percent of the important decisions were in Florida, I suggested moving to Miami. Shashi was delighted at the prospect of living by the ocean. Neil was heading for college, and he liked the idea of a fun place to bring friends on his breaks. But Samir had a meltdown.

His friends are his identity right now, and he was in the middle of high school; he couldn't bear the idea of leaving them. He was saying things like "You've taken my life away from me, the whole world away from me—when I go to college I'll never come home." Sad and furious, he grabbed the car keys and wouldn't tell me where he was going. I stopped him, the way I'd so often stopped his mother, and held him close. Pictures flashed through my head: Shamal bolting from my parents' house and walking all over Belgaum when I didn't arrive on the scheduled flight. Shamal hysterical when I bought the Mercedes, tearing out of the house. Shamal on the cell phone that last weekend, driving to Kentucky Lake ...

I canceled my afternoon flight to Philadelphia, where I was to attend a board meeting of the Bruhan Maharashtra Mandal of North America, an umbrella organization of all Marathi organizations. Then I called the BMM officer who was organizing the meeting there—I was now chairman of the board of trustees—and explained that something had come up at home. Samir and I talked all weekend. The more we talked, the more I realized, "If we give in and stay in St. Louis for the next two years, he's gonna flip the next time a change happens to him." Partly, I was incredulous. I'd lived through so much change, so much hardship and adversity, and my son couldn't stand to go to a fine town like Miami and live in a condominium and go to one of the top private schools there? If he couldn't handle something like that, I hadn't made him strong enough.

I decided that we would move. "Life is full of changes," I told him, "some planned and some unplanned, some you want and some you don't. If I teach the two of you anything at all, I want it to be that you should never resist change." He looked up and nodded, and I ruffled his hair. Then I said, "We've got to do this, but tell me how to make it better for you."

Slowly he started coming up with things that would help. "The more time I spend with my friends, the better," he said, so we planned some trips. He had limited text messaging on his phone, so I made it unlimited. I also told him that he could choose the school he went to, and he selected one with an international emphasis. It turned out to be more challenging and rigorous than his old school, and after a few bumpy months of trying to break into established cliques, he started to do really well.

"In a year, you'll be even happier than you were here," I'd predicted when we left St. Louis. He hadn't believed me, of course, but the following August he said that it was—not overwhelmingly, but by a slight margin—true. The international baccalaureate program at his new school was more challenging, and it demanded more writing. He'd made many friends, and he spent the summer working on a political campaign and learning to sail.

My hope is that the next time a change happens in his life, he'll embrace it.

I'm writing a book, not about Shamal's death but about her life. I'm writing it from both our perspectives, describing the same events from her point of view and then from mine.

My point of view is simple. Imagining hers is like squeezing through a narrow opening between mountains and then climbing really high and standing there looking down, with no railing. The world feels very distant, yet my heart races with fear. I fasten on certain details, keep my eye on them to ward off the dizziness. The air is thin and very clear, and there's jagged gray rock all around me.

Even in things I saw as cause for celebration, she found mortification. My mind looks for logic; hers was full of passionate loyalty, foreboding, and a sense of injustice that colored everything she experienced. I see now how much anger and sadness were trapped inside her.

But it is too late.

I still see Shamal's parents once a year—for the kids' sake but also because I feel I owe it to them. We rarely speak of what happened, but they always welcome me warmly.

I've met senators and congressmen, India's last three prime ministers, Asha Bhosle (India's most famous singer), John McCain. I've eaten dinner with Bill and Hillary Clinton (she was funnier than I expected, and warmer).

The first time I met the Clintons, it was through a mutual friend whose teenage daughter had died in an accident. He set up a foundation in her name, awarding scholarships for art education. The idea was, if young people get into art, they will relax their minds and release their creative energy and, as a result, actually do better in science and other subjects. Bill Clinton came to speak at my friend's fundraising dinner at the Ritz-Carlton in DC, and he did not charge a dime. Afterward, probably 30 people were waiting to have pictures taken with him. The way most politicians do these things is, they stand there like a robot with a permanent smile and you go stand next to them. *Click.* But Clinton was totally different. After each photo, he would actually walk a couple of steps and hold out his hand to the person next in line. He'd look into the person's eyes, ask his name, learn a little about him.

When he came to me, I'd brought the Hindi translation of my book, and he asked about my story. When he heard what it was about, he said that I should write it in English.

"I wanted to motivate youngsters in India," I explained.

"There are a lot of people here who can learn from your story, too," he told me pointedly.

Hearing about my friend's art scholarships made me think of Naushil. He came to see me last year, and we sat out by the pool, watching our sons swim and talk and tease each other just the way we used to. He is writing his second movie script for Bollywood, and he has written several plays in Hindi. It is good that he stayed in India.

It is good that I left.

I could never have done what I've done in India, I know that. The bribery and corruption would have made me insane. My directness would have offended anyone of importance. The calculated risks I've learned to take would have been misinterpreted; Maharashtrians talk about "sticking to" your job as opposed to "jumping into" a business, and most would have seen my actions as rash.

But I'd never had patience with the fearfulness of my culture. Its traditions, its relationships, its values, its arts, its language, its food!—all that I cherish, but not its fearfulness.

In a few years, I think, we will move to New York. When I no longer have to worry about the business at all, I want to be involved in the arts. Science was problem-solving, and I loved it, but I am ready to do something more creative—direct movies, maybe, or learn to paint. Art is food for thought; it is a different kind of enjoyment.

I give money to a hospital, to fund health care for the uninsured. We also support organizations such as the Juvenile Diabetes Research Foundation. Shamal would have done that. And I get involved—I don't like just writing checks, because it makes me feel oddly remote and grandiose. I'd rather see whether there's anything I, Shri, can do to make a difference. so it is hard work! At Thanksgiving, we collect food and clothes for the poor in our community. I host fundraisers to end child abuse for an organization in St. Louis, the Family Resource Center, which helps 10,000 children a year.

I'm also thinking of setting up business incubators in different parts of both India and the United States. Just like a premature baby, a tiny new business needs nursing and support. Entrepreneurs need a place where they can test ideas without losing their shirts.

I also want to do what I can to preserve the Indian arts. Parents in India now are so eager for their children to learn English and get an education that they forget that if the Marathi language dies, so does Marathi culture. I saw myself, after four years in the US, how easy it was for those words to slip away.

Any smart person can learn English. No one can re-create a lost culture.

When the economy fell apart, the kids worried that I'd be upset. But one night I overheard them talking about how hard times only made me try harder—which was exactly true. I'd already been plotting how to keep my company growing through the recession. Then they said something that made me feel really good: They agreed that even if I lost everything, it wouldn't bother me one bit. I'd go rent a small apartment and start a new company.

I hope and believe that they were right.

Now, Neil does say I've mellowed a bit. He told me one day at the airport, when a flight was delayed and it caused the usual tangle, "You're different now, Dad. You never yelled at us, but in a situation like this you would have been really impatient with the airline, fuming until you figured out an alternative. Now you're sitting there all relaxed, going with the flow!" I worried for a minute—had I lost too much of my edge? But he was grinning at me, utterly delighted by the change.

Our old parent-child roles are beginning to shift: When he comes home from college, he asks whether I've been eating well—he's studied enough to know the damage my diabetes could do if it were to go unchecked—and he and Samir challenge me out onto the tennis court to make sure I'm getting enough exercise! We all spend a lot of time together these days, whenever the boys are free. I've lost the desire to race around attending parties.

Shashi told me she loves our two-bedroom condo in Miami far more than the spacious house in St. Louis we're trying to sell. A terrace looking straight out on the ocean runs the length of the condo. "The boys probably don't like this as much as I do," she said, "but I love that we all see each other constantly when they're both home. There's no place for everyone to go off separately. In St. Louis, I wasn't even sure who was home and who wasn't. Now I get to see all of you all the time, not just at dinner. I think it is making us closer."

She's made friends at the Miami hospital where she volunteers, doing everything from working in the gift shop to restocking supplies in the emergency department. She hates to sit still. When I'm not around, she works out with a neighbor and she and her friends drink tea on the terrace, go to the beach, go out to dinner … Watching her, even I sometimes forget how different she was in Mumbai, so shy and constrained.

When I first wrote my autobiography, I wrote it for myself. Maybe I would let Shashi read it, I thought. Maybe my sons. But mainly I wanted to document the things that had happened.

My family read it, and a few friends, and the circle widened. Soon people were telling me that after reading everything I'd gone through, they had more courage. They urged me to publish the book. A few family members and friends, however, thought that I should not talk about

Shamal's death. They urged me to keep the family secrets, especially the dark ones.

But I'd had enough of secrecy and shame.

The Marathi first edition of this book came out in 2004, and it was a surprising hit. People wrote to me as if they knew all of us, asking after the well-being of my sons, Shashi, my brother and sisters ...

I did a book-signing in Belgaum, and one of the ladies said, "My mother read your book. She is 90 and really wanted to meet you but could not come tonight. We would welcome you if you could visit us."

"Of course I will come," I said, and took down her address. It didn't ring any bells, but when I got a little rickshaw and went there, the outside looked very familiar. It stood about three stories high, far taller than the houses around it, and the balcony was almost a full circle, beautifully painted. I stood outside for a minute, staring. Then I saw the railroad beyond the house, and it clicked: That was where I used to stand to look at this house. It was the biggest house in Belgaum, and when I was just a toddler, still hanging onto my mother's hand to walk, I saw it and told her, "Someday I'm going to have a house like that." She came to the open house for my biggest house and teased me by telling everyone there, several times, how I'd predicted this.

Now I walked in, enjoying the coincidence, and saw that it really was quite a modest house—maybe 4,000 square feet—compared to what I've seen since. But I never would have dreamed, back then, what I would see someday.

Later on the same trip, a well-known author in Mumbai was interviewing me at an event, and during the break someone walked up and handed me a note from a man in the audience. It read, "This is your former supervisor, S. D. Soman. I would love to talk to you afterward."

I was shaking a little bit, and there was sweat on my forehead. Mr. Soman! I didn't let him scare me when I was 24, but now he's read the book and I just finished telling my story about Mr. Soman to the audience ...

So after the talk, I was waiting nervously for him, and here comes this very short man, barely 5 feet, with a bit of a belly, wearing sandals and little round spectacles and looking very, very ordinary. He speaks softly, as though he could be my uncle, and tells me that he is proud of me. Then he gives me a hug.

What would I have done, I wondered suddenly, if Mr. Soman had been nice to me back at BARC? If he had given me a promotion, a cozy little job? I would have never come to the United States.

This leads me to a similar thought: What if my friend Guru had been kind after Shamal's suicide and said, "Here, let me handle the funeral arrangements for you, and my wife will watch the boys—you just go to work"? I would have learned nothing about Shamal, nothing about myself. I would not have grown close to my sons; I would not have become a leader in our community. I probably would never have learned how to delegate and so would not have been able to get my head above water and see clearly which businesses to buy.

At the time I just saw these people as obstacles, really high obstacles, in my way. Today I look at Mr. Soman and Miss Virginia and all the others and say, "They had a role to play. They didn't want people to manipulate the system; they were trying to protect it."

I have no problem with systems and their rules; I just like to bend them. As a young man, I was surprisingly self-confident, almost cocky. I was very ambitious, and somehow I always felt I was doing the right thing. Neil's right: I'm mellower now, and it's made me humble.

I'm still confident, though. It's that refusal to fear failure that keeps me going. I succeeded not because I was a genius or brilliant at business but instead because I had confidence to think I could overcome any obstacle. As a result, the obstacles only made me try harder.

And now I'm grateful to everyone who tried to stop me.

≈